TEATRO CHICANA

A Collective Memoir and Selected Plays

Edited by Laura E. Garcia, Sandra M. Gutierrez, and Felicitas Nuñez

Foreword by Yolanda Broyles-González

UNIVERSITY OF TEXAS PRESS AUSTIN

Printed in the United States of America
First edition, 2008

♾ The paper used in this book meets the minimum requirements of ANSI/NISO Z39.48-1992 (R1997) (Permanence of Paper).

Library of Congress Cataloging-in-Publication Data

Garcia, Laura E.
Teatro Chicana : a collective memoir and selected plays / by Laura E. Garcia, Sandra M. Gutierrez, and Felicitas Nuñez ; foreword by Yolanda Broyles-Gonzalez. — 1st ed.
p. cm. — (Chicana matters series)
ISBN 978-0-292-71743-5 (cl. : alk. paper) — ISBN 978-0-292-71744-2 (pbk. : alk. paper)
1. Teatro de las Chicanas (Theater group) 2. Mexican American theater—California—San Diego—History—20th century. 3. Feminist theater—California—San Diego—History—20th century. 4. American drama—Mexican American authors. 5. American drama—Women authors. 6. American drama—20th century. I. Gutierrez, Sandra M. II. Nuñez, Felicitas. III. Title.
PN2270.M48G37 2008
792'.08209794985—dc22

2008001834

Delia Ravelo Reyes
September 14, 1952–November 26, 2002

Timeless Warrior

For your love that touched our lives,
For your heart's universal compassion,
For your international humanitarianism,
a global citizen, union member, and proud worker,
Your spirit of light dances eternally in the depths of our abyss.

Teatro Chicana

intro
material method
results
discussion

CHICANA MATTERS SERIES

Deena J. González and Antonia Castañeda, editors

Chicana Matters Series focuses on one of the largest population groups in the United States today, documenting the lives, values, philosophies, and artistry of contemporary Chicanas. Books in this series may be richly diverse, reflecting the experiences of Chicanas themselves, and incorporating a broad spectrum of topics and fields of inquiry. Cumulatively, the books represent the leading knowledge and scholarship in a significant and growing field of research and, along with the literary works, art, and activism of Chicanas, underscore their significance in the history and culture of the United States.

CONTENTS

FOREWORD

Yolanda Broyles-González

Dear Reader:

You hold in your hands a recently unearthed treasure from the Chicana women's civil rights movement of the 1960s and 70s and 80s. In fact this volume is the single most powerful Chicana women's collective document from the era commonly known as *El Movimiento*. It reunites the voices of seventeen Chicanas and—by extension—of the varied communities and histories they came from. This volume is in fact two documents: It comprises a collective retrospective memoir, embracing the *historias*/lives of seventeen women who created a performance collective as they formed their own lives and organized to struggle for a new society. It is also a collection of performances (*actos*/plays) from that era of civil rights. The two parts of the book shed light on one another. Each individual woman's voice is preserved, and they all weave into one another to create a *Movimiento* women's tapestry. The collective was in constant change, and so was its name. It began as Teatro de las Chicanas in 1971, and then became Teatro Laboral in 1975, then Teatro Raíces in 1979. Their feminist collective and the performance pieces they created served as powerful consciousness-raising and organizing tools back then. Today they hold contemporary relevance, as well as historical significance.

I had heard of the Teatro de las Chicanas collective only by word of mouth, and only in bits and pieces. I perhaps met some of its *veteranas* at the 1980 Women in Teatro conference in San Jose, California. When they contacted me this year and invited me to write this foreword I felt greatly honored and enormously curious. As I read the manuscript I noticed that with each page my reading became slower and slower; I was clinging to each word; I was absorbed by the richness of heartfelt imagery, by each revelation, by each *historia*, by every poetic truth; absorbed by the hilarity, tragedy, and depth of each life-telling. I was also reliving many of my own *Movimiento* experiences.

And so I rejoice that such a book will now see the light of day. It is with great joy that I offer this foreword to the volume, in the spirit of a *partera* (midwife). With this foreword I introduce, I prepare and guide you, I open the door for you as you enter this vast Chicana feminist panorama.

The Social Context: Civil Rights and Liberation Struggles

> We dared to speak out . . . as women who were fighting for las Chicanas, for something bigger than ourselves: justice and equality.
>
> —LAURA E. GARCIA

Justice and equality were and remain utopian goals for Chicana women. The seventeen women in this volume provide eloquent testimony concerning their daily struggles to combat the full spectrum of social inequality, ranging from exploitative working conditions in the fields and factories to sexism and male supremacy; from sexual exploitation and homophobia to the humiliation and cultural assault upon U.S. Mexican children at every level of the educational system. For example, in this volume they courageously bring forward personal testimony concerning sexual assault and molestation. These sexual violences were submerged, taboo topics during the *Movimiento,* a liberation movement that had a penchant for overlooking the social oppression of domestic violence as well as its own violence against women.

The era from the late 1950s through the 1960s and 1970s was a time of intense social ferment. Local and also global transnational issues and movements inspired the *Movimiento Chicano* because they brought local injustices into clearer global perspective. Since the 1950s multiple liberation struggles against imperialism had raged in small and impoverished third-world countries of Latin America, Africa, and Asia. Struggles also raged in European contexts such as Ireland and Eastern Europe. Those liberation movements inspired local struggles, spawning solidarity groups and triggering a widespread political awakening. Local and transnational issues and struggles were often intertwined. For example, the disproportionate numbers of Chicanos dead in the Vietnam War cast a veil of mourning and then draft resistance throughout the *barrios* of the U.S. Southwest. At the same time, the United Farm Workers Movement in California waged a heroic struggle against the agribusiness giant. The farm workers established the first agricultural labor union in U.S. history and became the vanguard of the Chicana/o Movement at universities.

A great many Chicana/o university students at that time had experienced the oppressive conditions of the agricultural fields. Those conditions included widespread child labor, substandard housing, and generally inhumane working conditions such as pesticide poisoning, no toilets on the fields, and the indignities of racial and sexual harassment. In the early 1960s the injustices against farm laborers manifested themselves in a life expectancy of fifty-four years, an hourly wage of 86 cents, and life well below the poverty level. The United Farm Workers' 1965 grape strike and boycott, along with the UFW's 1966 landmark 280-mile protest pilgrimage from Delano to Sacramento, brought publicity to the moral and political determination of the nation's poorest. In the words of Clara Cuevas: "The farm workers' struggle was at the heart of the Chicano student movement, where most of the *teatro* women and myself got our feet wet." The UFW also grew into a transnational movement: UFW solidarity groups arose throughout Europe to block the retailing of boycotted produce such as lettuce and grapes.

The transnational north–south vision is evident in Teatro de las Chicanas productions such as *Archie Bunker Goes to El Salvador* and their performance piece entitled *E.T.—The Alien*. The *Archie Bunker* piece features Gloria Bunker, who takes on a journalism assignment in El Salvador and comes to understand the effects of the U.S. presence there. Her father, Archie, eventually has his eyes opened to the genocide and suffering caused by U.S. corporate imperialism. Gloria sets out to interview Salvadorans on the street. That theatrical device allows for the voices of Salvadorans to be heard in Spanish while journalist Gloria Bunker translates for English speakers. It also plays off U.S. mainstream popular culture: the Archie Bunker television series *All in the Family*. *E.T.—The Alien* also features an anti-imperialist transnational theme. The E.T. in question here is not a cute alien from outer space: it's Enriqueta Tejeda (E.T.), an economic refugee from South America whose land is taken over by U.S. interests. She is forced to flee northward into the United States in search of work and a better life. Her trials and tribulations—including her rape at the border—are still suffered by so many undocumented women border-crossers today.

This volume is a major contribution to a more inclusive history of the Chicana/o Movement. Even as the *Movimiento* was winding down—or taking on more subdued forms in the 1980s—the media and early Chicano Movement history were already anointing a select few well-known male names as leaders and spokespeople. They were Corky Gonzales, Cesar Chavez, Reies López Tijerina, and José Ángel Gutiérrez. Yet prominent women leaders—such as Dolores Huerta, Helen Favela Chavez, Francisca Flores, Betita Martinez, Manuelita Solis Sager, Rosa Rosales, Gracia Molina Pick, and the women whose words you find in this volume—have been largely ignored, or relegated to the margins of most books, to footnotes, or to an infrequent special issue of a male-directed journal.

Chicana women in struggle were quick to organize their own journals and newspapers from the late 1960s and 1970s. Among them were, for example, *El Grito del Norte* (1968–1973), *Regeneración* (beginning in 1970), *Encuentro Femenil* (beginning 1973), *Comisión Femenil Mexicana Nacional Newsletter, Chicana Service Action Center Newsletter, La Razón Mestiza*, and *El Popo Femenil*. I remember the day in 1973 when Dorinda Moreno placed in my hands a copy of her just-published collection of Chicana feminist writings *La Mujer—En Pie de Lucha*. It remains to this day a treasure trove, as do Marta Cotera's groundbreaking volumes *Diosa y Hembra: The History and Heritage of Chicanas in the United States* and *Profile on the Mexican-American Woman*. This volume now takes its rightful place among the primary documents of *El Movimiento*. Significantly, it is written and edited by a warrior women's collective and its publication is a profound addition to *Movimiento* history, Chicana/o theater, performance, literary history, and Chicana feminism.

Teatro: The Memory Arts of the Oral Tradition

> This was at the core of our quest, to learn with movement.
>
> —FELICITAS NUÑEZ

> The idea of an all-Chicana theater group to deal with the *machismo* we encountered and assert our place in the social revolution caught on like prairie fire.
>
> —LAURA E. GARCIA

In addition to print media such as journals, newspapers, and the flyers generated by *El Movimiento,* the memory arts of the oral tradition served as key organizing tools and a fountainhead of creativity. Civil rights organizers availed themselves of the performance forms rooted in indigenous cultures: musical forms, storytelling, *historia,* improvisational performance, and movement arts. This collection represents a prominent example of oral tradition now transitioned into print culture. The plays were created not as fixed, individually authored scripts but as living, changing, collectively crafted performances. Delia Ravelo recalls that "as actors joined and left, they always had the option of using their own words as long as the message came across." Change was a constant: "Change was initiated with each performance of a particular piece, when we would adjust and hone it depending on the actors needs and audience response."

Creation was a collective process of discussion, study, analysis, and finally improvisation, with human memory as repository and foundation. Human memory contains the lived experiences of the individual and each individual also shares in a memory system extending down through generations. Each actor is a living history, and these women actors drew from their life experiences first and foremost. There was a fluidity, and not a separation, between their life and their stage experiences. Within the collective improvisational process the social wisdom of the body emerges through movement and culminates in the creation of dramatic dialogue. As an exploratory process, improvisation involves a trial-and-error give-and-take system of rehearsal. Meaning is rehearsed through body movement until a play takes on form. "We all participated in discussing the ideas for the *actos,* writing them, rehearsing them, and performing them. Doing so helped us become stronger Chicanas" (Laura E. Garcia).

Plays then can take on an entirely different form from rehearsal to rehearsal and from performance to performance. The plays in this volume represent a moment in time, one moment's incarnation within a constant process of change. Each performance is a living organism and not necessarily a fixed text. Depending on who was able to show up, a performance could take a new course. Or a new political development would trigger a new play: "At times an issue would surface that required spontaneity, like when we got a call from Sandra Gutierrez on an issue that exploded in her hometown in the Coachella Valley. We wrote about the issue, memorized our lines in the car as we drove out to the site, practiced with our partially written dialogue on arrival, and performed. Talk about being troopers!" (Delia Ravelo).

As a collective, Teatro de las Chicanas was determined to focus its attention on gender problems as well as solutions. In their hunger for education they drew from print culture as well. Among the texts they studied were Karl Marx's *The Woman Question,* Anthony Bimba's *The History of the American Working Class,* and Bertolt Brecht's adaptation of Gorky's *Mother.* And although the Chicana women's civil rights movement had a complexion and economic experience different from the mainstream and predominantly white women's movement, these Chicanas also admired women like Jane Fonda and Angela Davis, as they read *Our Bodies, Ourselves*. They attended third-world conferences and sharpened their powers of analysis in multicultural ways: "People say knowledge is power. So we educated ourselves. We not only read about Emiliano Zapata and the *Adelitas* but we also read Frederick Engel's book *The Origin of the Family, Private Property, and the State*, which, by the way, became a bible to some of us" (Laura E. Garcia).

Critique of Chicano Movement Gender Wars and Sex Wars

> *¡Ya basta!* Enough with being put down by the *batos*—by men. Enough with the Vietnam War! Enough with the horrible working conditions in the fields! Enough with racism! We knew that if we didn't speak we were going to *reventar*. Yes, explode. There was a cry surging from the darkest corner of our souls, our *almas*, threatening to bust us open, like watermelons dropped onto the pavement
>
> —LAURA E. GARCIA

The centrality of Teatro de las Chicanas' focus on gender and women's powers—in addition to race and economic issues—was a marked departure from the dozens of other male-dominated *teatros* of that era. As a result they were feared, sometimes shunned by some, maligned by others. This group of Chicana intellectuals/performers triggered a great sense of insecurity among some adherents of the "nationalist" sectors of *El Movimiento*. Once renamed as Teatro Laboral, the Chicana collective was advocating for the workers of the world to unite while nationalists were pushing to uphold cultural boundaries between different ethnic groups.

Some *Movimiento* men even sought to censor or stop their performances. One of those times was at the 1975 TENAZ (Teatros Nacionales de Aztlán, the Chicano Movement's chief performance conference) in San Antonio, where the women were denied the right to perform. And although they affirmed their presence by taking part in the post-performance discussions, they were also not recognized at the conference: "Luis Valdez called out the participating *teatros* and had the individual representatives come to the front of the assembly to be recognized. We were not included" (Felicitas Nuñez). Virginia Balanoff remembers: "It seemed to me that most of the plays at the conference were about love affairs, gang warfare, mysticism, and Aztlán, but lacked specific direction on how to organize." As Teatro de las Chicanas worked collectively to reconstitute the centrality of gender, Chicano male opposition sought to affirm its heterosexist stronghold; men launched their homophobic defense play, using the term "lesbians" as an accusatory weapon.

Performance was one of the most powerful organizing and consciousness-raising tools of *El Movimiento.* Yet gender and sexuality consciousness tended to be underdeveloped in the *teatro* movement of that era. Virtually all *teatros* were male-led and male-dominated. Those male-led *teatros,* which typically featured both men and women, represented gender relations only inadvertently and to the detriment of women. Although politically progressive in some ways, acting ensembles—such as the famed Teatro Campesino or Teatro de la Esperanza—focused their attention on relations of economic class, race, and culture. A sustained consideration of gender was viewed as threatening, and it was dismissed as a divisive issue. During my own research residency with El Teatro Campesino—while writing my book *El Teatro Campesino*—I witnessed the exodus of women whose growth and voices were stifled. For the women of this volume, for example, the San Diego–based Teatro Mestizo, which performed only male-centered Teatro Campesino plays, proved limiting as far as voicing their experiences as women, their gender oppression and power, their economic class oppression, their sexual oppression.

In their quest for liberation the women of Teatro de las Chicanas proved resourceful, creative, and imbued with a deep sense of womanist history. Historically, these women figure among the first generation of Chicanas admitted into the nation's universities in large enough numbers to form a collective. Delia Rodriguez describes the quest for Chicana education in poetic terms: "[As children] . . . we would show up to class with tumbleweeds in our hair, with our clothes rumpled and dirty, and many times barefooted." Although the first women of color cohorts began entering university shortly after the Civil Rights Act forced the desegregation of higher education, Chicanas by the 1970s were still underrepresented, as they are today, in higher education. If anything, this volume speaks to how Chicanas' collectivizing efforts magnified their presence and power.

The dilemmas of Chicanas in higher education are enacted in a classic performance piece entitled *Chicana Goes to College.* Not only does this play expose how Chicanas are humiliated within the racist and sexist educational system and society, but it also enacts the sustaining power of women's collectivity. With a characteristic economy, two Chicanas join forces as they navigate a hostile university environment, helping and affirming one another along the way. Yet *Chicana Goes to College* also issues a critique of the Chicano

Movement, of the sexism and sexual violence against women internalized by so many men of the movement. In other words, a good measure of the hostility Lucy and Chona encounter at university stems from Chicano men, brothers in the struggle. Chicana gender oppression might have had its origins in Euro-American patriarchy and colonialism, but Chicano men absorbed sexist ideologies and the privilege of perpetrating sexual violence. For Chicanas interacting on a daily basis with Chicanos, it became clear that Chican*o* liberation could not happen without Chican*a* women's liberation. Teatro de las Chicanas exposed these problems in many of their performances.

In *Chicana Goes to College* there is a scene in which the two Chicana women attend a MEChA activists' meeting. That scene is a gender discrimination blueprint and a wake-up call. Right before calling the meeting to order the self-important (male) MEChA president states: "There better be some new chicks that volunteer to clean, cook, and type because we got so much work ahead of us." That is the extent of the male vision of women's roles within the liberation movement. The reality of sexism is often expressed with few words or only visually. When a MEChA member rapes Chona, the fact is never expressed with words. It is understood from the way Chona enters the room: "Her hair, make up and clothes are messed up. She is trying not to bust out crying." The reality of sexual assault in the *Movimiento* and of child abuse is a recurring theme in the personal memoirs of these women as well as in their plays.

In time the focus of Teatro de las Chicanas shifted from gender oppression and liberation to working-class issues. Their name change—to Teatro Laboral (Workers' Theater)—in 1975 reflected the new focus on working-class struggles and the need for unionization. Other important thematics were the struggle for bilingual education, the fight against drug abuse, the dangers of nuclear energy, police brutality, immigration, and U.S. imperialism. Yet gender issues never took a back seat. Their play *Salt of the Earth* intertwines both the working-class struggles of a mining community and gender issues. Such issues are inseparable in the collective's work.

In 1979 the Teatro de las Chicanas reorganized again under a new name: Teatro Raíces. The name Raíces (Roots) reflected the new sense of rootedness emerging from changed life circumstances. The membership was no longer university-based but now could apply its university education to the working world, to forming families, raising children, and living in communities. Felicitas Nuñez describes this new rootedness: "*Estábamos bien plantadas.*" In spite of putting down new roots, the collective still remained a street theater performing wherever there was a need: parks, garages, backyards, schools, and community organizations, even in homes.

The Deep Roots of Chicana Woman Power

> My yearning for understanding, universal knowledge, and equality also invited the disapproval of the overloaded testosterone males in the Chicano Movement. However, I was not alone, because the yearning to be a self-made woman was shared by most of the females who started out like me. . . . I found strength in las Chicanas; we regrouped with the sole purpose of revisiting our maternal roots and the fertile ashes of our history.
>
> —FELICITAS NUÑEZ

Teatro de las Chicanas women were predominantly rooted in working-class history and families. They were for the most part the first in their families to attend college. For most of them sheer survival had been an accomplishment.

Once at the university, they reflected on their greatest source of strength and power: their maternal roots. So in 1971 they organized a conference that brought their mothers onto the San Diego State University campus. That Seminario de Chicanas (Chicana Women's Seminar) further strengthened their resolve to organize as a women's collective, creating a free space where Chicanas were "nourished by the generous energy of women" (Felicitas Nuñez). With that conference they proclaimed their woman-centered and woman-identified social vision. At the same time they proclaimed and also celebrated womanhood in its myriad social, psychological, and spiritual aspects across generations. Teatro de la Chicanas was affirming and cultivating the connections between themselves—the young women who had left home and entered the university—and their mothers, who continued in a working-class existence. In spite of the separation, their mothers or other elder women in their lives continued to be a perpetual course of inspiration in their struggles. "I learned from my mother to use my hands to work, direct, and guide. My mother's hands blessed everything she touched, including me" (Felicitas Nuñez). "Mother" signified life principle, origin, matrix, foundation, strength, and protection from social disenfranchisement. At that conference they performed for their mothers, exposing the Teatro's strong stance against male supremacy and male ego.

The centrality of their mothers in the life of the collective is revealed not only in the eloquent and often poetic personal narratives, memoirs, and *historia* but also through the artistry and politics of their performances. Their play *Salt of the Earth*—the story of protracted labor struggles by miners in Silver City, New Mexico—begins with Esperanza, who is nine months pregnant. She protagonizes the birth of new labor relations, new gender relations, a new society. What is more, the play highlights women's collective organizing and agency. Esperanza's story and her relationship with her husband, Ramón, models the undoing of a hierarchical system of family authority headed by a man. Over the course of the play, the women's collective manages to effect a horizontal system of collectively shared authority.

Clearly, Teatro de las Chicanas, as a group of Chicana feminists, drew from the many sources of what I would call proto-feminism, the earlier role models of a more egalitarian society or of struggles to establish gender equality through organized resistance. Paramount in that egalitarian striving were the proto-feminist women warriors of the Mexican Revolution of 1910. They led troops, fought on the front lines, served as messengers, doctored the injured, and also had the additional superhuman responsibilities of carrying supplies, carrying the children, and cooking. These women have come to be collectively known as "*Las Adelitas*" or "*Las Valentinas*" after the *corridos* (narrative ballads) that have helped immortalize them. These warrior women remained a dominant inspirational force for Chicana feminisms for decades. In 1970 Felicitas Nuñez, Peggy Garcia, and Sylvia Romero, for example, mentored the San Diego group known as the Junior High *Adelitas*—manifesting their identification with the soldier women of the Mexican Revolution of 1910.

Some would shortsightedly claim that the gender segregation of the Chicana teatro collective was discriminatory, and it certainly came under unfair attack by male supremacists and homophobes. The womanist *teatro* collective deepened male insecurity in some sectors, bringing on clashes with some nationalists, and prompting slurs that tended to deploy (hetero) sexuality as a weapon: "You are lesbians." Yet organizing along gendered lines has ancient roots on this red continent. Since ancient times Native American sociopolitical formations have featured woman-centering. Chicanas (even if at times subconsciously) have adopted such gynocentric models.

Native American social organization offers powerful proto-feminist antecedents. The indigenous gendered division of labor in fact has secured women's institutionalized power within many indigenous societies for thousands of years. Women's sodalities were and are coequal with men's within traditional indigenous culture. Clan mothers have held and continue to hold central power in indigenous societies across the continent. The oldest democracy on what is now American soil—the Haudenosaunee (People of the Long House, or the Six Nations) in today's New York State—features the clan mothers as institutionalized coequal powerholders. Similarly, the Zapotec women of Oaxaca, Mexico, hold economic and social power by virtue of their gynocentric social organization.

The fact that the Chicana women *teatristas* sought to reassert and cultivate their own power by organizing themselves into a women's collective has a long-standing tradition in what is now the Americas. Vestiges of that ancient dynamic are visible in many of today's Mexican households. That dynamic often manifests during social functions where women gather in one room and the men gather in another. In more recent times, the separation not only keeps patriarchy at arm's distance—it also creates a free space for women and girls. In that space women can cultivate feminine energy and a feminist vision.

With regard to the tributaries of Chicana feminism, this volume reveals the complexity of its origins and its multiple sources of inspiration and power, including German socialist philosophers, mainstream feminism, black feminism, the Gay/Lesbian/Bisexual/Transgender movement, the *Adelitas* and *Valentinas* of the Mexican Revolution, the sorrows and lessons of poverty, the spirit of liberation that moved across the land, Vietnam, the *Movimiento* and its *teatro* movement, and multiple antipatriarchal impulses. Not surprisingly, Teatro de las Chicanas served as a free and generous space for Chicana sisterhood, embracing women of all walks of life, experiences, and worldviews. As one reads the memoirs of the seventeen women of this volume it becomes clear that the Teatro de las Chicanas was a crucible and a crossroads. It was a safe haven from the dogmatism of Chicano nationalism's narrowness.

This volume is a chorus. Its richness comes from the confluence of seventeen very different voices, of many class, sexual, cultural backgrounds, of many ways of thinking, of many different body shapes and hues. It is a primer on Chicana heterogeneity and it breaks stereotypes on every page. But at the same time that it manifested all this beautiful diversity, the Teatro de las Chicanas evolved "Points of Unity." The first was "Recognition, implementation and protection of the rights of women, equal pay for equal work." There was a common ground for all members, manifest not only in the Points of Unity but also laid down in the bylaws. Those documents, along with other press and flyer documents from that time, are included in this volume.

All of the women whose voices are reunited in this volume found the collective experience of Teatro de las Chicanas to be pivotal in their individual lives. That empowering experience of sisterhood was hugely transformative. All the women provide eloquent testimony of its lasting effects. In the words of Clara Cuevas: "They gave me the wings to fly and reach for the stars." Margarita Carrillo describes the bond: "There are also no words to describe the deep friendship that developed between us, the *teatro* women. Through the years we were each other's mother, sister, comadre." Lupe Beltran comments: "*Teatro* taught me to act out feelings. Real life taught me to hide feelings."

Kathy Requejo, for example, founded the very first UMAS organization at her high school in 1969. She joined the group two years later. She elaborates on not only the political powers that unfolded in the *teatro* but also the personal powers. With regard to the political she says, "It meant being viewed as a rebellious Chicana, a radical, and a feminist." With regard to the personal she comments on how deeply the women shared in each other's lives: "We helped each other out by taking care of each other's children. We have cried together over breakups, divorces, disease, and death. . . . Most of all, we shared in one another's dreams and aspirations. There is an umbilical cord that bonds us." The *teatro* was a healing force for old social wounds: "The women of the *teatro* gave me back my voice, which was taken away from me in kindergarten when I was told not to speak Spanish" (Virginia Balanoff). At the same time the *teatro* experience energized the women for lifelong engagement with social struggles. Through their engagement in the *teatro* several of them developed the lifelong courage to speak out in the political arena.

One of the most startling aspects of this manuscript is that it has taken several decades to come to light. What kept it from the printing press? Maybe the fact that the material was created in the performative living, breathing arts of the oral tradition? They did not use or need the print cultural medium. Maybe it remained unpublished because the post-*Movimiento* spirit of male dominance in academia sought out predominantly male-centered versions of the *Movimiento Chicano*. Maybe life's circumstances kept the treasure buried. In the ensuing years those young women became adult women, then elders. However, these many years gone by have greatly enriched the women's retrospective personal memoir. Those intervening decades have brought maturity, wisdom, and an entire life perspective to bear upon the women's retrospective narrative visions and remembrance of *El Movimiento*.

Teatro de las Chicanas was a utopian space, which every woman describes with strong images, such as "heart comfort" or "red handmade shoes." Each of the seventeen women reflects upon that experience with heart and with an immediacy unmatched in academic treatments of *El Movimiento*. Both in the plays and in the women's *historias* that accompany them, this book lays bare both the lofty visions and the nitty-gritty daily life of *El Movimiento*. It offers a rich remembrance of the day-to-day occurrences and challenges, and the creative struggles, in which women affirmed their dignity, power, and vision for social change.

ACKNOWLEDGMENTS

WE COULDN'T HAVE realized our collective dream without the encouragement, forbearance, and support of our husbands, partners, sons, and daughters. And we are grateful to our *madrinas*—Antonia Castañeda, Deena González, and Suzanne Oboler—the professors who mentored our progress every step of the way. Thank you for reading our rough drafts and believing in the value of this collective story. Your wisdom and kind words gave us the extra push to "get it done."

We say "thank you" to journalist Luis R. Torres and professor Steve Acree for their editing skills. We also thank friends and university professors Manuel Delgado, Gracia Molina Pick, and Maria Elena Ramirez for reading our stories and providing moral support.

And to Yolanda Broyles-González, who kindly agreed to write the foreword. Her insights on the history of *teatros* and the role of women encouraged us to tell our story.

If you find any mistakes in this book, the burden must fall on us, the women of the Teatro.

TIME LINE

1955 December 1. Rosa Parks is arrested for refusing to give up her seat on a public bus in Montgomery, Alabama. That led to the Bus Boycott, which was the catalyst for the modern Civil Rights Movement.

1959 San Francisco Mime Troupe is founded. This politically charged, radical theater group, which incorporated agitprop and *commedia dell'arte* styles, became a pioneer in social activist drama.

1962 César Chávez begins organizing farm workers. His initial efforts are sponsored by the Los Angeles–based Community Services Organization. The following years of strikes and boycotts are supported by students.

1964 September 29. At UC Berkeley the Free Speech Movement spawns a student strike that in turn galvanized the antiwar sentiments at university campuses.

1966 October. Black Panther Party for Self-Defense forms in Oakland to address discrimination against African-Americans. Their example is followed by formation of the Brown Berets for the Chicano Movement and the Young Lords for Puerto Ricans.

1967 Rodolfo "Corky" Gonzalez publishes the poem "Yo Soy Joaquín" ("I Am Joaquín"). The poem became an inspiration and a galvanizing force for Chicano leaders.

1968 March 3. The East Los Angeles student walkouts begin. Students of the Los Angeles eastside high schools—Garfield, Roosevelt, Wilson, and Lincoln—walked out to protest discrimination and inferior education in the schools.

1968 April 4. Civil rights leader Martin Luther King Jr. is assassinated in Memphis, Tennessee.

1969 The Third World Strike at UC Berkeley and San Francisco State College begins. Students demanded funding for educational programs for minority students.

1969 March 30. The Denver Youth Conference sponsored by the Crusade for Justice headed by Rodolfo "Corky" Gonzalez is held. The conference brought together Chicano student leaders from throughout the Southwest and the Young Lords organization from Chicago.

1969 April. *El Plan de Santa Barbara,* a manifesto, is written for Chicano political action and the formation of MEChA (Movimiento Estudiantil Chicano de Aztlán). This Chicano student organization at high schools and universities focuses on the educational concerns of Chicano communities and promotes self-determination.

1970 San Diego State College [now University] establishes departments for Chicano Studies, Black Studies, and Women's Studies.

1970 August 29. The third National Chicano Moratorium in Los Angeles. The massive anti–Vietnam War demonstration draws more than 30,000 peaceful protestors. The crowd is attacked by the police and a riot ensues. Hundreds are injured, two hundred are jailed. After the rampage, Ruben Salazar, a columnist for the *Los Angeles Times* and news director for KMEX-TV, is killed at the Silver Dollar Café on Whittier Boulevard. A coroner's inquest later establishes that he was killed by a Los Angeles County Sheriff's deputy. No one was ever prosecuted.

1971 Teatro Mestizo performs at San Diego State College. Their plays include *No Saco Nada de la Escuela* and *Soldado Razo*, written by Luis Valdez.

1971 March. Seminario de Chicanas is organized at San Diego State College by the MEChA women. The seminar for the mothers of Chicana students is the venue for the debut of a women-only cast performing *Chicana Goes to College.* The play, in three scenes, is about a Mexican-

American girl who leaves home to go to college and joins the Chicano Movement.

1971 April. Several women who will become members of the Teatro attend the Indo-Chinese Women's Conference in Vancouver, Canada, which spoke out against the Vietnam War.

1971 Fall. Teatro de las Chicanas is formed. In the following years they perform *Bronca* and *The Mother.*

Bronca is a one-act play that protests how young women are treated by MEChA male students in what is supposed to be a progressive organization.

The Mother, Bertolt Brecht's play adaptation, is set in the 1970s. The story is about unionization.

1971 Teatros Nacionales de Aztlán (TENAZ), a national organization of Mexican-American theater groups, is established in California.

1972 May. "Blowout" rocks the campus of San Diego State College. The confrontation concerns the use of the Educational Opportunity Program and Affirmative Action.

1973 United Farm Workers strike in the Coachella Valley. Blatant violence against strikers by paid Teamster "goons" shakes the community.

1974 San Diego State College changes it name to San Diego State University.

1975 Teatro de las Chicanas changes its name to Teatro Laboral. The group performs *Salt of the Earth,* an adaptation of the movie with the same title. The story, told in eight scenes, is about the miners' strike in New Mexico and the women who joined them as equals.

1975 Alan Bakke, a white male, files a lawsuit against affirmative action programs in the University of California system on the basis that he was discriminated against in applying to medical school.

1976 Teachers Socorro Gómez and Yolanda Almaraz lead a student strike at the Coachella public schools. Parents and Mexican-American teachers organize to defend students against teacher abuse. Teatro de las Chicanas travels to Coachella to perform an *acto* at a community meeting.

1977 Teatro Laboral writes *No School Tomorrow* in response to the Bakke debate. They perform the play for the San Diego Equal Rights Council on November 27.

1977 The Teatro women perform at the TENAZ Conference at UCLA.

1979 Summer. The women start up the *teatro* again, this time naming it Teatro Raíces. They perform *Archie Bunker Goes to El Salvador, So Ruff, So Tuff,* and *Anti-Nuke Commercial.*

So Ruff, So Tuff is a play about a mother and her son and daughter who have just graduated from high school. As the children wonder about their future, the play provides a glimpse into the welfare system and the world of drugs, police abuse, abortion, and unfair unemployment. The experience helps them to realize the importance of getting an education.

Archie Bunker Goes to El Salvador is a four-scene play about U.S. military aggression in South America.

Anti-Nuke Commercial is a one-scene play written as a television commercial that points to modern pollution that is destroying our planet.

1980 September 7. Teatro Raíces performs *This Is Your Life* in San Diego.
This Is Your Life is a "roast" of Nelson Rockefeller and capitalists in general.

1980 WIT holds a conference in San Jose in support of women playwrights, producers, and directors. Teatro Raíces members are invited to meet with WIT members at a workshop in Yosemite Park.

1981 Teatro Raíces performs at the TENAZ Conference in San Francisco.

1981 March. Teatro Raíces performs *Archie Bunker Goes to El Salvador* for International Women's Day celebrations in Chula Vista.

1982 March. *E.T.—The Alien* is written and performed for the International Women's Week event in San Diego.
E.T.—The Alien is an eight-scene play that tells the story of a female undocumented worker who illegally crosses the border into the United States in search of a better life.

1982 March 6. Teatro Raíces performs *So Ruff, So Tuff* at Machos Restaurant, San Diego.

1983 April. Teatro Raíces performs *Challenge to Learn* at Sweetwater High School. This is the last public performance by the *teatro*.

INTRODUCTION

THE *TEATRO* (THEATER) experience transformed the many women who were part of it, and the progressive street *teatro* movement of the 1960s and 1970s was, in turn, transformed by those women who contributed their talents and their hearts to it.

This book is about the women in the Teatro de las Chicanas, a grass-roots troupe that later operated under a variety of names, including Teatro Laboral and Teatro Raíces. For over a decade, beginning in 1971, the women performed at political rallies, at antiwar demonstrations, in high school gyms, at community centers, and at practically every imaginable makeshift venue. This ragtag group put on short plays about the issues of the day, from immigration to police brutality, to discrimination in the public schools and the emerging feminist movement. It was the time of the "Chicano Movement," coined to describe the social movement of Mexican-Americans in the Southwest against social discrimination.

The kernel of the idea for an all-woman *teatro* started when the women of MEChA decided to bring their mothers to the university campus setting. They organized the Seminario de Chicanas so that the mothers could understand what their daughters were going through in college. Several women wrote and performed *Chicana Goes to College*. As a result of that experience Felicitas Nuñez and Delia Ravelo undertook the formation of the Teatro de las Chicanas.

In those years the core of the Teatro de las Chicanas was Felicitas Nuñez and Delia Ravelo, but dozens of young women participated in the *teatro*. They all gave to the *teatro*, and in return the *teatro* experience, one of camaraderie, sisterhood, and solidarity, gave something special to the women who were part of it. All of those experiences were distilled in the cauldron of the socially and politically turbulent era that was the sixties and seventies.

Teatro de las Chicanas was started by students at San Diego State College. It was begun at a time when the Chicano theater movement was growing. The Chicano *teatro* movement began with the formation of El Teatro Campesino by Luis Valdez in Delano, California. The style of El Teatro Campesino was based on the experience Luis Valdez had had with the San Francisco Mime Troupe. El Teatro Campesino developed as an arm of the United Farm Workers union. It became an effective and accessible way to spread the word of the farm worker struggle.

And the *teatro* movement itself soon spread very quickly throughout California and the Southwest. By 1970 *teatros* had sprouted in scores of cities. Some were community-based. Many were based at colleges and universities. Some became much more polished than others. Some writers and actors in those early theater groups had aspirations of pursuing careers in "legitimate" mainstream theater. But most participants saw the *teatro* as an end in itself, serving the purpose of educating communities through agitprop performances featuring *actos*, or short, didactic skits. *Teatro* was an educating and politicizing tool.

The young women in San Diego also wanted to use the *teatro* for a political purpose. Felicitas and Delia were influenced by the leftist political ideals of the San Francisco Mime Troupe. They united with the objectives of the Chicano movement—social justice, bilingual education, unionization—but felt that they needed to go further politically by adding a voice to the definition of women's equality. They used "Chicana" in their name and years later changed the name to address the political issues of the day.

Teatro de las Chicanas wrote the *acto Bronca* in order to protest and reject the stereotypical role assigned to women in MEChA. They also performed *The Mother* to support unionization in the San Diego area. Teatro Laboral wrote *No School Tomorrow* in response to the Alan Bakke lawsuit against affirmative action programs in the universities. Teatro Raíces wrote *E.T.—The Alien* to raise awareness about the issues of the undocumented worker. They also wrote *Archie Bunker Goes to El Salvador* as a satire on U.S. involvement in Central America.

The women involved in the Teatro de las Chicanas found it a transformative experience. Most of the young Chicanas came from small farming communities throughout California. Most of them were the first in their family to leave home in pursuit of a college education. Some came to the college campus scared and not sure of what to expect. Others came with confidence, intending to embrace the college experience. But all of these women needed friends. They found that friendship and *familia* in the Teatro. What kept them together were political ideals.

The women of the Teatro de las Chicanas/Laboral/Raíces were diverse. Some came into the *teatro* for a school semester and some participated many years after leaving college. All of the women involved contributed something valuable, and the *teatro* contributed to the nourishment of their spirit. In the opening essay, *teatro* cofounder Delia Ravelo Reyes writes passionately about the hardships she and her family encountered and had to overcome. About the *teatro* experience Delia says, "The *teatro* awakened my senses in every imaginable way." The stories of the women in this book echo her sense of discovery and self-realization.

This book was prepared by some of the women who comprised Teatro de las Chicanas/Laboral/Raíces. Seventeen women tell their stories. The essays touch on such themes as self-discovery, burgeoning independence, sisterhood, survival in the face of enormous challenges, and political awareness and empowerment. While the essays reflect the personal growth and experiences of the individual women who wrote them, they also reflect a transcendent experience and reveal emotions and values common to all of the women who were part of the *teatro*.

In some of their stories the women talk about the sacrifices their families had made crossing the border for a better life in the United States. They talk about working in the fields as children and adolescents. Other women talk about abuses. Some speak about memories of being punished for speaking Spanish at school, or of having teachers Anglicizing their names and breaking their spirit. The darker memories include incest and sexual molestation as children. Painfully, the memories surfaced as the women regrouped decades later to write this book. Many felt that the stories needed to be told to help us understand the significance of young Chicana women banding together to speak about social injustices.

The book also includes some of the *actos* performed by the women. Some were adaptations of plays, movies, or television sit-coms, and others were written by the women. Some photos and other archival materials were also added.

This book project was started in 1999, and can perhaps be called a collective memoir. It contains the reminiscences of the strong women typical of the group, women who are today engaged in a variety of professions. The exciting days of *teatro* are far behind them, but the experience remains an important part of their lives.

This compendium invites readers into their lives and into the realm of the *teatro*. There are lessons to be derived from both excursions. We hope you enjoy the reading.

I

Recuerdos / Memoirs

1

Delia Ravelo

UP UNTIL I reached the age of six, "Paradise" was my domain in the small Midwestern town of Kenosha, Wisconsin, just north of the windy city of Chicago. My father worked in a foundry that supplied American Motors, and *Mamacita* worked at home. Yes, I was the eldest of three children and raised around the era of the Harry Truman administration. This was the birth and backdrop of my childhood. Even then I knew I was different from other kids although I couldn't tell you why.

My parents had accents like the other kids' parents, who were mostly Italian and German. The only discernible difference between the other kids and myself was the food we ate. While the Germans feasted on sauerkraut, the Italians enjoyed *manicotti* and *cannelloni*. They ate *focaccia* and we ate tortillas, feasting on *enchiladas* and *chiles rellenos*. I didn't understand the difference between parents born in Mexico and parents born in Italy. All I knew is that parents spoke funny English compared to us children, especially those of us who were members of our local Mickey Mouse club.

Our Mexican and Italian families were Catholic, attending the same parochial school and church, celebrating holy feast days, baptisms, communions, and confirmations—going through all the same motions of ritual. Our fathers competed against each other in the potato sack races at the annual company picnics while our mothers and we children cheered them on. When our celebration for the 4th of July came around we all gathered together at the same end of the park to watch and be a part of the crackling spectacular fireworks. Our lives seemed to mirror the Norman Rockwell covers of the *Saturday Evening Post.*

At least that is how I wanted it to be. Behind all this though there was a dispute between my parents. I can recall listening to them speak behind closed doors in muffled tones about the arrangement that had my dad's brother living with us. He was a prime example of Mexicans migrating into a Midwestern beginning. I knew my mother harbored resentment over this arrangement, but any matters of discomfort between adults were kept distant from us children. We remained cushioned and distracted in our plentiful world.

Nothing could have prepared me for my great fall.

The unfairness of the world came home to me when my father was fatally injured at his job at American Motors. An engine fell on his chest, crushing it. At the same time he suffered a heart attack. Since the doctor ruled that the heart attack happened before the engine fell on top of him, American Motors considered his death to be the result of a "natural cause." No monetary compensation would be paid. For as long as I could remember, my mother had battled with breast cancer, and with the death of my father, she battled on two fronts. She immediately sold most of our belongings and our beautiful home in Kenosha. We moved out of Wisconsin to be close to her relatives. My world shrank to a one-bedroom house in National City, a blue-collar suburb of San Diego, California. My younger siblings and I were unaware that this would be my mother's last earthly and most desperate mission.

Within a month of my father's death, *Mamacita* was also gone. She was taken by breast cancer. This became the marker and the scar of my seventh birthday. It took me a whole seven days to come to the realization that there were no fairy godmothers, no angels, no god in heaven, and no kindly strangers to protect us. I took over the responsibilities for my senile grandmother and two younger siblings while my maternal uncle dictated our lives.

I was at the mercy of adults and felt painfully lonely, so I turned to books. This is how I endured the loneliness and burden. I devoured books and *Life* magazine as if they were sweets. I read incessantly and for such long periods of time that I felt my head was going to burst. My headaches became so severe that I was taken to receive medical attention in Tijuana (T.J.), Mexico, to relieve the pressure of the bursting sensation. An incision to my head was made when

I was thirteen years old. But even the scar of this small incision could not scare or deter me from using written words to carry me away into the most perfect escapades. One moment I was Laura Ingalls on a cold prairie night warming up against the straw by the comfy fireplace and next I was Jackie Kennedy on a yacht, basking in the east coast sun and surrounded by the crystal blue waters of Hyannis Port. Lost in the world of words I became good at evading the sad and dreary life I led. This is how the wonder of words filled the void of my existence. This is how I survived.

The uncle with whom my siblings and I were left seemed to believe that all females were subhuman. I had known the feel of his belt for what seemed to be minor mistakes on my behalf, but most horrifying to me was his sweaty look of intense pleasure as he kept belting me. I was very careful not to cause him anger.

As protection, I started to gain weight and adopted the most homely facade, which was greatly embellished by my grandmother's black *rebozo*; this shawl enshrouded my upper torso. My only protection was my brain, and I needed to become invisible and unobtrusive in the adult world. As a child and in my present cursed situation I did not share with anyone why I felt different. What made a significant difference to me was being constantly aware of my surroundings and listening to my brain. I learned to ingratiate myself to teachers, priests, nuns, and any adult. I felt if I played my cards right, I would have access to their knowledge, their working skills, and sometimes their assistance, and possibly even a remote way to their heart.

I honed and created my survival technique by kissing the ass of any adult who crossed my path. Consequently they loved my impeccable manners. I didn't have the support, money, or means to go to college. And I knew nothing was free. There were a couple of teachers in high school who took an interest in me and encouraged me to keep my grades up. They arranged for a counselor to set me on a college prep track, so I could take the right classes and college entry tests. My survival tactics worked, but at the cost of playing a role. The price I had to pay was swallowing my pride and being my teacher's little Mexican peon throughout high school.

Shuttling between our extended family in Tijuana, the Anglo world of my teachers, and my home in the *barrio* known as OTNC (Old Town National City) became a juggling act. My conscious effort to keep all of those adults content and myself sane took all my energy. But I had my plan—I could not afford to not have one. My main goal was to attend college. Before my mother married, she had been a teacher in Zacatecas, Mexico. She instilled in me a love of learning and reading that remains to this day. Yet I can't remember my mother telling me I was supposed to attend college. My uncle would ridicule and chastise me if I said anything about going to college, but inside me I knew I would go.

In my plan every single juggling act, creation, facade, escapade, tactic, and remote chance of hope was a worthy attempt to reach my goal of attending college. All of my efforts came to fruition with the help of Lyndon B. Johnson's "Great Society War on Poverty," an indifferent high school counselor, and a few good and some condescending teachers. I was about to enter San Diego State University (SDSU) in the summer of 1970. My mother's family on both sides of the border didn't believe I should or would ever venture beyond their world of Mexican traditions, fatalistic Catholicism, and male supremacy. My uncle roared that I was not going to attend college or move into the college dorms. My uncle honed in on me—not my younger siblings, but me. He was out to break me down in some way if I would let him. I knew his world and I wanted out of it. College was my ticket.

Days before, in preparation and feeling great danger, I had arranged for a ride to the university dorms. I was raging on the inside, but in a supremely controlled act of disobedience I packed a shabby suitcase with my meager belongings, including my beloved books. I remember waiting, standing outside the house on the walkway, for my ride out of hell. My heart was pumping blood to every thinking cell in my body. I could see the neighbors in our small crowded community peering out their windows. They knew my uncle had raised me since the death of my parents. They knew my uncle was an angry and determined man. And they knew they would witness a battle. But they never said a word.

What the neighbors had not acknowledged or comprehended was that I also had an anger and determination of my own. In a showdown scenario worthy of a *telenovela,* my uncle came out of the house to drag me back into the house, pulling my long black hair and every body part he could grab, leaving his marks. Hairs were ripped off my head and caught between his clenched claws as I managed to push off and pull away with a rumpled torn shirt. I stood my ground. But this physical challenge was nothing compared to my mental resolve, my will, and my integrity. *I didn't feel a thing of what he was doing.* At that moment nothing mattered. He became nothing. I had to leave or die. If I were to return to my community, it would be on my terms, not someone else's. Nothing could stop me. My great passion was about being on my own, and education was my path to freedom.

And I made it.

As far as I was concerned SDSU was Harvard, a completely new universe. No longer beholden to adults in the *barrio* of OTNC, Sweetwater High School, or T.J., Mexico, I dove into my new freedom. As naïve, afraid, and inexperienced as I was, my horizons expanded into rapture! My life became an adventure. An interesting set of opportunities arose daily. I encountered a revolution in every sense of the word. I certainly received an education in my pursuit of knowledge. But the learning process in the classroom could not rival what was taking place outside the classroom. I learned from classmates, workers on the picket lines, and mothers who had lost their sons in the Vietnam War. Wherever I was, I savored the moment, becoming aware of all the numerous happenings.

Various national movements were reaching their apex. The first Women's Studies department in the nation had been founded at SDSU. The antiwar movement found a stronghold among the students; all this had been inspired by Mario Savio at University of California at Berkeley back in 1966. He was a great patriotic expressionist on behalf of freedom of speech, freedom of the press, the right of people to assemble peacefully, and the right to address our government with grievances. Ecological studies took a front row seat along with all nature and peace lovers, and the gay movement was rumbling in the distance. There were the Students for a Democratic Society and the United Slaves (US) organization, which was known on campus along with the Black Students Union. I was intrigued by all the grass-roots organizations—the Black Panthers, the Black Berets, and the Brown Berets—that were established in the student communities. And then, waving at me above everything, was this bright red flag with a white circle, centering around and contrasted by a black eagle, that represented the United Farm Workers (UFW).

I was bombarded by a plethora of happenings, options, and lifestyles. I moved away from the campus dormitory and chose to experience life on a rural reservation with my best friend from high school, Remedios. This was also a time of great respect and reverence for the Native American Indian movement. As a result of moving away from the dorms, Remedios married Sam from the reservation, and I got married to the reservation's canopy of brilliant stars. Whether my choices in experiencing my new freedom were good or bad, I was living my life my way and this made me content.

I had committed the ultimate rebellious act by coming to college and living as I pleased. Every secret whim I ever had was fulfilled during those first two years of college. Among those secrets was my desire to be an actor in a play, to perform on a stage, something like the Shakespearean literature that I had been exposed to in high school. What awaited me was more than I could ever imagine.

Teatro Mestizo was my first exposure to street theater. It was a student agit-prop theater group in the same style as the San Francisco Mime Troupe, which had won the respect and admiration of the public, including the sophisticated theater critics inside and outside academia. Students applauded the Mime Troupe's political stance against the Vietnam War and against the corporate greed of North America. At that time I had heard only about their street theater professionalism, but it didn't matter. I was in awe whenever Mestizo performed any play. Teatro Mestizo was based out of SDSU under the direction of Professor Ruth Robinson. This kind of theater, although it was entertaining, depicted the injustices and racism I had experienced in the Southwest of our nation.

Teatro awakened my senses in every way imaginable. It was live theater with a dose of popular Chicano culture, political criticism, and a mirror reflecting a society rife with institutional racism, economic disparity, male supremacy, and prejudice. I couldn't wait to see Teatro Mestizo or any of the other *teatros* making the rounds through the Southwest.

It was a great time for me. Most of the women in Teatro Mestizo were strong, articulate, intelligent, and talented. Most were associated in some way with the student organization on campus called Movimiento Estudiantil Chicano de Aztlán (MEChA). I felt less educated and less vocal next to these women, who I thought were powerful and in the front lines alongside the "heavies of *el movimiento*." But on the picket line for the grape boycott the loudest and heartiest voice, which earned her the title "La Heavy," belonged to Yolanda Flores. She had also gone to Sweetwater High School and had graduated a year before me. I identified and gravitated toward women like her and started to acquire my own voice in rap sessions and meetings. If Chicanas saw an injustice or disparity, they would speak out or act on it. I wanted to be one of them.

The Chicano Revolutionary Movement

The voice of the women within and around MEChA at SDSU was heard loud and clear. I had volunteered for cleanup duty, but when I signed up to be one of the guards at the high school conference, I was told that this job was not meant for women (although if someone fired a shot at someone like Cesar Chavez or Dolores Huerta, a female's body could also easily become a shield). I knew that women could be guards and perhaps even guardian angels. Let's switch roles, share the responsibilities, and be equals in organizing, I urged. Wasn't this what we were trying to communicate when we voiced our concerns over discrimination and injustices? The men in the group explained that there was not enough time to educate women to think politically. Were they telling me that women were incapable of being educated politically? I couldn't believe this type of mentality! So I became a student teacher for a political science class in Chicano Studies.

Chicanas in general were somewhat disillusioned by some of the revolutionary concepts inside the Chicano movement at SDSU, and, because of the inequalities, our wheels were spinning. There was a double standard among us; if one of us Chicanas chose to have a relationship with an Anglo man, or with a man of any other nationality, we would be criticized for being a traitor to the Chicano revolutionary movement. But when the men were dating Anglo women this was not to be taken seriously because they were "having fun." This double standard was justified by putting the *Chicanitas* on a pedestal. Supposedly, we were being saved for positions as wives and as the future bearers of the males' legitimized children. We were reprimanded for being outspoken and headstrong. The males called for a revolution that did not include women as equals. This exclusion was limiting Chicanas in the same way "The System" was limiting all Chicanos.

Not all males supported these views, but most remained quiet, smiled, and sometimes chuckled as they watched the spectacle unfold, in a "survival of the fittest" attitude. When a female finally had the floor to propose a valuable idea concerning the political or thematic direction of a conference, this idea would be flopped around until a male regurgitated the same thing. Women who were determined to guide and provide leadership within the Chicano revolutionary movement were viewed from one extreme as loonies who held lighted torches in one hand and a *machete* in the other. There was even a rumor that we Chicanas had a list of all the *machos* we were out to castrate.

This male supremacist attitude tended especially to undermine young Chicanas who were compassionate and wanted to be involved in the movement. In fact, even the word "movement" was used to demean us, and was made to allude to "sexual gyration." This one-sided male movement was great for well-deserved revolutionary party time and getting loaded on booze or drugs. Within this revolutionary movement were some of the most vocal male leaders and older "daddy" allies who gave birth to MEChA. It was those of this kind of narrow mentality within our revolutionary movement who had the most difficulty acknowledging and comprehending women's struggles.

Chicana Power!

We collided with the men with blatant disrespect, and I sang along with Aretha Franklin as she demanded R-E-S-P-E-C-T. In a supreme act of defiance, a woman's caucus was developed from this unfolding spectacle. We were not sure what to do but we were full of Anger with a capital A! F—k! This time we needed female unity. In 1971 we decided to host a seminar for our mothers, so that we could connect with them and share what we had experienced away from home. Most of us possessed about an ounce of rebellion—not enough to disqualify us from college or lose respect for our elders. We safeguarded and treasured this respect for elders inside and outside the classroom to a great extent. We were for the most part obedient daughters whose voices had been silenced at one time by parental authority. We were taught to be "seen and not heard" and although reluctantly we obeyed our parents' wishes, we were somehow also the "different" ones.

We were the daughters who obeyed but didn't blindly accept everything. For most of the Chicanas, attending college was a miracle that was made a reality by the sacrifice of ordinary people. The doors to higher education were opened to us because of educational opportunity grants, work-study programs, and loans. Chicanas wanted and opted for a better life through education. We had not meant to be disrespectful to our parents. We wanted future employment that was unlike theirs, that was better paying and more stable, and had safer working conditions. Yet as the "different" daughters we knew that our pursuit of knowledge was a rebellious act against the constraints of culture, religion, and the world we lived in.

The seminar/conference for our mothers was titled Seminario de Chicanas. We decided to introduce them to a variety of presentations, and *teatro* was amongst these. *¡Teatro!* I became unbridled, running wild with this concept. Finally, this was my chance to be in a play, and it was to be especially dedicated to our mothers.

I was more than ready to focus on this seminar and make mothers aware of our experiences without boring, disappointing, or scaring them away because as young women we had so much to say. Our mothers were more familiar with crying, praying, and singing in church, or so we thought. As their "different" daughters we walked in front of Safeway grocery stores singing *El Picket Sign*, and in our moments of fear we prayed in protest marches against the Vietnam War. We demonstrated on campus against the budget cuts affecting the Educational Opportunity Program, which benefited low-income students. Our cry was for red, brown, white, black, yellow, and green Power. As young women, some of the things we wanted to address were unfair labor practices and the unjust war. But in the midst of this ferment, the Chicanas took time out to reunite with their mothers and to question the *mucho macho* attitude within MEChA.

The *Teatro* Process

¡Híjole! None of us had any idea what it took to produce an *acto,* or play. Felicitas Nuñez had sung songs in Teatro Frontera and was a member of Teatro Mestizo. So she became to a certain extent the unofficial leader while I hung on to my thinking notepad, and I chose to get involved at this time as a writer only. We had to figure out the theme, the message to be presented at the Seminario de Chicanas, although Peggy Garcia preferred calling it the "Mother-Daughter's Tea Conference." We didn't own a teapot between us but we got the drift. We had to control our rage, even though we were angry about *machismo.* It was important to focus on a positive outcome for Chicanas.

We went for the familiar *acto,* a skit with a message that is highlighted by satire, exaggeration, and humor, and when possible embellished with a song. But the more exaggerated we made the *macho* image the more hilarious it became to us, especially because we had to play the male roles. We wondered how ridiculous this would look to the mothers but we hoped they got the point. We collectively brainstormed and made up a list of the ideas that we wanted to convey. Then we divided these ideas into three different scenes, producing an outline of what was to take place in each scene.

Honesty was the hallmark of this *acto.*

Whatever idea, message, or position we took on stage, we wanted it to reflect our reality. Each actor was to use her own words that made her, as the character, most comfortable. This made our voice come through with more clarity when each character was faced with an issue in the *acto.* It also made the play more credible because the actor was using her own vernacular, from "I promise to remain a virgin" to "I will kill myself if I don't go to college."

As the *acto* took shape each actor began to accommodate herself to a specific character. The play seemed to divide itself into three acts. The first scene was about the daughter still at home and conniving her way out. The second scene was about learning on a college campus. And the final scene was about young women in a Chicano student organization. These three scenes were put together as our presentation and called "Chicana Goes to College." So it came to be that the whole process of writing and performing our first play for our mothers was done from start to finish by a group of women in their late teens and early twenties.

Laughter for us signaled a release from tension when we performed at our Seminario de Chicanas, but we also felt our presentation became a success the first instant our mothers started laughing. We weren't sure that we looked or acted ridiculous playing the roles of father and political cultural *macho* characters, but it worked. I knew the *teatro* was a powerful avenue to communication. After the seminar there was an enormous sense of accomplishment and reunion. The mothers stayed and mingled with their daughters, and I felt a yearning in my heart for my *mamacita*. I felt a strong sense of belonging.

In a special way my mother was indeed present. I thought that we as young women demonstrated a love for our origins in a very unique way. As we resolved to continue our goal to improve and educate ourselves, we now knew that our pursuit for knowledge was not a curse, nor a shameful or rebellious act. Our pursuit of knowledge was nothing but our normal consciousness preparing us for the society we lived in. More, we wanted to improve society through our revolutionized minds.

I got hooked on *teatro,* and the next step was to provide relevant entertainment for potential high school recruits into the university. I was on a planning committee to organize the annual high school conference. I practically stood on top of the table to put forth my suggestion and insisted that our *teatro* be accepted as part of the entertainment. We also had to decide on a name, so on the spur of the moment we came up with, Teatro de las Viejas Broncas, which means "Wild Women Theater." I went laughing all the way to the SDSU Council to turn in the paperwork. But this time I was ready to be an actor, and there I was on a stage. Our group moved from a one-time performance to a whole different audience that applauded and cheered us on.

It was as if the group without a clue went from a minipilot to a full-blown program. We settled for the name Teatro de las Chicanas, whose goal, I saw, was nothing less than revolution. Being young and optimistic, I had no doubt revolution in this country would be occurring within my first two years at SDSU. Thomas Jefferson believed that an oppressed people should rebel until their civil rights are fully restored to them. His ideas made a lot of sense to me. At least, my mind was a revolution, and I loved *teatro*. The *teatro* became a propaganda tool for our expression to better the world and a forum to make a difference.

No issue was too small or too big, whether it was education, the war in Vietnam, male supremacy, discrimination, environmental concerns, or local issues. We still wrote as a group, and the *acto* was still written in an outline form. In order to present our ideas and fully understand the political message we were trying to convey we formed a study group. With much effort we would assign reading material regarding the issue agreed on. It would have been easier to be handed a written script that required no thinking or research. But no, I went out of my way to consult with an African American professor from University of California San Diego to make sure our interpretation of Juneteenth, which celebrates the end of slavery in our country, was politically correct. We did our homework on whatever position, idea, or message we had in mind. This meant increasing our efforts to make sure it was the truth and that we understood it in its entirety.

We wanted to be and had to be as flexible as possible, because, lo and behold, change is inevitable. Change was initiated with each performance of a particular piece, when we would adjust and hone it depending on the actors' needs and audience response. We would take turns introducing and ending our presentations. And there was always a question-and-answer period after each play. The audience had an open invitation for questions and discussion about what they saw. This is where our study groups came in handy, because we were armed with the knowledge to defend our position and at the same time we were open to new ideas or suggestions.

Eventually, through suggestive reasoning and trial and error, we did start to write dialogue instead of relying on an outline. These written lines became very helpful when the roles were taken over by a different actor, especially when the lines had to be learned phonetically. Also once these words were written down, then we could edit. Even a typo that was supposed to spell "lives" instead of "livers" was preferred because the liver could serve as a metaphor for the *teatro;* it was the front-line organ that fights a toxic environment. At times we would start out with a ten-minute *acto* and it would end up being a full-length play, evolving in the process like a child. But as actors joined and left, they always had the option of using their own words as long as the message came across. The message was always more important than knowing one's lines verbatim.

I, as always, was drawn and influenced by models of plays, movies, and books with a strong progressive theme. This was more the reason to use written dialogue. We took Bertolt Brecht's play adaptation of the book by Maksim Gorky, *The Mother,* and changed its context from nascent capitalism in early-twentieth-century Russia to contemporary San Diego in the early 70s at the height of North American imperialism. We also adapted a movie depicting the struggles of the Mexican mine workers and their families in New Mexico.

This was one of our most successful presentations. This film, made by blacklisted artists, is titled *Salt of the Earth* and can still be seen on late-night television. Its message about the danger of oppression ruining a community as well as an individual is just as powerful and important today for both males and females.

As the *teatro* grew we began to branch out, and many of our experiences were startling and even funny. In one instance Felicitas set out to drive most of the group to a performance at Cal State Northridge. Hilda and I went in a separate car filled with props, and while we made it to the performance, the rest got lost and never showed. Hilda and I ended up on the stage with the spotlight all to ourselves. We sang along with explanations in between while acting out the different roles and dialogues of each character. We must have looked more like a couple of comedians clowning around on the stage, picking out props, mimicking voices, and distorting our body movements. I say this because the audience was so attentive and laughing in response to our storytelling. And to the amazement of the gracious audience, we completed our dazzling performance.

Another time I was so bedazzled when a couple of representatives from a German radio station were sent out to California. They were pleased to see and hear our contemporary performance of *The Mother*. When I told Felicitas, she asked me if they were FBI agents. I had to laugh. We had heard through the grapevine that FBI informants were growing in number and infiltrating unions and everything else, including student activities. Whether I was gullible or not, and whoever the two men really were, they respectfully assured me that Mr. Brecht would have been proud of our efforts.

At times our efforts to be perfectionists or the times we barely made our schedules would also invite short tempers. If we got angry with each other and exploded right before a performance, this meant extra effort for the actor to play her role onstage. We did have our moments of jealousy, *prima donna* complexes, and ignorance, but we were true to our *teatro*'s message. At times an issue would surface that required spontaneity, like when we got a call from Sandra Gutierrez on an issue that exploded in her hometown in the Coachella Valley. We wrote about the issue, memorized our lines in the car as we drove out to the site, practiced with our partially written dialogue on arrival, and performed. Talk about being troopers!

The Whole Enchilada Process

Our *teatro* performed mostly in southern California close to the Mexican border. I developed some valued lifelong relationships with some of the *teatro* members, a couple of whom were male. Within our *teatro* we shared great moments of kindness for each other. And when Felicitas and I would talk and gaze at the night's canopy of brilliant stars, I knew kindness was reflected everywhere.

Every day with the *teatro* was truly emotional undiscovered territory. The impact of the learning process and the experience for most of us in *teatro* was beyond what we could fathom. In retrospect I see that my childhood and high school years gave me the impression that I was an actor even back then. Clearly, I joined *teatro* to continue being an actor. And I will never cease to be an actor in my lifetime. In *teatro* when I was an actor what became passionately real were my ideas, my positions, and my message. These real passions became my truth, and this is what gave me purpose and a mission in life.

Today I celebrate my life's journey, knowing I've made some big mistakes with grand style. Yet I would probably repeat those same mistakes if given a second chance. But regardless of, and perhaps because of, the different choices and different mishaps in my own life, I've been enormously blessed with the memory of my mother's love. And from this memory, right or wrong, I set out to live my life my way, learning and loving along my path.

The wonderful human beings who have crossed my path are as numerous and as real as my canopy of brilliant stars. I've had the honor of being heard and accepted by my fellow workers in the International Brotherhood of Electrical Workers Union, and by fellow volunteers in community organizations. My family has brought me great joy and pride. I hold dear my international buddies who crossed frontiers to make a difference in the world. The smiling little faces of children at the Tijuana orphanage keep me moving toward a kinder world. I cherish my long life and recent friendships with people coming from multiple nationalities, faiths, and socioeconomic backgrounds, all of whom share their humanity and love.

My earthly journey eventually will end and then my body will disappear and my brain will follow. But the passion, purpose, and rapture of my love will continue as an extension of my life and forever in my imagination.

2

Peggy Garcia

IT SEEMS THAT it's been many years since I have thought about my experiences in the Chicano Movement and especially the las Chicanas *teatro* group. I now reflect on this pivotal time in my life, when I questioned my place in the world and was searching for my independence. Why did I gravitate toward las Chicanas? They were a means of support. They were a collective body from which to learn about the world and the conditions revolving around me.

My wonderful Catholic Mexican-American parents were born here in the United States. They were proud of their Mexican heritage, but never let us forget that we were Americans first. As my father would say, "In this house we speak English." They were, in many ways, typical in their generational wants and desires for their female offspring of Mexican descent—marriage, a good job, or the convent. If any topic came up about the Mexican-American plight, it was in relationship to the farm workers' troubles. Both my parents came from small farming towns, and both worked in factories during part of their adult lives. They spoke of the unfair wages and poor conditions the farm workers had to face on a daily basis. Any participation in other causes was by mainly donating to their Catholic church, and I never saw them take up a picket sign because they considered picketing too radical for them.

When I attended Mesa Junior College in San Diego, California, there were opportunities for me to get involved with the United Farm Workers (UFW) movement, but I often felt I did not want this to consume my life, so I stayed at a distance. Besides, my desire was to travel the world and, at the same time, find ways to pay for college. I transferred to a four-year college in the fall of 1970, where I recall some memorable experiences.

On a beautiful warm day I found myself at San Diego State College. It was a welcoming day for new Educational Opportunity Program (EOP) students, sponsored by Movimiento Estudiantil Chicano de Aztlán (MEChA), which sounded like a militant name. There were so many Mexican-American students there that I almost thought I was in another country. Most of the young adults could speak Spanish and wanted to be identified as *Chicanos*. This title felt uncomfortable to me because I was used to the term *Mexican Americans*, but I had a desire to learn why the title *Chicanos* was so important to them. All who attended seemed genuinely excited about the camaraderie, the food, the music, and especially the enthusiastic guest speakers. The speakers were charismatic and encouraging. One of the speakers who impressed me the most was a very thin-framed beautiful dark-skinned woman. She was wearing crisp blue Levis that fit her tiny body perfectly. She had donned a traditional Mexican blouse, black boots, and no makeup, which only enhanced her natural beauty. Her name was Felicitas Nuñez. She spoke with much conviction and, it seemed to me at the time, with much common sense. I thought perhaps I could learn much from her.

Another strikingly beautiful woman who seemed to be working in the background with Feliz (as we later called her) was a Chicana named Silvia Romero (Chiva). She had raven-black, long straight hair, a small frame, and very exotic features. She kept to herself and took pictures of all the events happening during the conference. The third young woman who appeared to be helping Felicitas was a taller, more native-looking beauty named Delia Ravelo. She was loud at times and had a wonderful, catchy laugh. Her smile was coast-to-coast, and she attempted to make everyone feel welcome. Little did I know that with the support of these three women, I was to learn more about myself, my heritage, and the politics of our time than any college course could ever have taught me.

It was during an orientation for students interested in college that theatrical skits were used to introduce counselors, tutorial services, and even how to use the class schedule and catalogue. This was one of the student activities where I had volunteered my services. The skits incorporated the problems expressed by these first-time college-bound students and showed possible solutions. The first character I portrayed was a helpful Chicano, so I felt a bit more comfortable in this role.

I became more involved with *teatro* as an actor for the seminar we planned for our mothers. I was quite shocked at first that my mother would even consider attending this seminar, but since I called it the Mother-Daughter's Tea Conference this might have facilitated the invitation. Many times I would attempt to ask my mother questions about the new world I was discovering and she would pause and say, "*Ay, hija, no sé.*"[1] I was nervous and excitedly happy that she attended. The conference was a huge success, with a lot of discussion between daughters and mothers and about each other's desires and concerns. Memories of this cherished event will always fill my heart with tearful joy.

Teatro for me was a big part of and very connected to the events and adventures I experienced.

One adventurous trip I remember taking was with Feliz and Chiva. We spontaneously decided to take a break from our studies and go to the San Francisco Bay area. It was party time for us three Chicana women! We took very little money but had big plans to do "this and that." I was the only one of the "Three Stooges" who could drive my Volkswagen bug. Although I was full of excitement, after several hours of driving, I was ready for a break. The only way to get this help was for someone to change driving positions with me while the car was still moving, since my comrades were not skilled in the art of shifting gears.

Well, you guessed it, that's just what we did! As I was speeding northbound on Highway 5, Felicitas climbed over me, her butt in my face! I thank God she had tiny *nalgas* at the time, because I don't think I could have maneuvered under her. Besides being unable to shift gears, her sense of direction was poor, as we found out later. You see, we ended up in Las Vegas, Nevada! Don't ever fall asleep on someone who does not know how to shift and has a poor sense of direction. Leaving Las Vegas, we finally were on the road again, headed for the Golden Gate Bridge.

I believe we were attempting to stay at the local YWCA, but for some reason that I can't remember, it did not work out. For the life of me I don't remember how we ended up in Angela Davis' sister's house, but we did. Angela Davis, of course, was the controversial professor who was a member of the Communist Party U.S.A. What would my mother think? I vividly remember voicing my concern about being in the midst of such militant surroundings. You see, there were also some Black Panther members at the house and lots of communist propaganda about the apartment, and I felt intimidated. Chiva and Felicitas seemed to take everything in stride and reminded me that this could be a learning adventure. Almost as soon as I entered the apartment, I needed to use the bathroom. Feeling a bit nervous, I walked into another room. It was tidy and small and had a beautiful wood floor. On one side of the room a conference-type table was up against a propaganda-filled wall. The table itself had books, papers, and pamphlets stacked on it that, I am sure, were revolutionary in content, but since I had to pee so bad, I had no time to investigate.

As I turned to go out the door, something caught my eye. There on the beautiful wood floor was a long oblong-shaped box with the lid loosely on. On top of this box in big, bold black letters was written "USA Army." I could only imagine what was inside. My heart pounded, and I called for Felicitas in a much-determined manner. She responded immediately, and I exclaimed, "What the hell have you gotten me into!" She, in her famous political manner, explained that we could see this as a learning experience and to understand the conflicts and struggles of the working-class people.

During our less than two-hour stay there, the people of the house were very hospitable and tried to make us feel at home. I just felt scared and at first all I wanted to do was go home. When it was time to leave, I felt a sense of relief, not just because I had finally made it to the bathroom, but because I had come face-to-face with people who believed in their right to bear arms as we as students believed in the right to an education. However, we all believed in our right to freedom of speech. I had to challenge my own Democratic Party ideology along the way. Maybe I would not change, but I sure had a lot of thinking to do.

The next encounter was when I was introduced to Vicky, who was one of Angela Davis' bodyguards. Vicky was light-skinned with thick bronze hair and towered over the three of us. She drove us around the Bay Area, showing us the sights and sharing her bodyguard stories at times with a bellyful of laughter and a beautiful smile. Victoria had a powerful presence and I thought back then, Who would be foolish enough to mess with her shadow? I only found out later that she was a lesbian. This lay heavy on my heart, because my Catholic upbringing had always taught me this was against God and nature.

Yet Vicky was a kind person and did everything to make us feel comfortable. Not once did she push her sexual preference on us. Later Vicky came to visit us in San Diego and attended one of our annual High School Recruiting Conferences. It was funny observing her take out a guy to dance. She commanded in her broken Spanish, "*Tú me gustas. Baile conmigo*,"[2] and the guys danced. I felt so uneasy about many things, but I was learning to make the best of my experiences and to achieve a balance between accepting the rights of the individual and holding on to my family values.

On November 18, 1967, I lost an older brother in the Vietnam War. Our family, I am sure, was like other American families, not wanting a war but willing to fight if it was a just cause. At the time my family, relatives, and friends wanted no part of communism. We were ready to fight against it. Only when I started to attend college did I question my feelings about our involvement in the war in Vietnam. I still don't believe communism is the answer to many of our troubles, but I also have a lot of questions as to the necessity of going to war.

The Chicanas had a chance to go to the Indo-Chinese Women's Conference in Vancouver, Canada, which was held at the University of British Columbia campus to discuss ways to stop the war in Indochina; it took place from April 2 to 4, 1971. I had such mixed feelings about our country's involvement in this seemingly unjust war. The Garcia family had lost a young twenty-one-year-old member, and the pain was still deep. My father was never the same after losing his first-born son. He drowned his sorrows with alcohol and became quite bitter toward God and his country for a long time. The verse in the Bible about "laying your life down for your fellow man" did not seem to comfort my parents much through those first several years after Ray Jr.'s death.

So with a heavy heart, I went to the conference to listen, ask, and share feelings with other women, from another continent, who had also lost loved ones. Felicitas had encouraged us to take notes and possibly put a skit together depicting our government's role in the war and ways to end it. I can remember lots of tears shed by people from both sides of the fence at the closing of the conference. One tiny elderly Asian lady made a lasting remark which was translated to us as, "Please let us do all we can to stop our sons from killing each other. I do not want my leaders to tell my sons to kill your sons. I do not want your leaders to tell your sons to kill my sons." Many tears were shed that day.

Before we attended this conference, a strange and scary event took place that directly involved me. We were running around the Vancouver campus checking it out and meeting other women who had come to this antiwar conference. Most of us were dressed in our usual attire, which consisted of jeans, army shirt, black boots, and, since it was quite cold, a navy pea coat. I had chosen, for whatever reason, to wear a large, white, fake movie-style fur coat. The coat seemed more fitting for a disco scene and not the semi-militant look we normally wore.

We were huddled around each other just chitchatting and laughing when a rather large-framed, long-haired, dark-skinned Chicana approached me. She was dressed very much like the rest of us, and her expression was far from being friendly. She aggressively attacked me verbally, making comments about how phony I was and honing in on my bourgeois style of dress. She felt insulted by the way I was acting. She was loudly lecturing me on how I must not be from the *barrio,* and that this was not party time but a time for action.

I then noticed something silver moving rapidly back and forth near her waist, but not until I heard some loud moans and gasping from the other Chicanas did I realize what she held in her right hand. It was a rather large knife! And I am not talking about a pocket-variety type. She stood directly in front of me, and as she continued to criticize me, I yelled back at her, making comments about her judgmental attitude. As she stepped in closer, I could see she was much taller than I, and when she started waving her weapon of destruction around more, I was thinking I was a goner. She threatened to kick my ass with or without the knife.

Right before she got into my personal space, Felicitas stepped in between us. Now I am all of 5′3″ tall, and Feliz is shorter than I. I made no excuses for myself. Of course, my militant *amiga* Feliz did what she was known for: she educated. She was successful in defusing a volatile situation. This large, rude, militant-looking woman, who let everyone know she was from the *barrio,* was like a sponge listening to what Felicitas had to say. Although I do not recollect what words were actually exchanged, I do know for a fact that most likely I would not be here today if Miss Nuñez had not intervened.

This distant *carnala* never apologized to me. I don't believe we ever exchanged words again at that conference, but through gentle nods of heads and faint smiles, we came to understand each other's place in this time of global and related community issues.

Another trip we took was one that was quite an eye-opener for me. Carlos and Linda LeGerrette, who were loyal UFW organizers, invited some of us Chicanas to travel to Delano, California. This is where the Filipino farm workers first gained political momentum and the Mexican workers joined hands in struggle. Safeway grocery stores were being picketed to boycott table grapes. This was something I wanted to attend. So we went to see what we could see and listen to what we needed to hear. There was a story to tell and a message to expose, and we were going to do this through Teatro de las Chicanas. Felicitas had all of us understand that we were to help out in whatever manner needed by the staff for Dolores Huerta and César Chávez.

Of course all the Chicanos agreed, and they all felt that they could handle any task presented to them. It seemed unusually hot the day we arrived, but we dared not complain too much because we never heard the *campesinos* utter a word of discontent about the climate. They all treated us so well and made us feel like we were special. There was going to be a meeting that we were going to attend, but we first wanted to help the farm workers with their duties. Feliz had met with some of the workers beforehand and had known of some of the jobs that lay ahead. She asked for volunteers, and I agreed to go with her, not knowing what I would be doing.

It did not take long to figure out what my job would be. Felicitas and I walked several yards from the main meeting place. As I walked closer to a building that looked like a very badly chipped cement bungalow, the heavy smell of disinfectant and human feces began to surround me. The odor became more pronounced the closer I got. Feliz did not answer my questions right away, but just kept gesturing to me to come along. The outside of the building had a couple of half-dead–looking trees near the one-door entrance. The exterior was a light gray color, and all around the building there was evidence of needed patching and repair. The dry dirt was hot to the feet, and even when walking gently, you would cause small amounts of dust to fly around.

I found myself coughing from the dust and wanting at the same time to hold my breath from the smell coming from this building. As I entered the mildly dark room, I immediately searched for a light. There was none. I then went to go moisten my lips with water from the nearby sinks. No water flowed from the first faucet I attempted to turn on. The second sink had both faucets broken. The third sink had no hot water handle, and the cold water faucet trickled with minute amounts of water and could not be turned on any further to allow more water to flow. The smell of fecal material by this time was strongly encompassing me no matter what direction I turned.

I felt an urgent need to open a window, but once again there was none to be found. I kept thinking what a poor job someone did in the construction of this bathroom. As I turned to face the direction of the commode where all the smell was coming from, I almost tripped. The uneven, cracked cement floor was the reason why I almost lost my balance. The floor was like this throughout the whole inside of the building. I quickly noticed that there were no doors on the three toilet stalls, but what made me really gasp and take several steps back was what was inside the toilet bowl.

I could not believe my eyes, nor could my nose accept the smell. All the toilets were full of human waste! My first inclination was to complain and attempt to flush this disgusting debris far from my sight and smell. I was wondering where Feliz had slipped away to and couldn't wait to tell her about my discoveries. Then she reappeared, walking toward me but without stopping to listen to me. In fact, she handed me one of the shovels she was holding and a bag, and showed me what to do. I still had to prove to myself that the limited water supply and flushing mechanism were not quite synchronized.

I said, "Felicitas, you have got to be kidding. Do we have to shovel this shit?" She calmly said yes and explained how the farm workers have many labor issues they are trying to address, and one such issue was the unsanitary conditions they live under. I guess I remember my parents sharing a few concerns about this, but I never witnessed this degrading condition firsthand. We continued to talk while cleaning out the commodes and taking the debris to the waiting trucks. All the time I kept thinking that no person should have to live and work under these conditions. I knew somehow that a play would be written to help expose the truth about the conditions many of the migrant farm workers worked and lived under.

The final experience I will address here is a lesson in lack of communication between Gracia Molina Pick, an older respectable community leader and professor, and us as young students. She had been instrumental in getting us to the Canada conference, yet we couldn't grasp the importance of her inviting us to crown Gloria Steinem as an "Honorary Chicana." Chicanas from the neighboring colleges throughout MEChA Central attended this mini-conference at the home of Gracia.

We were going to discuss women's issues and investigate who in the mainstream political arena might be sympathetic toward those issues. One of these issues was abortion. When the *teatro* first started forming, Delia Ravelo had strongly encouraged us to read *Our Bodies, Ourselves* by the Boston Women's Health Book Collective. Most of us agreed with what was written but a few of us objected to the "the right to an abortion" section. I wanted to express my opposition, and as pro choice as Delia was, she encouraged me to voice my concerns.

Gracia's home was located in exquisitely beautiful La Jolla. This was a prestigious and affluent section along the beautiful Pacific coastline. She had small finger foods and drinks available for us, and I was in awe of all the women who did attend. Gloria Steinem was a beautiful woman. She was small framed, taller than most of us. She had absolutely beautiful porcelain skin and long, straight, light brown hair, and she wore no make-up. She wore large tinted glasses, but this did not distract from her wide brown eyes. Her smile was that of a model and it seemed to be perpetual. I'm sure her presentation would have been worthwhile for most of us to hear but we did not hang around for long after Gracia crowned her Honorary Chicana.

I had never heard of this term; unfortunately I was more accustomed to the derogatory labeling that came from *machos*. As I said, we were confused. I remember Feliz standing up, voice a bit cracked, shifting from side to side. We felt we were not consulted and left out of the process of putting this event together, and therefore we did not understand the meaning of the crowning. It was a short to-the-point statement and several of us walked out right after. Gloria's smile broke only to show disappointment. Gracia was more vocal, reminding us of how ungrateful our actions were.

Our action was a big mistake, because we cut ourselves off from a very valuable source. What ignorance to not have requested a meeting between Gracia and those of us who were not clear before this event took place. Boy, did we think we were so militant.

Those of us who walked out gathered around our car to discuss what our next move would be. Teresa Oyos, who was involved intermittently with the *teatro*, suggested we go skinny-dipping at the coves of La Jolla beach. The Chicanas from University of California, San Diego (UCSD) were Maria Blanco, Martha Salinas, and Yolanda Catzalco. Yolanda also did a couple of presentations with the *teatro*. We were all laughing at the suggestion. After much giggling and debating about our reservations concerning this activity, we decided to "go for it." I was raised with the message "It is better to conceal than to reveal," which was playing on my mind as we drove to the site where we would join the great mother, water.

As a group we did so much together, such as classes, travel, fundraising, that it just seemed a little odd that we had so many reservations about this all-women activity. We found a locale where the water appeared fairly calm with tall rocks surrounding three sides. We must have smoked some marijuana before this adventure, because my recollection of our behavior was that we were constantly laughing. We were frustrated about the previous event that had occurred but somehow the laughter, the comradeship, and the soothing ocean water that massaged our naked bodies were healing.

This is the first and only time I have participated in this type of escapade. During our skinny-dipping affair our dialogue went from Chairman Mao, to local MEChA activities and concerns. Oh, what a night! I'm sure thirty years later, if we the original skinny-dipping women would repeat this activity we would not need a chemical agent to make us laugh as far as our naked bodies go. Oh well, gravity does exist.

Along with gravity are the lessons we hope to learn from life. Gracia Molina Pick has forgiven us. We have the privilege to once again embrace Gracia and hear her words of wisdom. Along with gravity, life, and wisdom is death. On November 22, 2002, Delia Ravelo left this valley of tears. Now she rains down to bathe our bodies and fertilize the earth.

In my life, I mostly cherish the deep and lasting relationships with the women who were a support group for each other. I do hope and pray that every woman is blessed with true friends. Proverbs 17:17 states, "A true friend is always loyal." This has been proven to be true between las Chicanas and the women in the *teatro* from its inception. The Chicanas were friends who knew you as you were, understood where you had been, accepted who you became, and still gently invited you to grow.

I am sure there are many more reflections that I could share about Chicanas and the *teatro*. Maybe my memory is on vacation, or maybe I want to keep some things private. The fact is that my reflections make me feel very blessed.

Notes

1. "Oh daughter, I don't know."
2. "I like you. Dance with me."

3

Laura E. Garcia

Who Was the Teatro de las Chicanas?

"*Son unas putas y lesbianas, lo que necesitan es una buena cogida*" (You're a bunch of whores and lesbians. What you need is a good screw). This is what some of our critics would say about the Teatro de las Chicanas. And even my closest friends would ask, "What's a nice girl like you doing with them?"

We were "Chicanas," members of the new breed of *Valentinas* and *Adelitas* of the 1970s. We were young women with revolution brewing in our blood. *¡Simón que sí, ese!* That's right, man, ready to fight any injustice, *a la brava* (at the drop of a hat). We were the first generation of Chicanas who had gotten the opportunity to go to college. Away from home and the watchful eyes of our parents, we shed our cortex of shy and meek *chavalas* and found our identity: Chicanas!

We were *rucas del Valle*—Felicitas, la Chiva, and I were from the Imperial Valley, where tomatoes, lettuce, sugar beets, and cabbage grew in abundance. Sandra, Virginia, Hilda, and Margie were from the sweltering Coachella Valley, with its 100-degree weather that was perfect for the harvesting of table grapes. Kim, Micaela, Angie, Lupe, and Lupita were from the San Joaquin Valley. Then there was la Cubanita, the mulatta girl who spiced up our ensemble, and our sister Delia, the beautiful and gentle Chicanita from Kenosha, Wisconsin.

The Teatro de las Chicanas was the first all-female Chicano theater group of our times. We came from traditional Mexican families, and most of us were raised in one of the agricultural towns in California. We grew up at a time when girls were expected to do "girl things" like make tortillas, cook, wash clothes, and clean house. This was after a day's work picking tomatoes, grapes, strawberries, or whatever was being harvested that season. Our upbringing typified almost every Chicana's upbringing in our generation—whether you lived in Calexico, Brawley, Coachella, Fresno, Gilroy, or Merced. That is, until we began to break the mold.

The Teatro de las Chicanas embodied las Chicanas' rebellion against the one-sided version of the *Virgen de Guadalupe*—meek, submissive, eyes respectfully glued to the ground. With our clamor we hoped to get the other Guadalupe, get her out of the house and into the streets fighting for *La Causa!* That's right, the cause. We wanted to get out the Guadalupe who not only felt our pain, but also stood up, unafraid, ready to speak her mind and stand her ground. This other Guadalupe felt strong because she was fighting for justice and the liberation of *los de abajo*. In our skits we promoted her spirit, the one that galloped on horseback or jumped onto running *vagones* during the 1910 Mexican Revolution.

People say knowledge is power. So we educated ourselves. We not only read about Emiliano Zapata and the *Adelitas* but we also read Friedrich Engels' book *The Origin of the Family, Private Property, and the State,* which, by the way, became a bible to some of us. We learned about the women of color's triple oppression, as women, as workers, and as national minorities. We all participated in discussing the ideas for the *actos*, writing them, rehearsing them, and performing them. Doing so helped us become stronger Chicanas. This acquired knowledge unleashed us like wild horses. Once unleashed, we were bad! We had style! We had the walk, we had the talk, and we felt invincible. We made a statement of our liberation wherever we went. We were always in full force and full gear: tight bell-bottom Levis or straight-leg button-fly Levis; halter tops (and yeah, bra-less), or long embroidered Mexican dresses; *rebozos* and *huaraches* bought in Tijuana, Baja California, or *T.J.*, as we called it.

Our looks reflected our personalities and our moods. Some, like Feliz, Chiva, and Delia, opted for the "natural" look. Mind you, "natural" is in quotations because in one of our *teatro* tours, one of the *rucas*—and I won't mention who—hauled along a bag full of lotions and creams, lip gloss, nail polish remover, and nail polish she used to acquire her "natural" look. Others like

Margie and Micaela preferred the *chola* urban look. Margie was the master blaster. She would spend hours for the look: pencil-thin eyebrows, white eye shadow, Betty Boop false eyelashes, and for a final touch, layer after layer of black mascara. These girls looked great! Then there were the wannabes like me, who preferred the *chola* look. But no matter how hard I tried, I couldn't get my Chinese eyes to match theirs. So I went *á la naturelle.*

El Picket Sign . . . War, What Is It Good For?

Songs like "El Picket Sign" and Marvin Gaye's "What's Going On" signified our times.

El picket sign, *el* picket sign *lo llevo toda la vida,*
[The picket sign, the picket sign, I'll carry it all my life]
El picket sign, *el* picket sign *conmigo toda la vida . . .*
[The picket sign, the picket sign with me all my life]

Okay, this is the Chicano version.

War, What Is It Good For? Absolutely nothing . . . mmm, Say It Again

The early seventies were years of social turmoil and a time when new ideas sprouted up to challenge old ideas. My generation took to the streets—the chants of "Black Power!" "Brown Power!" "Yellow Power!" "Red Power!" "Free love and Peace!" roared through the university campuses, shaking the foundations of all existing institutions of government, church, and family.

¡Símon que sí, ese! That's right man. We were proud of our *abuelitos* who wore *huaraches* and our *abuelitas* with their *rebozos.* Of course we later learned that some of the things we called "culture" our parents called "poverty." We were proud to have been raised eating tortillas, beans, and *chiles jalapeños.* Yes, the *campesinos* needed a union too. It was about time, don't you think? Most of us knew what it was to strain our backs picking tomatoes, grapes, or whatever other vegetable or fruit people put on their table. So yeah, the idea of a United Farm Workers union was all right with us. As for the equality of the sexes, it was a given. Maybe the Chicanas spoke more heatedly about our rights, but some of the *batos,* our young men, did too. Like my *abuelita* used to say, "*A empujones y a jalones.*" Pulling and pushing them, but the men would follow.

I was a prime candidate for *la causa.* Even at home I had begun questioning the way things were. The sixties were the years when cities like Chicago and

Detroit were up in flames, not to mention the Watts Riots in Los Angeles. For the first time in U.S. history television brought to our living rooms the drama being played out in the streets of our country. Once after seeing the news and seeing the images of angry blacks on the screen, I asked my stepfather, "Why are the blacks so angry?" He looked at me and said, "If you had suffered the injustices they had, wouldn't you be angry?"

The *teatros* used the street-theater form, most popular in Latin America. We also used Spanglish, a mix of the English and Spanish languages, which reflected our culture. We were youths of mixed cultures caught in the middle and claimed by neither culture—neither American nor Mexican. We created our own distinct culture, a distillation of the two. There were three ingredients that gave birth to the Chicano movement in the late 1960s and into the 1970s: First, the civil rights movement of the blacks, which inspired us Chicanos and gave us renewed hope that we could and must make change. Second, the green body-bags carrying our dead brothers, cousins, and uncles that were arriving daily from Vietnam. Last, President Johnson's "War on Poverty," which enabled poor students to have access to higher education. These three ingredients, mixed with a legacy of social repression, made the young Chicanos on college campuses fertile ground in which new ideas of liberation could germinate and take hold.

The Vietnam War was a defining factor for me. I can't deny that I had first swallowed the lies and believed we were fighting for the ideals of democracy. Yet as the body-bags started coming home I began to question, like so many others, the values and morals of a country that was fighting for democracy abroad and yet was poisoned by racism and prejudice at home. Yeah, somehow their democracy did not ring so true.

In October 1969, when I was sixteen years old, I moved from Brawley to San Diego. I came to attend the High School Equivalency Program (HEP) in San Diego State University (SDSU). The aim of HEP was to assist children of migrant farm workers who had dropped out of high school. The HEP student was taken to the college campus and sat in classes to attain the General Education Degree (GED). The hope was that the students would then enroll in college classes. All room and board expenses were provided—and to top it off, we were given a weekly stipend of ten dollars. Who could refuse?

I found out about HEP through my sister, who had left home the year before. The two requirements for HEP were that applicants be from farm worker families and that they be high school dropouts. I met the first requirement, but to meet the second requirement I dropped out of school the first month of my sophomore year. It hurt to drop out of school. I had been an honor roll student since the fourth grade, only a year after coming to this country from Mexico. In fact in seventh grade I had the honor of attending a luncheon sponsored by the Lion's Club for all "straight A" students. My picture together with those of eight or nine other students appeared in the Brawley newspaper. Though my parents didn't make a big fuss over me, I knew they were very proud. My stepfather gave my mother some money to buy material and make me a dress and to buy a new pair of shoes for the occasion.

Many years later my mother gave me a box with all my school papers, Valentines I had received, the pink honor roll cards I got, report cards, and, yes, a yellowed newspaper photo memorializing that event in my life. Let me provide a bit of context. That was a triumphant moment for me; I was fourteen years old and I had only been here in this country three years. You cannot imagine the humiliation and embarrassment I had gone through in those three years. When I came to the United States from Mexico I was eleven years old. I was a very cocky young girl, though very shy. My cockiness and bravado came from doing very well in school and getting good grades in Mexico. I was also the youngest in my class and because of that I was used to getting a lot of attention from my teacher and my classmates. When I started school here I did get a lot of attention but for the opposite reasons. I was the oldest in all my classes and I didn't speak English.

Because I didn't know English I was put in third grade. It was a common practice at the time to put Spanish-speaking children behind two or three grades. This was a humbling and humiliating experience. I felt like screaming, "I'm not dumb, I just can't speak English."

It wasn't easy to be the laughingstock of your class just because you didn't know English. I would wait until I couldn't hold it any longer to ask for the simplest things such as going to the bathroom, because I knew the other kids would end up laughing at me. My third-grade teacher was a nice woman; it would pain her to see my embarrassment, so she would forever be telling my classmates to "hush."

Other teachers were not as nice. Once in recess I was speaking Spanish to the only girl in my class who spoke Spanish. A teacher supervising the school ground turned to me and sternly said, "English! English!" and grabbed my arm and hauled me to a nearby tree and told me to stand there until the end of the recess.

But my worst year was seventh grade. I was the class representative for one semester. This was not an elected position. It automatically came to you when you got straight A's. My teacher would sometimes tell the class that he couldn't believe I was an honor roll student with my limited English.

Once we were given an assignment to do a speech in front of the class. When the teacher called my name I hesitantly stood up. The topic I chose was the history of Mexico. I desperately held on to my cards and stammered painfully through my speech at a speed that would have been difficult to understand even if I spoke perfect English. I finally ended and rushed to my seat. Then I heard the teacher call on one of my classmates, "Yeah, Joe, what is it?" With a devilish smile Joe said innocently, "Mr. Johnson, I didn't understand a word she said." I glared at Joe, but I never imagined what came next. "Laura, go to the front of the class and give your speech again." I wanted to run and hide. I looked at my teacher pleadingly. But by his look I knew he wouldn't budge. Angry tears were burning my eyes. I passed by the door and hesitated; it would have been so easy to leave. So, I turned and looked at the class, particularly Joe and Mr. Johnson. I began my speech, this time more slowly and deliberately. As I finished the bell rang, and I ran out of the class. It was then that I promised myself that no one was going to break me, no one.

When I left home and went to the HEP that was located on the campus of SDSU, my mother didn't say much. Brawley's population was made up of ranchers and farm workers, and those who serviced them. The majority were farm workers who toiled in this desertlike valley that was made fertile by modern water irrigation. My mother and I knew that Brawley, a desert town twenty miles from the Mexico/U.S. border, with a population of a few thousand, didn't have much to offer to its youth. If I was lucky I would get a job at one of the dime stores lining Main Street (which was two blocks long), such as Ben Franklin or Newberry's. At worst, I would end up working in the fields surrounding the outskirts of Brawley. Unemployment and illegal drug use are rampant; many young males experience both. And many, many more females get pregnant by or before the age of fifteen. No, I would tell myself, I had to get out. I had to go out into the world and see what the world had to offer and what I had to offer the world. Some might say I had been watching too many *novelas*. But I knew there was something in me that genuinely sought a better, more fulfilling life.

It didn't take long for me to join the Chicano Movement in earnest in 1969. How do you join a movement? Well, it was easy then because of the times. This was a time of the civil rights and national liberation movements. These movements took physical form in Cesar Chavez and the farm workers of California who were organizing and fighting for a union. We weren't just fighting against something, be it racism and prejudice or repression and exploitation, we were fighting for something: the right of farm workers to unionize, civil rights, and equality. It was for union rights and better working conditions for the farm workers. There were protests, marches, meetings, and conferences almost every day of the week it seemed. HEP students were the foot soldiers of the Chicano Movement at SDSU. Any organizer—whether of a protest at the Tijuana/San Ysidro border, the UFW grape boycott, or a demonstration against the governor of California (then Ronald Reagan)—knew that all he or she had to do was to provide transportation and the HEP students would jump on the bus. "*El* picket sign, *el* picket sign *conmigo toda la vida....*"

These were the times when at practically every university and college campus in California, Arizona, Colorado, New Mexico, and Texas where there were Chicanos there was a *teatro* or a *ballet folklórico,* or both. As Yolanda Broyles-González explains in her book, *El Teatro Campesino: Theater in the Chicano Movement,* the *teatros* were the medium Chicanas and Chicanos used to speak their piece and educate *la raza.* TENAZ (Teatros Nacionales de Aztlán) was formed in 1971, and it linked the *teatros* together into a network. At TENAZ's helm were the Teatro Campesino members, particularly Luis Valdez. Teatro Campesino for the most part wrote the *actos* that the other *teatros* in the Southwest performed. The *teatros* used the street-theater form, most popular throughout Latin America, but which had roots in other theater traditions, including Italy's *commedia dell'arte.*

At SDSU a number of Chicano and Chicana students established Teatro Mestizo and Teatro de las Chicanas. I joined Teatro Mestizo in 1971. The skits (or *actos*) Teatro Mestizo performed were progressive for the time, such as *No Saco Nada de la Escuela,* a skit about the racist educational system. *Los Agachados* is a story about an immigrant couple forced to cross the border and endure injustices in the hands of the ranchers. *Soldado Razo* is an anti–Vietnam War skit about grunt soldiers. My cry in that skit—"*¡Mi hijo!*"—as the dead soldier's mother was so convincing that it brought tears to everyone's eyes. I knew it wasn't my acting that brought out the tears, but that the skit hit home with so many people. Many of our young Chicanos were being killed in Vietnam. Chicanos represented over 20 percent of the casualties of the war, though we were 6 percent of the U.S. population.

Teatro à la *Chicana*

Yet as good as the *actos* we performed in Teatro Mestizo were, they still portrayed women in the traditional roles of "*no sabe nada*" girls—girls who didn't know anything. So when Felicitas approached Lupe and me to join the Teatro de Las Chicanas, neither of us hesitated. The idea of an all-Chicana theater group to deal with the *machismo* we encountered and assert our place in the social revolution caught on like prairie fire.

I had met these Chicanas soon after I got to SDSU, though some of them were already in their junior or senior year of college and I was just getting my GED. The Chicanos and Chicanas on campus immediately took the HEP students under their wings. We were invited to meetings, protests, and marches. Some of us joined MEChA, the Chicano student organization, while others joined the Brown Berets and the UFW Support Committee on campus. But it wasn't until the Seminario de Chicanas we gave for our mothers in 1971 that I became seriously committed to the Chicanas' ideals of equality and class struggle.

The *seminario* was organized by the Chicanas for our mothers. Unfortunately, my mother couldn't come because of work. Through songs, plays, and dance we opened our hearts to our mothers and related our experiences in college, and how and why we had become Chicanas! (The term *Chicano/a* was not a very popular one with my parents' generation; they preferred either Mexican or Mexican American). As I sat there cross-legged on the floor, listening to the presentations, watching as a group of Chicanas whirled by in black leotards and tights and flaming colorful capes and saw the *acto Chicana Goes to College*, it began to sink in what we were about. I was then eighteen years old.

It wasn't long after the *seminario* that the Chicanas formed the Teatro de las Chicanas. At the first meeting I remember attending Delia Ravelo, Maria D. Roman, Peggy, Feliz, Gloria Bartlett, Lupe Perez, and Yolanda were there. The next school year brought us Virginia, Sandra, Clara, Kim, Micaela, Lupita, and Angie, while Gloria Bartlett, Maria D. Roman, Peggy, and Yolanda left. The year after brought us Margie, Hilda, and Cubanita, and then Kim, Micaela, Clara, and Angie left. That's how the cycle went: each school year would bring in a new crop of Chicanas, as some of the others left because they had either graduated, married, had kids, or dropped out. September was our harvest month. It was the month we harvested new Chicanitas into the *teatro*.

Chicanas would join the *teatro* not because their calling was acting (though for some it was), but because the *teatro* fit us, and this is where we felt welcomed and found camaraderie with our *carnalas*—our sisters. I know it fit me.

I was that Chicana who, when she ventured to speak, spoke in a lingo of broken English and Spanish. Although a U.S. citizen (my mother was born in the United States before my grandparents were deported in the 1930s), I had been in the United States only for about six years. So the *teatro* was a safe place to begin breaking my silence and finding my voice. It was the same for everyone; we dared to speak out not as la Lupe, la Feliz, or la Chinita (as they sometimes called me), but as women who were fighting for las Chicanas, for something bigger than ourselves: justice and equality. I knew that because

I was a member of the Teatro de las Chicanas people might not like me, but they respected me. They knew that behind me or with me stood my *carnalas.*

I joined the *teatro* in 1971, my freshman year. This was also the year that I found out about my grandfather's sexual advances in the family. After that revelation it was like someone had shined a spotlight on a dark and hidden place where my brain had stored his sexual advances toward me. All of a sudden his grandfatherly caresses made me feel dirty and betrayed. He was the person who my mother had trusted with our care while she worked in the United States.

I felt shattered. To ease the pain of his betrayal I began drinking; Jose Cuervo became a "good friend of mine," and reds (downers) became my daily regimen for a while. They all gave me an "I don't give a fuck" attitude. They didn't relieve my hurt. Why am I now revealing something so painful? Because in life we all experience moments of betrayal and tragedy that make us vulnerable. At these moments some of us might fall prey to drugs or alcohol or some other suicidal behavior. So we need to know what can pull us out of self-destruction. For me it was fighting for the ideals we Chicanas were fighting for—equality, not only for my gender but for my class.

Later, much later, I found out that at least one-third of the *teatro* members had been physically and sexually abused by a family member, a neighbor, a friend. What's sadly ironic is that the violation of what's most sacred to the human spirit (of a man or a woman) is in most cases covered up, especially back then, barely at the beginning of the women's revolution. In the *teatro,* though we didn't always openly talk about it, we gave each other strength and encouragement in whatever way we could.

For example, Cubanita (she really is Cuban like her name says) had a caring disposition. Cubanita couldn't stand seeing any of us quiet or withdrawn. She would come up to any of us when we looked down and would say, *"No estes triste, sonrie"*—don't be sad, smile. If this failed, she would start poking you in your side, until you couldn't help but to break into a smile, feeling warm inside knowing that she cared.

People either loved us or hated us. And it wasn't just our performing style like they used to tell us. We knew it was our politics, since in our *actos* we spoke against the cultural nationalism that prevented the working class from uniting, and for class unity. What gave us the idea we could act? Nothing and no one; on the contrary, almost everyone said we were bad actors. But we couldn't care less. On the contrary it only made us more defiant. We had something to say, and we were going to say it, no matter how we said it. *¡Ya basta!* Enough with being put down by the *batos*—by men! Enough with the Vietnam

War! Enough with the horrible working conditions in the fields! Enough with racism! We knew that if we didn't speak we were going to *reventar.* Yes, explode. There was a cry surging from the darkest corner of our souls, our *almas,* threatening to bust us open, like watermelons dropped onto the pavement.

In our own ways we were all struggling to rip off the gag that muffled our cries against the rape our spirits had suffered either by the hunger pangs of poverty or by the sexual and physical abuse we had endured. The *teatro* helped us channel our anger and restlessness. It was the battering ram we used to knock down the walls of our silence. It helped us find our voice, and we intuitively knew that once we had our voice we were closer to our liberation.

We all performed and sang in the *teatro.* Some of us also contributed in other ways. Delia loved literature. Delia's trademark at that time was a *rebozo* and her shining long dark hair. She was one of the principals in writing our *actos* and coming up with ideas, though we all participated in one way or another, since the *actos* were a collective effort. She introduced us to Bertolt Brecht's adaptation Gorky's *The Mother.*

Lupe was from Fresno, and she was the *teatro*'s treasurer. She was in charge of turning the *teatro*'s plans into reality by submitting proposals for funding to the student body and raising money. With this modest financial support we toured several campuses in California. One time we even went to Salt Lake City, Utah, where we were videotaped for the University of Salt Lake City archives.

Then there was Sandra, who I met in biology class. Her family came from Pancho Villa's state of Chihuahua, although she was born in Coachella. She was one of the *teatro* members who, at seventeen, had the body of a full-grown woman—breasts stretching out through her T-shirt, and wide round hips. Ironically she almost always played the role of a *bato* in the play *The Mother.* What Sandra added to the *teatro* was her open and frank way. Sandra was the type who stood tall and didn't seem to know how to lower her eyes in meekness. *¡Que chingona la Sandra!*[1]

Felicitas was the driving force behind the *teatro,* but her leadership was different from that of the "political heavies" who told us what to do. Felicitas relied heavily on the group deciding what needed to be done. She pushed us to take on responsibilities that we wanted to do but we thought we couldn't. For example, MEChA was organizing and sponsoring a high school student conference in 1973. Out of the blue, she told me, "China, I think you should be the chair of the organizing committee." "Me?" I choked on the words, "No way," I said. "Yes way," she responded. I don't have to tell you who won.

At this student conference we performed our *acto Chicana Goes to College,* the same *acto* that we performed for our mothers at the *seminario*. I was playing the role of Teresa's daughter. This was the first time I had ever performed and my legs were shaking. I told Teresa this, and she told me I would be okay. And I was. But if she hadn't held my hands so tightly throughout the play, I don't think I would have made it.

This *acto* portrayed women breaking the stereotypical female role. We used satire to make our point by poking fun at the guys for their *machismo*. But this *acto* was also a challenge to everyone speaking revolution because one thing is the talk and another the walk. One thing was saying we had the same rights as the *batos;* the other thing was to believe it. We had to break the pattern of the *batos* doing security and the *rucas* (the women) doing the food. We had to break the pattern of the *batos* being the chairpersons for this and that committee, and the *rucas* being the secretaries. Do you get my drift?

It was that same year that we wrote our most infamous *acto* and a real favorite of mine. This *acto* definitely put us on the scene as a *teatro* fighting against *machismo* and for revolution. This was *Bronca*, with its chorus "*BroncaBronCabrónCabrón.*" What is *bronca?* "Let's duke it out" or "wrangle." What is *cabrón?* It has so many definitions, including "motherfucker," "goat," or "asshole," depending on the deed. When you say these two words together at a quick pace, the two words run into each other and *bronca* changes to *cabrón*. Pretty clever, huh? Well, at least we thought so. Some thought we were a bunch of *malcriadas*. Just plain rude!

I loved the costume for this *acto*. We dressed all in black—black turtleneck, black trousers, black boots. When this *acto* was performed in an indoor auditorium with stage lights, it was very powerful. To set the mood, seconds before we appeared the auditorium lights would go off. Then, with all eyes on the stage, the lights would be turned on gradually, as we streamed in one by one: right foot crossing over the left one, left foot stepping sideways to the left. We would be snapping our fingers to set the tempo, whispering in chorus *broncabroncabroncabronca*, gradually raising our voices from a whisper to a crescendo. *¡CABRÓN!* We would strike a pose and freeze. Then one at a time we would break our pose and speak our piece. My role in this *acto* was *conciencia*—consciousness. I still remember my lines. Lights on me, stepping forward I would start:

[Serious face, looking at the audience I would start in a somber voice.]

Carnales, the *machismo* hurts man and woman alike.

[Raising a fist I would look to the right.]

The *machismo* is a tool of the oppressor.

[Looking to the left I would say]

We know that men are not our enemy.
The oppressor is!

[Pleading voice, hands reaching out.]

Brothers, unite with your sisters to fight the oppressor.

[Raising voice a pitch or two.]

Down with the *machismo*!
Brothers, unite with your sisters to fight the oppressor.
We are both members of the same class: the working class!

[Fist up!]

Only by women and men uniting as equals can we attain the liberation of our class!

[Hands extended, looking at the audience.]

[At the end of each actor's speech we would whisper, staring from side to side as if looking for that cabrón.]

Broncabroncabroncabronca broncabroncabroncabronca

Do you think the *batos* would hear our message? Shit, no! Most had the opinion that what we needed was a good fuck. Of course, maybe our doctrinaire drill tone didn't help any or us calling them assholes. Yet our message was like opening up a version of Pandora's box. Once said, it couldn't be put back.

When we finished each performance we took the opportunity to recruit new members to the *teatro*. This was how Angie, Micaela, and Kim joined. They were second-wave Chicanas and while most of us spoke Spanish, these girls spoke *nada*. At least Virginia and Clara spoke *mocho*, broken Spanish, but they spoke none. It was also a time to clarify the points in the *acto*. "No, we weren't against the men. No, we know men are not our enemies. No. . . ."

But the ones who were really on the hot seat were our *jainos*—our boyfriends. They had to explain why they were with Chicanas like us! To their credit they would stand by us. After all, they were revolutionary men of the times. I sometimes could hear my babe explaining our performances, "Man, you don't understand, you're not listening to what they're saying. All they're saying is that there has to be equality. No more bullshit of the guys being the heavies in MEChA and them being the secretaries," although on our way back from the performance, he would get on my case for being so damn confrontational.

As we came to understand Marxist analysis more, our plays began reflecting this, and we moved from just being against the *machismo* to being for the working class. For example, we rewrote the play *The Mother* in Chicana style. This play is about the political growth of a woman in Czarist Russia in 1905. Her son, Pablo, was killed by the Czar's soldiers for passing out leaflets urging the workers to organize against the working conditions. After his death the mother commits herself to the struggle and continues her son's revolutionary work. She uses her ingenuity and uses the leaflets to wrap the tamales she's selling at the factory gate. *"Ándale, cómpreme unos tamalitos"*[2] (I would say it in the singsong voice I heard from a *tamalera* seller in Mexicali where I grew up). Then under my breath I would whisper, "Don't throw the wrapper away, *muchacho,* read what it says. Strike!"

In *The Mother* the song we sang for the son's funeral was the Che Guevara song *El Revolucionario.* I loved to sing this song, although I couldn't carry a tune (and I wasn't the only one). This song inspired me to continue in the struggle in spite of whatever difficulties I went through. For there was no greater tribute than to die *por la causa*! I still remember some of the words:

Comandante Che Guevara, tu muerte no ha sido en vano.
El fusil que tu llevaste ya lo llevo aquí en mi mano.
Yo quiero que a mí me entierren como revolucionario.
Envuelto en bandera roja y con mi fusil al lado.

Commander Che Guevara, your death has not been in vain.
The weapon you once carried, now I have it in my hand.
I want to be buried like a revolutionary,
Wrapped in a red flag with my weapon at my side.

What the *Teatro* Meant to Me

The *teatro* bonded us. We got so much nourishment from each other that some of us became almost inseparable, particularly when it was party time. Parties, *parrandas,* were for the most part held in someone's dormitory room, at someone's house, or at the Centro Cultural in Balboa Park. After a few *cheveres* and *toques de mota* we were ready for anything and everything. At times we would get so loud that we bordered on becoming obnoxious. This was Delia Ravelo's doing. She riled us up with her *grito*, "*¡Que vivan las Chicanas!*" We would roar back, "*¡Que vivan!*" *Esa Delia.*[3] Mind you, not all the *teatro* members would hang out together. There were the ones who had boyfriends, and they were "busy" ever since we had discovered the birth-control pill. But the rest of us were, in the main, loose and on the prowl. We would strut our stuff with pride, "Didn't I tell you we were bad?"

Yet, near dawn, when the party was about to break, you would find la Feliz in one of the rooms strumming a guitar and singing, *La Llorona.*

Todos me dicen el negro, Llorona, negro pero cariñoso,
Todos me dicen el negro, Llorona, negro pero cariñoso.
Hermoso huipil lucías, Llorona, cuando del templo salías,
Ay de mi Llorona, Llorona de azul celeste.

Everyone calls me the dark one, Llorona, the dark one but the affectionate one,
Everyone calls me the dark one, Llorona, the dark one but the affectionate one,
You wore a beautiful *huipil*, Llorona, when you exited the temple,
Woe, my Llorona, Llorona of celestial blue.

Once I heard this wistful song, I knew that the curtain was about to close our night's performance. The sorrowful lament in her voice would draw us together like a magnet. No matter what I was doing or where I was at the time, once I heard the sound of her voice singing *La Llorona,* I would follow it, only to find the others there amid the shadows of the room. I would look at my *carnalas;* before the world we stood, as fragile as dry leaves, young women barely in our twenties. This was the other side of these bad, brave girls.

Tears would wash off the grime of old, caked makeup, eroding away our masks of bad girls. We would all stand there in silence, *carnales* and *carnalas,* listening, trying to shake off the memory of past heartaches and humiliation. How do you erase the fact that your gender is the unwanted one, that because of your position in society you have only been good for a fuck, a slap on the face, or as an animal of burden?

Our spell was broken and released to a higher level by the deviant snapping of our fingers as we sang *picarosamente* (mischievously), "Hit the road, Jack, and don't you come back no more, no more . . ." We would roar with laughter, singing at the top of our lungs and shouting out the pain in our broken hearts, yet confident that we would have liberation. Yeah, hit the road, Jack, and don't you come back no more.

As I look back at the years I spent in the *teatro*, I must say they were the most defining years of my life. These *carnalas* changed me. In their company I cast aside my shell of a meek, *no sabe nada* girl, and became a *revolucionaria*. The metamorphosis was almost magical: gone was the shy girl—I had become an *Adelita*, a revolutionary woman like my counterparts in the 1910 Mexican Revolution.

Nurtured by my sisters, I gathered strength and courage. I left the *teatro* in 1975, but not the love of my *comadres*. It is their collective strength and love that I carry with me today. It has given us the confidence that, this time too, we will survive, as we bend over to pick up the pieces of failed relationships, endure the loss of loved ones, or fight for a brighter future.

In the *teatro* we discovered that we are eagles able to fly high in the sky, though at times we have been forced to walk. But, yes, we know that when we take to the skies, spreading our wings, with the wind caressing our faces, "O world, beware, behold the sight of *las que sí saben*—the ones that do know."

Notes

1. Sandra is so tough!
2. Come on, buy some little tamales from me.
3. "Long may they live!" That Delia.

4

Gloria Bartlett Heredia

I'M FROM CALEXICO, a border town in the hot and harsh desert of California's Imperial Valley. I started college in the late 1960s, at a time when there were very few Chicanas at San Diego State College (SDSC). (A few years after I enrolled, the name was changed to San Diego State University.) I was one of the minorities in all senses of the word, though I was well assimilated and I studied diligently.

There were five of us children when my mother died at thirty-seven years of age, and our father was not present in our lives. Mexican women who were my great maternal aunts brought me up. They were relatively young for having children who had children; they were barely in their fifties. But their thinking was old—very traditional. They were from the old school, and that was the lifestyle I absorbed. I could relate to Latino culture, and this is what Teatro de las Chicanas had a lot of: culture, music, dancing, and plenty of parties.

Frankly, I got involved in the *teatro* because I thought it would be fun. I liked doing *teatro* because as a young girl I was very shy and even in college I was shy. *Teatro* helped me overcome that shyness. But I liked being around people who were boisterous and spoke their minds. Maybe it was because I wasn't like that that I was attracted to these women who voiced what they were thinking. I do believe that as a group, as women, we were tired of being put down, of being treated as "less than." I felt that I didn't want to be like my mom, yet I did like a lot of her values. I did want to be more educated.

I wanted to be more independent. I did not want a man to provide for my food and shelter. And if I didn't have a man to support me I still could make it on my own. All of us in the *teatro* group felt this way. We didn't want to be under someone else's power. In the Mexican culture the women overtly don't make many decisions for the family. Well, that was certainly true in my family.

At first at SDSC it seemed things were going to be the same way—women were not the decision makers. For instance, in MEChA, the student organization, we were always the helpers—helping the guys to be successful at the conferences. I didn't mind doing this entirely because I am a helper. I'm not the person who necessarily relishes the limelight. The women involved in the *teatro* knew that we needed to change things. We needed to set an example for the younger Chicanas coming to college. We wanted to say to the younger Chicanas, "It's great that you are in college, stay in college, you can do it; you can be successful, and you don't always need a man for this." So our *teatro* was one way to communicate a need for change.

In the *teatro* I liked playing the roles of characters who were different from me. After all, isn't part of the essence of acting becoming something you are not? I once played the role of a male racist teacher. I think the girls must have picked me for the character because of my blue eyes and light brown hair. In the *acto* the racist teacher would correct Mexican students in a way that belittled and embarrassed them in the classroom. I would also make degrading sexual remarks to the female students. Of course, we exaggerated the characters a lot to get the point across. Through our *actos* we revealed how we were made to feel like second-class citizens in the United States.

It was fun performing, going to Tijuana and other places and seeing people's reaction to our skits. They were so surprised and curious. After our *actos* people would ask questions and we exchanged ideas. The *teatro* was almost like a family and we usually had a good time wherever we went and in whatever we did, including rehearsals. I don't know how I found time because I was still completing my postgraduate studies and working on my teaching credentials. But it was easy to keep my involvement in the *teatro*. My boyfriend at the time was a friend of the men who hung out with the women in the *teatro*. I was also rooming with some of the other *teatro* women.

I attribute who I am today to my college experience, and a big part of that was my work with the *teatro*. I'm a college counselor and have been working at San Diego City College for thirty years. I have taught classes on personal growth, but my major occupation has been in academic counseling. I assist students who are transferring from a two-year to a four-year school. For a lot of my students community college has been like a stepping stone from the *barrio,* looking for a life outside of drugs or, alcoholism, or just a different overall lifestyle.

Today, as I look back, I see that we Chicanas/Chicanos accomplished some rather remarkable things. We have made a difference as a result of our endeavors in the social movement. Today there are Latina doctors, for example. This is wonderful! I met a Mexican woman from East L.A. who was a cosmetologist, was married, and had two kids. I was awed by her determination to become a doctor.

Back in Calexico there has been some research that shows that 80 percent of Latino students who graduate from high school there end up going to college. This percentage is just as high as it is in Beverly Hills. One reason for this is that in Calexico there are many Mexican teachers who live in the community. They know the parents and grandparents of the students. The teachers know where these students are coming from and what they are going through because these teachers have been there. It's been really phenomenal what has happened in Calexico as far as the community is concerned. It used to be that Calexico had only white mayors, and recently there have been Mexican mayors and other elected officials. The face of politics has changed since I went to school.

The *teatro* experience has also helped me deal with my shyness. I remember there were a lot of people present in the activities we got involved in. On one occasion a group from Mexico City, Los Mascarones, were there. They were a very professional theater company and had an international reputation. Seeing them perform was so intimidating to me! But now, because I've addressed big crowds before, the fear of speaking to big groups is lessened. If I could perform in front of Los Mascarones back then, I can overcome my fear of speaking out now.

In particular, the *teatro* experience helped me in working with people. In the *teatro* we all worked well together, although there were occasional clashes. For a while when I first started working we had a women's group. This was positive, especially for the younger women, who were kind of lost in a college environment, as I was when I first started at San Diego State College. Through the *teatro* I've become who I am.

5

Teresa Oyos

Las Chingonas

We were *morenas . . . como la tierra*[1]
We were *güeras . . .*
like the color of wheat which nourishes us . . .
A few of us were tall and slender, like the lofty eucalyptus trees . . .
Most of us were closer to the ground . . .
Some of us were beautifully full and Rubenesque . . .
Some of us were petite and compact for easy travel.

We all learned to speak up and use our voices,
¡Que viva la Raza! . . . ¡Que viva la Chicana! . . .
We carried picket signs at Safeway,
Boycott lettuce!!!! Boycott grapes!!! Boycott Safeway!!!
We demonstrated to get Chicano Studies at UCSD, SDSU, and San Diego City College . . .

We took our *madrecitas* to Tijuana for lunch,
My Nana never forgot that Mother's Day . . .

She enjoyed talking to Henri Chavez' mom and for years after would ask for
"*La Señora*" . . .

We traveled all the way up the breathtaking West Coast to Vancouver,
Canada . . .
Felicitas sang *La Llorona* while we ate whole-wheat tortillas in the back of the
van . . .
Híjole . . . so many wonderful women were at the Third World Women's
Conference.

We were forever changed by listening to our Vietnamese sisters,
Who had traveled so far to share their excruciating stories . . .

Peggy and I were afraid to go into the bathroom
Because there was a gang of big ole' lesbians and they might try
something . . .
I was sooooo curious and terrified of myself and my undiscovered attraction
toward *mujeres* . . .

Nos dejamos caller las greñas[2] en "El Teatro de las Chingonas" . . .
I mean "Teatro de las Chicanas" . . .
We were baaaaad . . . we had *ovarios* (ovaries)
We comforted one another, *con abrazos de* encouragement . . .

We had meetings and more meetings. We agreed and disagreed . . .
Platicamos del movimiento, del machismo[3]
Platicamos de Cuba; César Chávez; Dolores Huerta . . .[4]
Platicamos de lesbianas . . .[5] what do they do anyway?

I had no idea that I would end up in the healthiest relationship ever, with an
amazing woman named Rose, for seventeen years . . .

So many memories have been rushing through my mind . . .
Rosalva, who called me from a concert,
"Teresa, I'm with the guys from Malo, they want you to go party in T.J. with
us . . .
you've gotta go!"

Arquelio, my boyfriend, wouldn't LET me go . . . *que pinche lástima . . .*[6]

And those fantastic dances organized by Linda Legrette . . .
All of a sudden I would be dancing, then I would hear Rosalina singing her sultry rendition of *Sabór a Mí*

Maria Sanchez . . . do you remember when we first moved into the house on Island Ave.?

Pintamos la cocina[7] bright green and blue,
I wanted to paint a large arrow but you said that was too *gabacho* . . .
so I painted a few large drops instead . . .

Then there was my tough-love lesson,
You were all waiting for me in the living room . . .
Pissed off because I hadn't enrolled my daughter in kindergarten,
You all told me how you felt . . . especially Rosalina . . . well . . .
Later that evening when Gloria Bartlett got home, I cried the blues to her. . . .
She simply replied, "*M'ija*, how dare they tell you the truth?"

Gradually we all moved out of that old creaky house on Island Ave. . . .
That old creaky house where everyone would call to see where the parties were . . .
That old creaky house with the red light bulb on the front porch . . .

That old creaky house in which my gorgeous baby sister Norma; with the wild, long, curly brown hair . . .
Would love to cha-cha to the song "Pillow Talk" before we went out partying at 11 P.M.

The day I moved to the *huelga* (strike) house, I was in the blue and green kitchen, overwhelmed. . . .
Just starting to pack . . .
Chiva (Sylvia Romero) walked in with a shocked look on her face. . . .
What? Was I supposed to be all packed and ready to go?
"Teresa, you live in Disneyland!"
She helped me finish packing while we waited for the guy with the truck.

You all gave me the precious gift of honesty . . .
You all taught me by your examples of strength, courage, and assertiveness . . .

In all your humanness . . . you treated me with respect and compassion, because
honesty is compassionate!

You all began the process of peeling back my layers of protection . . .
My layers of hard-ass shell . . .
the shell that it has taken so many years of recovery to dissolve . . .
The softening of that shell came from many *curanderas* . . .[8]

Curanderas como mi abuelita y su cariño . . . y sus dichos . . .[9]
Curanderas como Rose and her loving gaze,

from those beautiful eyes with the long eyelashes . . .
Curanderas that I met at Alcoholics Anonymous and Narcotics Anonymous meetings . . .
Who helped me recover . . .
Curanderas whispering to me while I sat by the ocean or under a big oak tree . . .
Curanderas como las Chicanas, who told me I looked beautiful sitting in the rocking chair . . .

Wearing that long sleek blue dress with the tiny white dots. . . .
The dress I wore because I was feeling self-protective . . . I wanted to cover up . . .

Cover up my body.
Cover up the pain . . .
I might have been thinking. . . .
Am I really only worthwhile as a good piece of ass?
A good piece is worth a trip to Mexico City . . .

A good piece is worth getting the rent paid . . .
A good piece is worth magnificent silver jewelry . . .
A good piece is worth a lovely red lace dress . . .
A good piece is worth exquisite orange boots. . . .

Was all that stuff worth feeling like the "Golden Pussy"?
The Golden Pussy Syndrome has taken tenacity and self-love to overcome . . .

To overcome the childhood sexual abuse,
I had to get help from women and men who had been through similar and worse trauma. . . .
To overcome the childhood sexual abuse,

I had to write angry letters to my Tío and then to my Dad.
I had to tell them about my healing process and how it took every ounce of strength and courage to face the truth. . . .
To know it was not my fault!

The healing took many years, it felt like my skin was being pulled off in little strips,
It felt like my *tripas*[10] were

SLOWLY. . . .
being pulled out of my body . . .

My Higher Power, the Great Spirit has helped me become a whole person. . . .
As I sit here tonight in my comfy rocking chair. . . .
In my sacred place, my room, my sanctuary . . .
Mi casita . . .

The place I've never gotten drunk in . . .
The place I've never smoked weed in . . .
The place I've never brought a one-night stand to . . .
The place I celebrate my sobriety . . .
celebrate my spouse,
my daughter,
my granddaughter,
mi familia and my extended family . . .

The place I come to nurture myself through my drawings, my journaling, talking on the phone,
and making love. . . .

As I sit in my comfy rocking chair, I am grateful for las Chicanas and the seeds that were planted about thirty years ago . . .
The seeds that continue to blossom through this labor of love.

Notes

1. Dark-skinned women like the earth.
2. We let down our hair.
3. We talked about the Movement, male supremacy.
4. We talked about Cuba, César Chavez, and Dolores Huerta.
5. We talked about lesbians.
6. What a fucking shame.
7. We painted the kitchen.
8. Healing woman.
9. Healing woman like my grandmother with her affection . . . and her sayings.
10. Intestines.

6

Kathy Requejo

COMO UNA GALLINA *Sin Cabeza,*[1] I rushed around frantically. It would be a three-hour drive to San Diego, California, from the Los Angeles area. I had promised to meet my *comadres* in Old Town San Diego for lunch. This would be the first reunion of the Teatro de las Chicanas. The last time I had seen *mis comadres* had been close to twenty years before. I had stayed in contact with a couple of the women, but the entire group had not seen each other since their last performance in the 1980s, an eternity ago. I wanted to reminisce about the good old days; as I rushed out the door I reached for some old tapes by Daniel Valdez and Los Alacranes, celebrated Chicano singers and songwriters from the sixties and seventies.

I started on my journey south. The traffic was heavy, moving very slowly. Like a snail, I inched my way across the City of Angels. The mountains on the east formed a silhouette against the hazy sky and the weather was sweltering at 90 degrees. In the distance a mirage kept appearing and disappearing. I became tense with anxiety. If I did not relax I would never get there on time. I put the tape by Daniel Valdez into the tape player and the first song began to play. I began to hymn along with the song "Primavera."

Now the wait of winter's gone,
and once again we see the sun.
And the birds come out to sing . . .
To tell the world she's home again.
Primavera. Pri . . . ma . . . vera

I settled back into my car seat and relaxed my grip on the wheel. The music began to permeate my body and the lyrics began to flow. I thought a few more songs like this would send me back into the past. *Primavera. Pri . . . ma . . . vera.*

My mind began to drift, "How did my involvement begin with the Teatro de las Chicanas? What attracted me to this group? Who were the women of the Teatro de las Chicanas, and where did they come from? Why did they call themselves las Chicanas?" My vision became obscured and I found myself in the center of a mirage.

"El pueblo unido jamás será vencido!"
"The people, united, shall never be defeated!"
"¡Que viva la Huelga!"

I remember that the *gritos* (chants) rang out as militant Chicanos jammed into San Diego State University auditorium for a rally to fight against injustice. Las Chicanas, having performed, shouted into the audience and waited with anticipation for a response. The "Chicano clap" followed, indicating the crowd's approval of the performance. The clapping would start off very slow and would change into a faster, louder clap sounding like beats of thunder. The crowd stood whispering among themselves. These Chicanas jolted the men who were being portrayed as backward *machos. Los viejos,* the older men, stood with their arms crossed and with a look of disbelief shook their heads. But the women stood tall with their heads held high, *"Híjole, estas son unas Chicanas con huevos"* ("These were women with (big) balls!").

I am unable to put a finger on when I was recruited, or by whom. It happened one day at a performance when someone failed to show up, and I was recruited on the spot to perform. This was my grand initiation into the Teatro de las Chicanas. What brought me into this group of liberated, rebellious, radical, boisterous, progressive women? *Mujeres locas*, in the eyes of the *machos*, who were nothing more than a bunch of Chicana feminists. Women that wanted to wear the pants in the family. To belong to the *teatro* meant that one would expound political fervor. I wanted to be part of this group. I wanted to prove to the world that I was a liberated woman and could make it on my own.

I spent all of my life searching, for truth and happiness.
'Cause I just want to be as free as the wind,
And know the reason why, I'm living . . .
'Cause I don't want to be confined anymore,
I don't want to be afraid to live . . .

—*ANSWERS*, BY DANIEL VALDEZ

To put this in perspective, I would have to begin with where I came from and the events that occurred in my life prior to the Teatro. I was born and raised in the small town of Carpinteria, California. The community is located approximately one hundred miles north of Los Angeles, and approximately fifteen minutes from Santa Barbara. The town is nestled between the mountains and the ocean. On the horizon are the Anacapa Islands. This community was once rich in agriculture, with lemon and avocado orchards blanketing the hills. Growing up in a small community meant that everyone knew each other and their families.

We were a family of nine children. My father worked two jobs to put food on the table and to keep a roof over our heads. My father and grandfather picked lemons and worked at the local lemon-packing house. They would come home covered with green stains on their hands and clothing. The smell of the green dust from pesticides brought a stench into the small house. Sunburned faces. Wrinkled lines etched into my grandfather's forehead from squinting all day. Tired bodies from working hard left little time for play with the children at the end of a long day. Our family was poor, and the only way out of poverty was to become educated. My grandmother and mother emphasized this to all of their children.

Up to California from Mexico you come,
To the Sacramento Valley to toil in the sun.
Your wife and seven children, they're working, every one,
And what will you be giving to your brown-eyed children of the sun?

—*BROWN-EYED CHILDREN OF THE SUN*,
BY DANIEL VALDEZ AND SYLVIA GALAN

At the age of sixteen I was selected to participate in a program called Upward Bound. This program was created for disadvantaged minority students, exposing them to higher education at the college level. This was my way out, a summer camp where I wouldn't have to deal with my younger brothers. It meant freedom! I would be free at last!

I ventured to the University of California, Santa Barbara, spending the summer of 1968 in the dormitories with forty-nine other students. There were students of different nationalities who had been recruited from the neighboring cities around Santa Barbara. The sixties were a time of race riots, and our civil rights struggle became a movement that began to explode within our society, whose foundation of was racial discrimination. I returned to high school a changed person. I had a new understanding of where I fit in, and what I needed to do to force change and make things happen. The baby snake had shed its outer skin and had returned with a new one. The snake had become a rebellious rattler.

The political and social knowledge I had gained was phenomenal. These teachings turned me into a political activist. I returned that summer to run as a student leader my senior year. The atmosphere of the late sixties encouraged me to participate in making history. Chicano students throughout California were marching and making demands for quality education. Student blowouts, or strikes, were occurring at the high school level. Protests and activism were at the peak of social awareness. A void existed at my high school, and someone needed to pick up the banner and run with it. I was destined to raise that banner. With the help of my history teacher, the first United Mexican American Students (UMAS) chapter was started at my school. It was then that I became aware of the fact that I had the ability to raise people's consciousness to a higher level of social awareness.

The UMAS chapters joined forces with the Movimiento Estudiantil Chicano de Aztlán (MEChA) chapters from the nearby colleges. I graduated from high school in 1970 and attended Santa Barbara City College for two years. I became politically involved, joining other Chicanas from MEChA to form a Chicana committee. Our internal struggle soon focused on fighting the *machismo* within the Chicano movement. As the saying went, "Chicanas were fighting not only against imperialist oppression, but against male supremacy within their own *raza*." Chicana women in general were triply oppressed: as a people of color, as earners of a low income level, and as women.

On August 29, 1970, I joined thousands of men, women, and children in East Los Angeles, to march in protest, shouting, "*¡Que viva la Huelga!* Boycott grapes! *¡Que viva César Chávez!* Chicano Power!" We were peacefully marching to protest against the Vietnam War and on behalf of all the young Chicanos who had been killed in the war. As the marchers peacefully protested against the injustices that existed in society, a deafening shot rang out. The peaceful march turned violent and chaotic; men, women, and children were screaming, crying, and running for safety. Burning gases in our eyes and noses, and batons flying in the air ready to strike if we got too close. Many of us are convinced the police started the violence.

All my life I had been taught to obey the law. This illusion ended when I saw men, women, and children beaten by policemen who had been hired to serve and protect us.

> War . . . what is it good for? Absolutely nothing!
>
> —SUNG BY EDWIN STARR

In 1974 I transferred to San Diego State University to prove to my family that as a Chicana I could attend college without ending up pregnant. I needed to prove the myth wrong. It was difficult because the 1970s were an era of drugs and free love. I was finally on my own and could come and go as I pleased. I became a woman with *huevos*—one who was not afraid to express her thoughts, take chances, and seek new adventures. I was ready and willing to experience whatever life had to offer me.

I became fascinated with and ultimately drawn to the *teatro* group. Joining the Teatro meant taking a position on social issues that were not being addressed by the other *teatro* groups. It meant being viewed as a rebellious Chicana, a radical, and a feminist. The Teatro struggled to perform at universities and colleges to deliver their message. During this time an internal struggle was taking place within Teatros Nacionales de Aztlán (TENAZ). This was the organization that represented the different *teatro* groups on a national and international scale. Regardless of the opposition to our group, las Chicanas continued to make appearances. The working-class communities of San Diego and San Ysidro became exposed to our slogans. Las Chicanas would appear at community functions in Logan Heights and other *barrios* in San Diego. While we were changing from the Teatro de las Chicanas to Teatro Laboral our message evolved from becoming liberated as women to working-class issues of organizing into unions, fighting for bilingual education, protesting the abuse by the *migra,* and police brutality.

> In the year 1970, in the City of San Diego under the Coronado Bridge, laid a little piece of land, a little piece of land the Chicano community of Logan Heights wanted to make into a park . . . a park where all the *chavalitos* (children) could come and play so they wouldn't have to play in the street and have to worry about getting run over by a car; a

> park where all the *viejitos* (old folk) could come in the *tarde* (evening) and just sit down watch the sun go down; a park where all the *familias* could get together on Sunday afternoon and celebrate the spirit of life itself; but the city of San Diego said *chale* (no way) we're going to make a highway patrol substation there. La Raza of Logan Heights almost twenty years later is known as Chicano Park. It began in 1970 under the Coronado Bridge, in my barrio in San Diego, where my people began to fight for Chicano Park . . . Chicano park . . . under the bridge . . . under the bridge . . . Chicano Park . . . under the bridge . . .
>
> —BY RAMON (CHUNKY) SANCHEZ, LOS ALACRANES MOJADOS

Life as a member of the *teatro* meant being devoted to the *teatro*. It meant spending precious time rehearsing and going to meetings. The majority of time the role I played in the *teatro* was that of the announcer. I would introduce the *teatro* as well as give a short summary of what the play was about. It meant that in the delivery of the introduction, I had to prepare, excite, and motivate the audience before the performance.

The title Teatro de las Chicanas signified that there were no male actors, therefore a few of us would take on the role of a male. I would dress in jeans and a *cholo* shirt. My long black hair pulled up and covered up with a black beanie. A mustache or goatee painted on my face. With a cigarette in my hand I would stride over in the *bato loco* walk, *"Órale, ese."* The two Chicano brothers would exchange the Chicano handshake. The *bato loco* would take a drag from the *mota* and pass it on to his *hermano*, and the *batos* would begin to converse. Our plays dealt with drug abuse, education, strikes, immigration, and community issues. My favorite was the *Mother* adaptation of the play by Bertolt Brecht. I was not an actor or a singer—few of us could carry a tune. No harmony, no lessons, simply *a la brava*.

> *Migra, migra, pinche migra . . .*
> *Déjame en paz.*
>
> —*MIGRA*, BY SANTANA AND MANÁ

During the time I spent with the *Teatro de las Chicanas*, I came to appreciate certain life values. The greatest value was the friendship that developed among all the women who passed through this group. There are memories of pride and joy when we were successful, or of disappointment when we failed to come together as a group. There are memories of anger and frustration when one of us would bail out, of jealousy and hypocrisy when one of us took the leading role, or of fear and nervousness when one of us failed to remember her lines. Yet we all had the same goal—to get through the play with the least amount of screw-ups and to get our message across. In the end we would prevail and the clapping would begin. We had no pretensions. We were not a threat to the Royal Shakespeare Company. We were in it because of the importance of the message.

Our time together did not consist solely of practicing and performing. Our friendships developed deeper as women from different avenues of life drawn together for social and political reasons. We experienced together the joys and happiness of getting married and becoming mothers. We helped each other out by taking care of each other's children. We have cried together over breakups, divorces, disease, and death. We listened and gave advice to each other. Most of all, we shared in one another's dreams and aspirations. There is an umbilical cord that bonds us.

¡El pueblo unido jamás será vencido!
¡Que viva la Huegla!

El *grito* became softer and faded into the background of my mind. I glanced at a sign as I sped past it: Old Town next exit. I had finally arrived in San Diego with time to spare on that day. I looked at myself in the mirror, powdered my nose, and put on some fresh lipstick. I found the restaurant, and some of the Chicanas were already there. *Abrazos* and *besos* were exchanged. I sat down and glanced at everyone. We had come a long way. A touch of gray hair, a few more pounds, and signs of lines on our faces revealed our age. It was time to catch up on each others' lives, exchange pictures of our families, and reminisce about old times. Tomorrow we would perform once again for Las Chicanas reunion.

Some thirty years after having solidified my independence with the *teatro*'s support, I still visit my sisters in San Diego. The *teatro* group no longer exists but the women do. The umbilical cord that kept us together can never be broken, for it is the core and the essence of what we are today. This umbilical cord helped define our life, our being, our morals, and how we view ourselves in this society. Many of us have taken a different road, but we always come back to where we feel the most home-heart comfort. When we come together it's like we were never apart. We start where we left off.

If anyone were to ask me today whether I would do it all over again, I would answer, YES! Life is about the people you meet along the way who inspire you, educate you, transform you, and help you become the person that you are. I feel honored and privileged to have been part of the Teatro de las Chicanas. I would like to say to all my sisters out there who may happen to read this. I thank you for your friendship, *mis comadres*, "*¡Las Chicanas por vida!*"

Notes

1. Like a chicken without a head.

7

Clara Cuevas

I GOT A SURPRISE call from Felicitas after twenty-five years, inviting me to a *teatro* women's reunion. Her call was most welcome, and it set me thinking about the social and political issues swirling around me as a student in the late 60s and early 70s. Why did I join el Teatro de las Chicanas? At first I wasn't sure why I was so drawn to this particular group. I suppose I saw the fight in their faces, and later I witnessed the courage in their hearts. Although I had lost contact with most of my *teatro* colleagues, I often wondered how each of us came to be involved with the *teatro* and why it was so important for us to unite and express ourselves in this way.

I'll never forget the day I was to be interviewed by this group of Chicanas in their typical "uniform" of blue jeans, men's long shirts, and boots. Well, there I was, this chick from Northern California, wearing a long colorful shirt, a short, midriff top, and open sandals with my long hair, waving at their militant style of walk and talk. They wanted to know why I wanted to become a part of them.

I could feel their eyes checking me out. I thought they might be thinking, "What the hell is she doing here?" We talked; actually I talked, they asked lots of questions. Basically they wanted to know about my background and why I had an interest in joining. Even though we seemed like we were from different parts of the world, my excitement, enthusiasm, and concerns for the *causa* must have satisfied the group. In any event, I felt more comfortable as the interview proceeded and my political background slowly unraveled into a tapestry of common issues and concerns that matched their goals for *teatro.* I could sense that my political perspectives and interests were intertwined with those of these girls.

I say "girls" because this is how our parents perceived us. Going to college was expected of me, my siblings, and cousins. We had all heard my uncles' weekly sermons about the importance of getting an education. My uncles were World War II veterans, and their perspective on life was based on discipline—and they were strict. Their philosophy was ever-present at our weekly gatherings at Grandma's house, where we would all gather after Sunday mass. There the real sermons would begin, and I must say that we were all listening, because all of my cousins—from every family—have a college education. This is unheard of in Mexican families! However, my going far away to college was a struggle at first.

The first college I attended was sixty miles away. I had to come home every weekend, thereby proving to my father that I was still his little obedient girl. Finally I proved to my parents that I could survive on my own, and I decided to attend San Diego State University.

This college was eight hundred miles away. I was swept up into a whirlwind of confusion, joining in the demonstrations against our government's war in Vietnam. Many young men were being drafted and destroyed physically as well as mentally. On the home front the farm workers were in the forefront among issues of social injustice. I certainly grew out of my girlhood within this chaos. We were all struggling for an identity within ourselves and at the same time struggling to overcome the injustices established by society.

The farm workers' struggle was at the heart of the Chicano student movement, where most of the *teatro* women and myself got our feet wet. Dolores Huerta, the cofounder of the UFW, came from my hometown of Stockton. She became a hero for me because of her strong voice in the movement at a time when there were hardly any women who held important political positions. It was as if lightning had struck this "Sleeping Giant Machine" known as *la Raza.* And we finally awoke to find this ache in our hearts to demand justice for our people.

It was as if my own aching heart had been especially awakened by the voice of strong women. I joined *teatro* to demonstrate and voice my concerns in the form of acting. I had found a home away from home. I felt our bond of sisterhood was so powerful I could overcome any obstacle in my life. As I thought about Felicitas' call I struggled yet again with memories of my own sister and the abusive relationship that took her life. I had been struggling to let go of the past as it related to my younger sister, Arlinda. I had to stop my lingering heartache from clouding my optimistic sense of the future. Ten years had gone by since her tragedy and this incident had to some degree embittered my views regarding issues of women's independence and empowerment.

My sister was being stalked and intimidated by her estranged husband for months. She tried to go on with her life yet was constantly looking over her shoulder and hoping that he would understand that their relation was ended. But he was persistent, slashing her car tires outside her workplace and committing other similar acts. He was never caught doing any harm to my sister or her car tires, which at the time made the police powerless to arrest him. They suggested Arlinda put a restraining order on her husband, and she did. This action enraged her possessive husband even more.

My sister was aware he kept guns in his house, and the palpable atmosphere of fear and tension surrounding her escalated. She got to feeling safer at her workplace and dreaded being home alone with her children. I was willing to help when I became aware of what was happening and also advised my sister to go into hiding as an extreme measure. Arlinda, with her four children, went to a women's shelter seeking help and protection. But she was able to support her children and her income was over the limit, so she was turned away because she was not destitute.

Not long after this, I got a call from my mother, who barely, in quivering words, forced herself to say, "Arlinda has been shot." I screamed, "No! No! No!" banging the telephone on the table and focusing my anger and blame at the police for their inaction and the women's shelter for their lack of compassion. The death of Arlinda carved a deep wound in her children and the children's extended families. The children's father was convicted of first-degree murder, and they lost their thirty-two-year-old mother. The pain of Arlinda's loss could not be erased and the pain followed both of my parents to their graves.

The infamous O. J. Simpson trial for the murder of Nicole Brown Simpson brought to light the fact that domestic violence crosses all walks of life. Today the doors to women's shelters are more open, regardless of the victim's status or wealth. Our society was forced to realize that domestic violence is a problem that needs attention.

My feeling of sisterhood was revived when I reunited with the members of this all-woman *teatro* in July of 2000. I was very nervous at first, but the big hugs and kisses that we exchanged at our gathering comforted me. I met members who came into the group after I moved up-state and then there were the familiar faces. We had taken on some weight, wrinkles, and plenty of silver hair, reflecting our accumulated wisdom.

I felt this magical power of energy as each of us retold our story as if it were yesterday. I could clearly see the strength and courage that it took these women to decide to make a difference in their young adult lives. The women's faces melted into one another, reliving their life through laughter, tears, joy, and sorrow. At our break we released our passion into the song "*La Llorona*" and this singing transported us back in time. What a privilege for those of us present, to have come full circle. I knew my sister Arlinda was with us.

Today I use this common bond of the *teatro* and the powerful memory of my womanhood to accept the pain of love for my sister Arlinda and counter the obstacles in my life. I live to show those around me that "Yes! Life is not fair and love is painful. One must have faith and be strong in order to deal with life and continue with love." I move forward as an experienced and educated middle-aged woman, feeling a lot stronger about making a difference for our future young females and all our children. As for the *teatro* experience, I will always keep a special place in my heart for the women I met and worked with. They gave me the wings to fly and reach for the stars.

8

Virginia Rodriguez Balanoff

IT WAS A blast being in the Teatro de las Chicanas! I would not trade my eighteen months with those charismatic women for anything in the world. I grew by leaps and bounds during that time. The *teatro* women helped me transition from a sequestered *Mexicanita* living in the sticks of a desert town, Coachella, into a woman taking charge of her life in big-city San Diego.

I felt like the misfit of the Teatro de las Chicanas because I spoke Spanish poorly at that time. After being chastised in kindergarten for speaking Spanish, I spoke only English. During the next twelve years of my education I did not speak Spanish at all. I didn't realize how much Spanish I had lost. I was not aware that Spanish words could have double meanings. In listening to the *teatro* women converse, I was not always catching the double inferences in their jokes.

I started participating when the *teatro* had already been functioning for a few years and already had a cohesive group that functioned well together. I was originally invited to watch them perform at a Movimiento Estudiantil Chicano de Atzlán (MEChA) meeting. Wow! They were explosive! Dynamic! Powerful! I liked these women. You could feel their energy in the room. It beckoned you to join in with their "Down with *machismo*" attitude. I am a *macha,* an assertive woman, having grown up with six brothers. What woman would not be assertive, having grown up in that family dynamic? I could relate to their confrontational skit, "*Bronca (rough) . . . Bron . . . cabrón . . . cabrón* (male goat/cuckold)" jives. Anyway, the Chicanas invited the women to a group meeting after their performance. Although I do not remember exactly all that was said, I recall it made a lot of sense and that I wanted to hear more.

Most of the women of the *teatro* were students at San Diego State University (SDSU) who were finishing their General Education Degree and planning to go on to higher education. I was finishing my second year of college. They knew a lot more *bromas* (slang, nouns, joking words) that I had not been privy to in the past. I remember I was really trying hard to keep up with some of the double inferences of common Spanish words. For example, *tapada* means covered or constipated, but also means an ignorant female. It was a true learning experience, not only in college, but the new experience of being away from home. At home I was always chaperoned everywhere by at least two brothers. But now these women had two-plus years ahead of me on *independencia*—to the max. They were showing me ways to put men in their place and stand up for myself. I felt like a nerdy Poindexter trying to get hip real quick.

Eventually, I met up with some of the women of the Teatro de las Chicanas at a party. We all enjoyed socializing together. I enjoyed their company. They were so comical and fun to be with. The *pelotas* (balls) on these women reminded me of a Sor Juana or César Chávez or a Martin Luther King Jr. They had the courage to stand up for what they believed in, and I wanted to be more like them. It was then that some of the women invited me to try out for the *teatro.* Boy, did they find a gullible woman in me! They quickly snatched me up and gave me a script to memorize by the next *teatro* meeting the following week. I let them know I had no theatrical experience. They let me know they did not have theatrical experience either when they started in the teatro. I just hoped I would not let them down.

The script I was given was Bertolt Brecht's translation of Maksim Gorky's *The Mother.* It was about a mother trying to justify her son's death and show that he was not lost in vain by organizing workers for whom her son was killed. We adapted the play to our Mexican cultural experience. In the play the mother sold tamales wrapped in a flyer with union propaganda. The flyers said, "Join the union to get better wages and better conditions." I could relate to this. Every summer our family worked picking grapes or some kind of fruit. It was dreadful, dirty work.

I started working with my family picking plums at the age of four in San Jose. I remember this trip so distinctly because we were working for "back

Members of Teatro de las Chicanas (1975). *Front, left–right:* Laura Cortez Garcia, Margarita Carrillo, Maria Juarez; *back, left–right:* Lupe Perez, Felicitas Nuñez, Virginia Rodriguez Balanoff, Hilda Rodriguez, Delia Ravelo, and Sandra Gutierrez. Courtesy of Felicitas Nuñez.

Members of Teatro de las Chicanas (May 1973). *Front, left–right:* Felicitas Nuñez, Peggy Garcia; *back, left–right:* Delia Ravelo, Maria Pedroza, and Lupe Perez. Courtesy of Felicitas Nuñez.

Teatro de las Chicanas performing *Chicana Goes to College* at San Diego State College at the High School Recruitment Conference (1973). *Left–right:* Gloria Barlett, Laura Cortez Garcia, Delia Ravelo (back), and Lupe Perez. Courtesy of Laura Cortez Garcia.

Attendees of the Seminario de Chicanas at San Diego State College (1971). Courtesy of Felicitas Nuñez.

Delia Ravelo Reyes. Courtesy of Michael Reyes.

Teatro Raíces performing *Archie Bunker Goes to El Salvador* at the International Women's Day celebration, Chula Vista, California (March 1981). *Left–right:* Guadalupe Beltran, Felicitas Nuñez, and Evelyn Diaz. Courtesy of Felicitas Nuñez.

Teatro de las Chicanas members on their way to a May Day celebration in Los Angeles, California (1975). *Front, left–right:* Hilda Rodriguez, Yolanda Catzalco, Maria Juarez; *back, left–right:* Kimberly, Micaela, Lupe Perez, and Laura Cortez Garcia. Courtesy of Laura Cortez Garcia.

Felicitas Nuñez playing the role of "La Muerte" during a community protest against the closing of the Natividad Center, Salinas, California (1976). Courtesy of Felicitas Nuñez.

Teatro de las Chicanas members Kimberly and Laura Cortez Garcia performing in *The Mother,* San Diego State University (1974). Courtesy of Felicitas Nuñez.

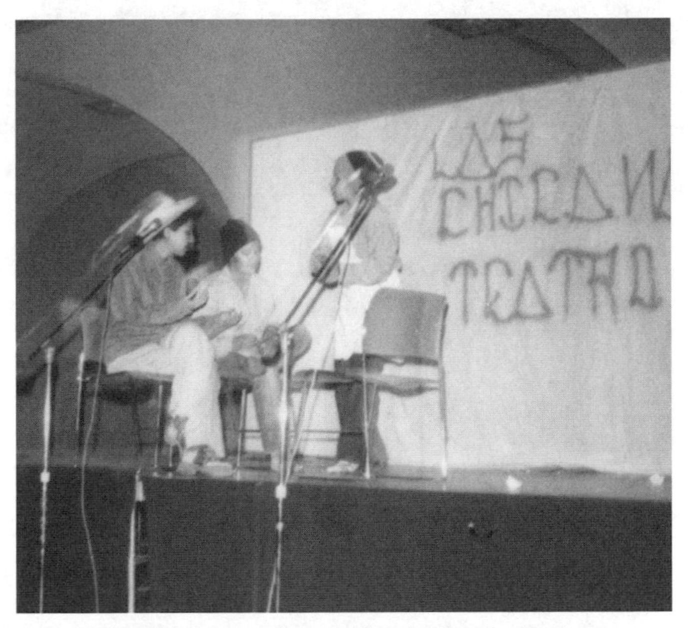

Teatro de las Chicanas members performing in *The Mother*, San Diego State University (1974). *Seated, left–right:* Guadalupe Beltran and Clara Cuevas; *standing:* Yolanda Catzalco. Courtesy of Felicitas Nuñez.

Teatro Mestizo performing *The Militant (1973). On stage, front:* Enrique Ramirez; *back:* Felicitas Nuñez. Teatro members on the left looking on include Angel Carrillo, José Aguiar, and Ernesto Hernandez. Courtesy of Felicitas Nuñez.

to school" money and I was going to start kindergarten. I was so excited. My parents always wanted us to feel we were contributing to the family. Even the youngest were given converted lard buckets to pick up salvageable fruit that had fallen off the tree. The objective of the youngest siblings—ages one, four, and five—was to fill one box by the end of the day. In grade school I seriously thought every family picked fruit every summer in the hot blazing sun, getting diarrhea from eating too much fruit sprayed with pesticide.

If we children were hungry, lunchtime was when our stomachs said so! We couldn't wait for my mother to wash up and make tortillas and fry up the beans. When my two brothers and I were hungry, we turned over our red tin lard buckets, sat down on them, and proceeded to eat fruit from the box—fruit we had just picked, pesticides and all. We didn't know better. When I grew up I joined the United Farm Workers and learned that things could be different. I learned that, by law, I should not have been out working the fields before the age of sixteen. I could definitely relate to the play *The Mother.*

The women in the Teatro de las Chicanas who gathered to perform this play with me were Sandra Gutierrez, Felicitas Nuñez, Laura Cortez (China), Maria Juarez (Cubanita), Guadalupe Beltran, Susan and Irene Aranda, and Hilda Rodriguez. Our goal was to perfect the script to perform for the community and for the upcoming Teatros Nacionales de Aztlán (TENAZ) conference that was to take place in San Antonio later that summer of 1975. At the annual conference *teatros* participated and gave each other constructive criticism. Unfortunately, we had put in our application to participate late. Usually every *teatro* group that had applied for past conferences was accommodated, but this time the rules were strict.

As I recall, we did not get a response. Felicitas, being the *macha* woman she was, said, "They got our money. We're going anyway." So there we were, a van full of eight women, on our way from California to Texas through the desert to criticize and be criticized. Out of the eight of us women who had practiced only four could make it to the conference, but at the last moment we were able to get Margie Carrillo, Raquel Luna, Becky Nuñez, and Irma Mendia to go. We were still short of actors, but once we got to the conference we would recruit from the participants to fill in on the minor roles. This had been done in the past and we were quite confident that we could pull through with our play.

Little did we know that we were in for quite a ride.

Traveling the interstate was an experience. I had never been out of California, except to visit my *tía* (aunt) Rosa in Mexicali. Believe me, there isn't much to see in Mexicali or along the way. If you've seen one tumbleweed you've seen them all. I had never been traveling by car to another state. I volunteered to drive the first nightshift because I was wide awake from all the excitement. There we were in our Daisy Duke hip-hugger cutoffs and halter tops in the blazing hot weather headed for Texas. Some of the other women had boyfriends and husbands. They were kissing and hugging goodbye before we shoved off, for what seemed like hours. Boy, what a fuss it looked to me. We were only going to be gone for a week! The way they were all smooching, you would have thought they were going to another country for years.

As it turned out, much of the drive was beautiful. The night had so many twinkling stars as we got farther into the desert. We also had spectators along the route as well. When we pulled over into an Arizona truck stop to gas up and use the bathroom for the first time, you would have thought that Arizona truckers had never seen Mexican women before. I never saw so many gawking eyeballs in all my life. I thought, "Did I pee on myself or is something showing that should not be?" No, we were all dry and intact. Who knows what they were looking at. All the truckers stopped eating and followed us out and watched us pile into the van.

Lucky for us that we were being looked at because on top of it being an unlit pitch-black road, we were unaware that the damn exit sign was covered up by tamarack trees. I passed the exit three times. Finally we were able to get out when the truckers stood in a line and pointed to the exit area, otherwise I would still be going back and forth! We laughed and said "Thank you." As soon as we left, the word must have gone out that the "beaver (vagina) wagon" was on the road. Truckers from all over were kind enough to "high beam" us when the highway patrol was nearby or if there was road construction up ahead. So, on the whole route "trucker guardians" essentially escorted us. I'll bet they thought we were a traveling brothel. To their dismay, we were just the Teatro de las Chicanas determined to get in some acting, and determined to be heard.

By sunup I was in awe. I had never seen such beautiful pillar mountains like those in New Mexico, such rich red brick color, touching a baby-blue sky. In the sky, hawks circled the mountains . . . or were they eagles? It was too hard to tell from that distance at a moment's glance. I had to keep my eyes on the road. For that moment in time, I felt I was looking at western artwork, like the ones on the walls of the restaurants or banks in Coachella. All the skies I had seen in the past were smog-filled and had too many lights to see the stars. I was enamored of the beauty I thought only happened in artists' minds and was then placed on canvas. I never believed such beauty in nature actually existed. It was then that I realized I was in dire need of sleep. I let Felicitas know my shift was over and she took over the driving.

On our way we stopped at the house of a *compadre* (someone's godfather) to rest. I had no idea where we were, since I had just woken up. Felicitas was calling ahead to let the conference coordinators know we were on our way, like it or not. She had all the documentation that we had signed up with paid receipts to boot. We expected to participate.

There was opposition when we got to the conference to sign in. The workshop coordinators were not going to let us participate. Felicitas started ranting and raving. She could be heard across the whole county, yelling that the *machos* would not let a women's theater group perform. At least, I was convinced she could be heard throughout the whole county. We embarrassed them. They did not want to be seen as chauvinistic or sexist, so they compromised. They would let us participate with the criticism, but not perform. I did not understand it all. Felicitas said it was because of the content of our play. They were probably afraid of what it had to say, that it might raise the consciousness of the other theatrical actors. If all the theater workers performed political plays on organizing, the Mexican community would be armed with knowledge to change their own lives for the better. The fact is, of course, many *teatros* were rooted in progressive politics.

It seemed to me that most of the plays at the conference were about love affairs, gang warfare, mysticism, and Aztlán, but lacked specific direction on how to organize. Only stereotypes of Mexicans were being portrayed, it seemed to me. Plus, there were these strange men, one who looked like Bozo the Clown, taking pictures of us, our van, and our license plate, which made me suspicious that Felicitas was right. We never performed, but participating in the conference opened my eyes to other Latino communities and their experiences and how much they needed more direction.

What I hated most about myself, but I did not realize it till this experience, was being such an emotional person. I started to cry when Felicitas was arguing with the conference coordinators to allow us to perform. Little did I know that my emotionalism was just the right touch to bring the conference coordinators to their knees. No one can stand to see a crying woman without trying to comfort her. Some of the male actors were sneering at the conference coordinators. I mean BIG male actors.

If the coordinators did not let us participate, they were going to get their ass kicked. From the spectators' view, it seemed as if I was crying because they were keeping us out of the conference. (I had almost immediately left the room because I did not want to be seen crying.) Shit, I was crying because Felicitas was standing her ground and proving them wrong, point by point. She made me so proud! I could never be as ballsy as Felicitas. She kept her emotions in check. Man, that woman had *huevos!* I thought for sure she was going to deck those *macho* assholes. Certainly, she had more *huevos* than all the men at the conference put together. Either way, we stayed for the conference criticism, but never performed.

My following *teatro* experiences were not quite as dramatic as the Texas tour. After traveling to the TENAZ conference I performed several times in San Diego. We were not polished actors. Many of us forgot our lines at times. I think it depended on how late we had been out the night before or how busy our school and work schedules were. Sometimes we got stage fright and others would ad lib to prime the partner who had forgotten her lines. We all grew from the experience. I also knew we were not a very good performing group, despite the good script.

Looking back twenty-five years, I regard the *teatro* as a group of lively outspoken women who had the courage to stand up and say what was on their minds. They acted out exaggerated stereotypes to help the audience laugh at themselves and see the error of their ways. The best part was that they gave answers to move men and women forward, whether it was on personal or political issues.

I've thought about what the *teatro* experience gave us, and what I contributed in my own way. One thing that comes to mind is *cariño*, a deeper sense of friendship that transcends time and space, which is innate to the Mexican culture. Without this friendship we'd wither away. In high school I felt so alone, pulled away from my friends to be placed in a "college prep" group because of my demonstrated academic potential. I was in a school that was ninety-eight percent Mexican, but I was the only Mexican female in my classroom. I think the schools meant to integrate all the classes—black, white, Asian, and Mexican—but the only place I felt truly integrated was in physical education. I missed my friends. That experience made me quieter, knowing only one other Mexican—a boy—was in class with me.

When I went to college, it helped having other Latino social groups to provide support, getting each other through the mandated core curriculum. I think this innate social need for friendship drew me to the *teatro*. Performing the *actos* in the *teatro* taught me to stand up for what is right and not be quiet about it. The women in the *teatro* gave me back my voice, which was taken away from me in kindergarten when I was told not to speak Spanish.

How has the *teatro* experience contributed to my development? I am a registered nurse. The experience of speaking in public taught me to stand up for my patients and make sure their voices are heard. For example, I have spoken up for breast cancer patients whose doctors were pushing for mastectomy, the complete removal of their breast. The patients wanted to wait until the biopsy results were available to see if the mastectomy was necessary because they would rather have the less invasive lumpectomy. At the hospitals, nurses were having multiple miscarriages from being overworked and exposed to chemicals or germs that were toxic to the fetus, no matter what trimester of pregnancy.

The registered nurses led our union to demand that OSHA standards were followed when it came to nursing assignments in order to protect our pregnant staff. I let my manager know that it was hard to keep my patient's temperature under 102° when the room temperature was 101°. Also an important battle involved my standing up for my first amendment right to speak Spanish to my Spanish-speaking patients when my hospital supervisor was demanding that I only speak in English. The *teatro* helped me put a voice to the feelings of what was right in work situations and gave me the courage to correct the situation.

Besides giving the *teatro* a warm body, I gave them my experiences from having worked since age four. I gave them someone who knew her lines and the pretense that I could act. I was a good and faithful friend. I believe it is in true caring for others that we can change the world. If we truly cared, we would work hard to ensure people were fed, warm, in good health, employed, and treated with dignity. Then and only then will we truly love our neighbors as ourselves. I believe this was conveyed in my acting. So it starts with one little Chicana actress trying to instill hope in the world.

I think the most valuable lessons learned while in the *teatro* involved the kindred spirit with other women. We sought to liberate ourselves from the chains of backward conformity and to stand up for equality. We learned to speak up when things had to be said—especially for those who cannot speak up for themselves. We also learned, believe it or not, when to lay low and eat crow for the well-being of others. These *teatro* women taught this country-bumpkin streetwise lingo from many cultures. For example, someone called me a "brick house." I thought they were insulting me but they were actually paying a compliment to my physical good looks. It was a bang of a cultural awakening.

I believe that the will and sincerity of these women could run a nation given the chance. It is from seeing their courage that I had the courage to be active in unions and speak out on behalf of my patients and in the political arena. Let the caring start with me and spread to others. I personally feel I have contributed to my workplace and community. I try to spread hope and try to change things where I can. I try to remain the optimist because I believe good prevails over all. I try to share this caring with all I come in contact with, and they in turn can transfer it to others.

We can instill hope and caring in others, one person at a time, by letting them know we care. I feel this deep in my heart and soul. That feeling of caring, I consider to be the Latin passion I have for the world. I believe we all have that spirit hidden somewhere in us. It just has to be kindled by someone's good deed. So, what's holding you back? What lights your fire? Lay down those barriers on the chopping block and blow them away and get moving to care!

9

Sandra M. Gutierrez

QUERIDA LIZELLE,

Next year you will be filling out college applications and visiting university campuses. Then you will wait anxiously for that thick packet to come in the mail from your favorite university. As you complete high school and prepare for college, I want to share some of my experiences as a young woman with you. Some of the most exciting and enriching times of my life occurred when I was in college and in a women's theater group.

Thirty years ago when I was a freshman in college I joined something called Teatro de las Chicanas. This was at San Diego State University (SDSU) back in the early 1970s, when tortillas were handmade and not store bought. My college experiences with the *teatro* were formative in my personal, political, and intellectual growth. In view of all that, I thought I'd share some of those recollections and memories with you. (I bet you never knew that your *tía* used to carry picket signs and defiantly raise her fist at rallies and mass demonstrations—some of which were angrily declared to be "unlawful assemblies" by cops with bullhorns and billy clubs.)

What I remember most about my days with the *teatro* are the feelings of camaraderie and mutual support that we felt—all young women trying to make our way in the world, all young women who proudly called ourselves "Chicanas." And even that was a bit bold for the time.

You have to understand that the world thirty years ago was quite different from what it is today. And I'm not talking about the fact that Janis Joplin was on the radio instead of Christina Aguilera! Taking a stand as a Chicana took a bit of courage. And that's what I remember about working in the Teatro de las Chicanas: We felt courageous. We were emboldened. It wasn't all seriousness, of course. We had a lot of fun. But underlying it all was a sense of cooperation and mutual shoring-up among women who shared similar dreams and aspirations. We wanted "social justice" and fairness—although that may seem a bit corny today. I'm not even sure the word "corny" is in your vocabulary.

As I look back on it now, it was Laura Garcia who introduced me to the *teatro*. There wasn't anything dramatic or momentous about it. I was in a biology class with her and husband, José. Their son, Emilio, had just been born. His birth more or less coincided with my introduction to the *teatro*. Anyway, Laura just casually asked me if I wanted to be in a little play that she and a few other women were getting ready to perform. Simple as that.

This was, I think, in my fall semester of 1973 at SDSU. (*M'ija*, that was fifteen years before you were born—*imagínate*.) And I think I just answered something like "Sure, why not." I remember that at that time I was really lonely, didn't have any family nearby and not many friends. I needed money and had gotten a work-study job at Casa Justicia in National City. It was a nonprofit organization that advocated immigrants' rights. That was important because that's also when I was introduced to some of the Chicano Studies classes. It was a time, for me, of accelerating awareness and consciousness about the world around me.

I mean that I was a young college student trying to survive and at the same time trying to reconcile some of the contradictions that I saw all around me. And the Chicanas I began to associate with, particularly in the *teatro*, were women from backgrounds much like mine. They were working-class people coming from agricultural communities in either the Coachella Valley or the Imperial Valley. We came from *mexicano* families that were filled with all of the riches of our culture, and all of the *pendejadas* and *tristezas* that characterize working-class, oppressed *mexicano* families.

So in that biology class Laura asked me if I wanted to be in this play and maybe join this group of Chicanas using *teatro* as a political tool. It wasn't anything grand, as far as "theater arts" are concerned. *M'ija*, I think they just needed an extra warm body at the time, someone to help fill the stage.

We did a version of the play *The Mother* by the radical German playwright Bertolt Brecht, who adapted it from the book by Maksim Gorky. It's a trippy play. I recommend you check it out when you have a chance. The ideas are old, but they are timeless and eternally relevant. You have to understand that back then, in the seventies, there were lots of things going on—culturally and politically, I mean. There was still momentum from the movement against the war in Vietnam. César Chávez and the farm workers' struggle was of intense and palpable concern to a lot of us. And the whole Chicano artistic movement was picking up steam. Poets, songwriters, muralists, and a good number of *teatros* were flourishing.

As far as the Teatro de las Chicanas was concerned, what we lacked in theatrical training and sophistication, we more than made up for with *ganas* and determination. And hey, we were all fine looking women at that time. *¿Qué más quieren?*[1] *M'ija*, remember I wasn't born middle-aged!

In the play *The Mother,* I remember playing the role of a young man. We put our hearts into the delivery of our lines. This was because the play was rooted in a political frame of reference, something we viscerally related to. It existed for a political purpose, not some artsy frivolous objective.

We wanted to communicate a message. It was fundamentally a Marxist/Leninist message aimed at working-class Chicanos and *mexicanos.* My understanding and my grasp of such things were evolving at the time. And my work in the *teatro* (and believe me, I was not a major player in any way) was part of that gradual but accelerating learning process for me. It was a matter of learning and understanding. Of opening my eyes. Of being able to attach a system of analysis to the things I saw around me—poverty, discrimination, sexism.

And, *m'ija,* sexism and feminism were big issues to us in the *teatro.* It was a big deal to me. And part of my personal evolution. You must remember that, although you and people of your generation take many things for granted and assume a great deal, things were not always as they are today. Not by a long shot. We were a feminist Chicana theater group. That was not an easy pill for many people to swallow back then.

One of the biggest forces deriding Chicana feminism was—in my view—hopelessly insecure Mexican men. There were battles in those days. And some of it was very unpleasant. I mean, they called us "lesbian bitches" and things that I don't care to repeat. Our strength, our solidarity as women, our devotion to a political perspective aimed at economic fairness and humanism, threatened many people. But that only made us women more secure in our conviction that we were doing the right thing—even though we freely admitted then (and admit now) that we didn't have all the answers.

We used to have *choques* and *chingazos* with a particular faction that existed in those days. They basically were the "Nationalists" who didn't share our class-based frame of reference. The Nationalists wanted Chicanos to struggle only for Chicanos. "White causes" like the women's movement were not supported. The Nationalists supported the UFW, but not other labor struggles. In some ways these clashes between rival Chicano/a groups may seem silly today, but back then it was pretty serious stuff. Yet we were not discouraged and we drew sustenance from the way our audiences cheered after a performance. It was very gratifying. We rehearsed discussion points and were prepared to answer questions from both *señores* and *señoras.* Their appreciation helped us continue our work. And it helped us improve, I think.

When I think back on those days, I immediately conjure up the faces of the women who were there with me. They played a more active and long-term role than I did in the *teatro,* but our experiences united us. I remember Laura and Felicitas and Delia, among others. Then later Virginia joined the troupe. I really liked these women. We developed a strong bond from being in the "trenches" together. We knew we could count on each other. And there was a quiet strength and reassurance that came with that. It felt good.

Again, these were formative years and transformative experiences for me. I came to SDSU from a working-class world. Our schools in Coachella were 80 percent *Mexicanos,* and we were not expected to go to college. I was one of the few who took some "college-bound" classes, but wasn't counseled about how to get to college. I was not as academically prepared as some other people were. But I had confidence in my abilities and I was centered in my self-identity.

My self-confidence came through to the other women. They asked why I was so self-confident and I realized that it was because of my mother's (your Nana) firm guidance and love. My mother always had confidence in me and she protected me from harm. Now, as an adult and mother, I understand the sacrifices she made to ensure my growth as a strong woman. She made sure I was educated, had plenty of books to read, and had a strong work ethic. She protected me from physical or sexual abuse. How did she do that? She made sure we left family parties before people got drunk. She made sure we were not alone with young uncles capable of sexually abusing us. Unfortunately, *m'ija,* such things happen.

My mother expected me to succeed. When I voiced a desire to go to college, she figured out how to fill out the forms and secure financial aid, and she got me a place to live with a cousin. She ensured that I was able to go to college.

The rest was up to me. And I was eager to learn and to explore! Being a part of the *teatro* fit in perfectly with that goal for me.

And, as I said, we believed in the politics of what we were doing, but it wasn't all deadly serious stuff. We had lots of fun too, as I mentioned. And that's part of the value of the experience for me. We performed mostly in community centers for audiences of working-class people. But we would "put on a show." No matter how "bad" we were, like forgetting our lines, we'd support each other and prompt the next sequence of action on stage. The audiences always seemed to love us. Partly, I think, they just appreciated that we were there and had reached out to them.

I remember this one time we were going to do a performance on a hot summer afternoon. Somehow we ended up at the house of a wonderful woman, Diane Flowers. We turned her house into a giant collective dressing room. We were scrambling to take a quick bath, put on makeup, pull on makeshift costumes, and do our hair. Elbows in each other's faces in front of every mirror we could find. Even though we considered ourselves "political stalwarts," we were having fun.

I learned then (as I believe now) that you can have fun *and* occasionally bury your nose in a book. It was a great time for me, although there were knockdowns and disappointments then, too. But overall it was a terrific set of experiences. My brain was opening. I was meeting new people, exploring politics and philosophies. The *teatro* and corollary experiences helped me continue to develop a personal strength and self-assurance. That part of the *teatro* experience was of great value to me. "Friendship" is a word that comes to mind when I think of the *teatro*. The value of friendship. While it's true that today I'm no longer in touch with some of the women from the *teatro*, I have this sense that we are all still sending "vibes" of support—positive feelings—toward each other. I know that sounds hopelessly "seventies" to you, Lizelle.

If we hadn't had the Chicano Studies program and the *teatro*, I don't know if I would have made it. That mutual support was very important. "Back-up" was invaluable.

And for me, the work with the *teatro* dovetailed with my rapidly increasing interest in and awareness of politics. I dropped out of SDSU and went home to the Coachella Valley. I eventually got my bachelor's degree from Azusa Pacific University. In 1975 I joined the United Farm Workers (UFW). The work I did with the union provided learning that has lasted a lifetime. I became a shop steward for my crew and tackled breaches of contract in grievance procedures. And won! I later was elected to the Comité del Rancho (Ranch Committee). We decided that with work-related and community issues, we would fight for the local members in their own communities. It was in Coachella that the *teatro* entered my life again. This time we needed the *teatro*'s help to expose an injustice that occurred at the local elementary school.

A young Mexican child was slapped, very hard, by an Anglo teacher. The teacher had been teaching in the school for many, many years and believed in slapping children to discipline them. No one had ever challenged her until now. There were a couple of young Chicana teachers, Yolanda Almaraz and Socorro Gómez, at the Coachella public schools. Yolanda witnessed the slapping of the child and challenged the teacher's right to slap children. The Anglo's teacher's response was to slap Yolanda and told her to go to hell. Yolanda immediately brought the outrage to the attention of the school principal, who pretty much told her he would do nothing and upheld the "slapping policy." The issue was taken to the school board. Yolanda and her friend Socorro were refused an audience. There was no option but to call a school strike.

The Chicana teachers and parents came to the UFW asking for support. Now, we in the UFW were very familiar with strikes, picketing, and challenging local oppressive policies. We had been picketing the local liquor stores that sold Gallo wine and had been getting arrested and tear-gassed for our efforts. So the UFW members had the *ganas* and *huevos* to take on the "slapping policy."

The UFW parents pulled their children out of school, as did many other parents. We all marched in front of the elementary school. Several of us made an appointment to meet with the MEChA chapter at Coachella Valley High School. Within ten minutes into the discussion, "Walk out!" rang through the corridors. A handful of us adults corralled about a hundred students and walked several miles back into Coachella. What a day!

I called the *teatro* to come perform at a community meeting. The next day they were there, ready to perform a skit about the slapping incident and the outraged response from the community. Delia Ravelo had written the script in the car on the way. And several of the women were from Coachella, so they were ready to perform in their home town. The performance was a hit. The *teatro* was a hit, and many parents later came up to thank me for arranging their appearance.

We, along with the parents, teachers, and students, later attended a school board meeting. The tension was thick in the air, and some board members made stereotypical racist and inflammatory remarks. However, we persevered once a threat of a class-action lawsuit was mentioned. You know it—we had young Chicano lawyers ready to go to work! *M'ija,* victory is so sweet, especially for those parents who never thought they could change anything! The teachers, Yolanda and Socorro, had been threatened with losing their jobs. They showed their courage and bravery in leading the fight. The parents knew that their children were in danger of being blacklisted. In our collective power, we negotiated the resignation of the "slapping" teacher, our Chicana teachers kept their jobs, and the parents felt empowered in shaping the educational experience for their children!

In the *teatro* we had a sense that we were doing something right, something significant. We wanted to accomplish things. For the right reasons. And for me the *teatro* was, in a sense, a catalyst for my eventual work in community organizing and politics. Others went in other directions, but I think the experiences with the *teatro* were important springboards for whatever they did next.

The best aspect of all of that for me, as I told you, was the camaraderie. You know—the sense that we were doing this together. I remember that warmly. And it helped me in my understanding of the world around me. I'll be eternally grateful that I had the chance to work and learn and grow with the women who were in the Teatro de las Chicanas. I wish the same kind of valuable experiences for you, Lizelle.

So, *m'ija*, when you get that thick university packet in the mail complete with its letter of acceptance, welcome it with open arms. I encourage you to boldly step forward and embrace the wonderful college experiences that are awaiting you. It will be a blast! Make the most of it. I hope you develop the kind of fulfilling relationships in college that I was lucky to have.

All my love,
Tía Sandra

Notes

1. What more do they want?

10

Margarita Carrillo

TEATRO DE LAS Chicanas. Just recalling the name brings a smile to my lips, and why shouldn't it? The name speaks for itself—a theater group of Chicana women. Above all, the *teatro* educated me at that time in ways I would never have imagined. I learned things my mother certainly hadn't taught me in my twenty-two years. From these women I learned to stand up for myself and be proud of who I am.

I left Indio, a small agricultural town in the Coachella Valley of California, with my best friend Cindy when we were seventeen years old. It was Cindy's idea to leave for San Diego and join the High School Equivalency Program (HEP), a program aimed to help high school dropouts get their General Education Diploma (GED). Ironically, I had just finished the twelfth grade!

Three days before graduation my counselor told me he had made a mistake. He had made me take the same Spanish class twice, once in my freshman year and then again in my senior year, with different teachers of course. He realized it when reviewing the class list before graduation. The counselor said he regretted to tell me that I did not have the mandatory courses to graduate with the class. He recommended that I go to summer school to take the second part of Spanish and then get my diploma. This meant I couldn't walk with my classmates onstage at graduation.

I was in shock and walked around in a daze for weeks with mixed emotions and confusion. And I was embarrassed and humiliated. The saddest part of the story was that my mother wouldn't even go see the counselor and speak on my behalf. I didn't have her support due to the fact that she didn't speak English and never got involved with school activities. She always thought teachers knew best and thought I had probably "asked for it." I felt alone, bitter, and frustrated, and there was no one to turn to for help. I was helpless and lost, and for the second time education had failed me.

I had been in third grade the first time I felt hurt and stripped of my self-identity.

I remember it was a spring day; it had rained the night before and my nostrils were filled with the cool breeze of the morning and the smell of blooming flowers. It felt good to walk into class after morning recess with my classmates speaking Spanish. I spoke Spanish because, although I was a Mexican American, I did not know too much English. At home everyone spoke Spanish, making it difficult for me to grasp the English language fully and to speak it fluently. As I was taking off my light sweater and we were walking into the classroom, my friend Becky was telling me who was in tetherball. A girl named Marjorie Thompson went to Mrs. Adams, our sixty-year-old teacher, and told her that "Margarita" had taken some writing paper home to do homework.

In those days school materials were hardships for the teachers. Every pencil, paper, and book was accounted for. Teachers had to pay out of their pocket for extra paper. No student was allowed to take anything home. And God help the student who did, as I later learned! Without thinking, Mrs. Adams turned swiftly around and the first Margarita she saw was I. She came towards me, calling my name angrily as I stood there and watched with big terrified eyes and my heart beating so fast I thought it was going to burst. I saw her big old hand raise and felt it come down hard against my little eight-year-old cheek, making my head snap back.

I felt a burning sensation in my face as the pain spread like fire, and the backs of my eyelids stung as hot tears ran down my face. All I could do was squeak in such a low voice that I could barely hear myself, "It wasn't me!" Mrs. Adams had forgotten in her anger that there were three Mexican girls with the same name, Margarita. It was only then that Miss Goody-Two Shoes, Marjorie, told her with a shocked face that it was Margarita Flores, not Margarita Luna (my surname then), who took the paper home. Mrs. Adams realized what she had done and went pale. She didn't know what to do; I could only stand there with big tears streaming down my face, saying in Spanish, "I want to go home, I want my mama." Mrs. Adams got her purse and gave me 25 cents, which was like giving me $10 dollars! She told me to buy some ice cream, not to tell my mom, and that she was sorry. Mrs. Adams waited for lunch recess, then went to the school office and changed our legal names on our student school records. That day three small girls' names were changed to Margie Luna, Margaret Flores, and Maggie Hernandez.

My mother never questioned the fact that I became "Margie" overnight. I learned then that a child of eight has no power to stop a teacher from changing her Spanish name to an English name for her own convenience. Needless to say, Margie stuck with me throughout my life. It was forty-three years later that I went through the work to change my legal documents back to Margarita and get my real name back!

But at that time in 1970 I would have gladly accepted a high school diploma with the name of Margie. I had to leave home to obtain a diploma. I had a GED within months, followed by my entrance as a freshman to San Diego State University (SDSU). But I was still not out of my mother's shadow or brave enough to say "no" to her authority. She came down to visit me one day, found out I lived in a co-ed dorm, and felt I had changed drastically—to her, for the worst. But to me I felt the change was for the best. "Rebellious," she said, and "outspoken against the government." So we packed my bags and back to Indio I went. I dropped out of college to work as a maid at a country club hotel for eighteen months. It was no big deal for my mom; she was happy that I would be able to help out financially. You see, she was a single mother with five more daughters at home.

My heart was sinking. I was slowly dying. I had returned to nothing but hard work and weekend parties. There had to be more to it than this! At SDSU I had been exposed to many things—the Vietnam War and how to protest against it, the farm workers' fight for unionization, and women fighting for equal rights. I had to get out of my mother's shadow. So I got married.

I married Manuel, who I had met in HEP. After our marriage we left Indio and headed back to San Diego, where I ran into the Teatro de las Chicanas.

At first, as a married woman with a newborn child, Tania, I was content with just being that, a wife and mother. I was content doing the routine house chores and waiting for my hard-working husband to come home. I made all kinds of hot homemade meals and baked. My mother used to say, "*Una buena mujer hace una buena esposa y madre en la cocina*" ("A good woman is a good wife and mother in the kitchen"). Manuel invited his friends from HEP to come over to visit and eat. One of the friends was Merced, who had met a young, quiet girl named Clara. Clara and I hit it off really well. She was going to SDSU to become a teacher. Clara was a Chicana who, compared to me, was raised to be confident and independent.

She talked to me about activities and a *teatro* she was in. About a month after we moved to San Diego, she invited me to go with her to a rehearsal after I told her that I knew some of the women from afar and that I liked what they did. It turned out to be better because now the old members in the *teatro* had moved on and had been replaced with my dear old friends from HEP. It was like seeing family again. I was ecstatic, overwhelmed with happiness. Clara of course didn't know I had known them all at the same time I had met Manuel and Merced. She didn't know we had all been very close in our learning experiences at HEP.

What I saw in the *teatro* women shone a new light onto what I wanted in life, and illuminated what I lacked in experience. Secretly, I hungered to be like Felicitas, a beautiful *morena* with long wild hair, and a woman who had the guts to say what was on her mind—another Adelita. Adelita was seen as a loose woman by some, but for me she was an icon of the Mexican Revolution. Felicitas was a woman of many talents—as an artist, boy could she paint! And sing! She had a beautiful voice; my favorite song was "*La Llorona*." Yes, she was assertive, a knowledgeable leader, and into women's liberation.

And then there was Delia Ravelo. Shy at first but a firm, positive person, her smile would warmly surround you, making you feel important and wanted. Above all she was very intelligent and politically involved. They were out to change the world for women, fighting for a cause we all believed in. Yet some like me hid behind the mask of a hardcore *chola* with Betty Boop eyelashes! The mask hid me, kept anyone from hurting me or seeing my low self-esteem. I was trying to look tough so that no one could guess I was just plain scared.

The *teatro* women tried to recruit me that very night!

I didn't join the *teatro* that night or for a while longer. I wouldn't participate because Tania was only six months old and it had been three years since I last saw them. I didn't know how they had matured. I know I did change, from the girl of nineteen to a twenty-two-year-old good wife and mother. The *teatro actos* seemed more radical to me and yet I kept going back to the weekly rehearsal meetings to observe them. I learned what was happening on the various college campuses they attended. I was also becoming aware of working-class oppression from their *teatro* skits.

Gradually, I was getting to know the *teatro* women very well and trusting their judgment. It was when Tania turned three years old that I became a full member of the *teatro*. I was told I'd done enough observation and acting as a substitute and that I needed to become a full member. After I joined, they actively recruited Hilda into the group, who had also been reluctant because she had a baby boy, Ray, at the time.

I was scared and yet very willing to join the *teatro,* but my upbringing cast a shadow over me. In many ways I was wet behind the ears. But then my friends Laura, Delia, Felicitas, Lupita, and Cubanita, had turned, amazingly and passionately, into great leaders of the *teatro*. They sent a message sharp and clear, and with a driving force, about who the Chicanas were. And what the 1970s had given them—"equality of the sexes," Chicano Power, and women's liberation. In the middle of it all was Manuel, my husband, encouraging me to learn and grow with these women, who felt like they were big *chingonas,* with an attitude of "Don't mess with us!" It was hard to grasp everything they had to offer me. I learned from the *teatro* women while carrying around my daughter Tania. I wanted her to see and learn as well. At that time Manuel was involved with the United Farm Workers, walking picket lines and carrying Tania as well. Boy, we had a lot to offer society.

The *teatro* women never questioned my Spanglish, or my acting abilities, which were less than I desired. Delia had to prod me along whenever I forgot my lines. She attended rehearsals with a *rebozo* and her child, rehearsing with the baby sucking gently on her nipple. Delia was a mother figure to me, even though I was a year older. Every time I was on stage, part of me liked the excitement. I was sending a message to the young people, and part of me was scared to death of making a mistake. Of course there was no room for making mistakes—Felicitas would have us by the neck! It was very clear we were there to send out a message to the young people to stay in school no matter what.

We wrote our own scripts, and I was the only one who questioned everything we did. Later it was another member, Hilda, who did the questioning. Felicitas would get exasperated that it took time to explain why we were doing or saying things, but I needed to understand our message before I went out there and performed for the audience. I remember one *acto* that, years later, still embarrasses me; it was called "Challenge to Learn."

The play was about a girl coming out pregnant and the guy didn't want to acknowledge that he was the father. Since we didn't have male actors, just women, Delia had the role of "Johnny" and I was "Rosa." I forgot my lines onstage and "Johnny" had to prod me along. He loudly said, "Anyone could be the father because maybe they pulled a train!" (A train meant that I had been gang raped.) Boy, real tears came to my eyes and I really wanted the audience to know only one man had sex with me! I forgot it was acting! And my emotions were real as I told "Johnny" that, and also told him I wasn't going on welfare but would finish school instead without him.

I remember that teenagers afterward came up to speak with us. I was still feeling emotionally drained, yet felt pleased when I heard them say how true it all was and how they could identify with what we had presented about a girl coming out pregnant. Some parents were pleased that their children could take the message seriously coming from us. The parents listened and were aware of the problems teenagers were facing. It was because of these moments that I do not regret my work with the *teatro.*

We wanted to make a difference. We may not have succeeded in changing society overnight, but I do see more Latinos staying in school and more women working in a man's world. You see, women are more aware now and know their rights. There are more bilingual teachers to teach Spanish-speaking children. I smile and believe that the audience of teenagers of long ago heard our *teatro* messages and have become these women.

There are also no words to describe the deep friendships that developed between us, the *teatro* women. Through the years we were each other's mother, sister, and *comadre.* As we matured into women so did our friendships. We cried together, laughed together, and told each other our deepest secrets, and now thirty years later we still get together once a year and update others on our accomplishments, failures, and disappointments. We understand each other so well. The *teatro* experience also helped me understand my mother and our difficult relationship.

It was years later, after being married and having children of my own, that I learned of my mother's sheltered upbringing. I realized that she really didn't know *how* to help me while I was growing up. My grandfather told me that he had raised nine children when my grandmother died. My grandparents and their children were all born in Texas, my mother being the fourth child. At the time of my grandmother's death, my mother was in the third grade. My grandfather didn't know how to take care of so many kids and work at the same time. He worried about his six daughters and three sons. He decided to take all of them out of school and into the fields to keep a watchful eye on his daughters while he worked.

The family joined twenty other families in the migrant stream. They traveled city to city in a caravan, from Michigan to Florida and back to Texas. The children all worked in the fields, but the younger ones ended up sleeping or playing in the fields. The children grew up without a mother figure and without an education. My mother had no idea of the hard life ahead of her.

She worked until she got married. Basic survival needs were what consumed my mother.

My mother was married by the age of twenty and, like her mother, had six daughters when my father left her. She was a single mother at the age of thirty. She didn't speak English and didn't have a job. She got on welfare and stayed home to take care of my sisters and me. I was the oldest and in the fifth grade. My mother didn't have the support of her family either. My father's family stopped all contact with us when he left.

My mother's family added to her anxiety and fear by telling her that it was not easy to be a single mom of so many girls. They told her we would probably all come out pregnant or run away. So my mother protected us like a mother hen, tucking us under her wing and keeping us in her nest. I realize now she did the best that she could under very difficult circumstances. She did what she thought was right, based on a very limited frame of reference. As we grew older she really didn't talk to us. We were just children in her eyes. Adults spoke with adults, and children spoke with children. She believed that the school system was designed to educate us in every area. I suppose she was just embarrassed and timid to tell us the facts of life. She just wasn't knowledgeable enough about the world to teach us. How could she be, given the very limited options and opportunities she had?

My mother later met the *teatro* women and saw me perform with them. She told me that she saw something in me that she lacked herself. We then talked about the changes that women were making in society. She loved talking to Delia, Cubanita, and Hilda. My mother told me that she liked seeing how we interacted with our children, teaching them and explaining things to them. My mother and I can now sit down like good friends and talk about women's liberation or why women should be equal to men. She doesn't necessarily agree with some things, but she admires us and is proud that we turned out to be close to our children. I believe she is proud of me, too.

I suppose there are thousands of girls out there who are still being told by their parents and teachers that they do not need a high school diploma or a college degree. They are told that as women we are expected to marry, bear children, and take care of the home and that our husbands are our providers. They are still being told that we don't need a brain of our own to think and make decisions because our men will do it for us. To this kind of thinking and advice, I say "Bullshit!" You do need self-respect to be your own person, and you don't need a man to survive in society. We need to be proud of ourselves as women.

11

Hilda Rodriguez

I FIRST SAW women's theater perform was one evening at a MEChA meeting in 1973. They called themselves the Teatro de las Chicanas at the time. I was appalled by their presentation, titled *Bronca.* They looked more like male rebels, dressed all in tight black pants, black fitted shirts, boots, and long hair. I could say some of them were sexy looking. But why in the hell were they calling for "equality"? Women can get what they want by going through the back door, isn't this true? I thought they were unnecessarily confrontational. And when I learned that some of them were already living with their boyfriends and having wild parties I thought these women were also shameless. How shocking! They were "enjoying sex without a license."

But their message would continue ringing like bells in my mind: "*Hermanos, hermanas, únanse*—Brothers, sisters, unite!" I think they were trying to tell the males that women are people too. I did not know what to think; I had already been living on this side of the border for six years. I did not understand the meaning of their struggle, and besides it was foreign to my traditional Mexican upbringing. But why were these loose women shouting for "equality" on a university campus? Where did they come from? I knew where I had come from.

I was fifteen years old when I came to the United States in 1965 and enrolled in Coachella Valley High School. I was placed with other students who did not speak English. We were referred to and mocked as "*chuntaros*" or "*alambres*"[1] by mainly first-generation Mexican Americans born and raised in the United States. To us they were "*Los Pochos*," who spoke no Spanish or broken Spanish but made fun of my accent when I attempted to speak English. Even within my group we would make fun of each other. I would question why and regret that my father brought me to a land where my own people belittled me, but my internal feelings of insignificance exploded outward when the high school counselor told me, "According to your low SAT scores you are not qualified as a student for college. It will be too difficult for you."

It was as if I was being sentenced to a life of self-defeat, and being told that I had no intelligence or will for higher education. The exams for getting into college were not geared for Spanish-speaking students like me. And still worse, classroom instruction was not geared to strengthen my skills to prepare me to face the challenges of higher education. At the time I may have been too isolated, ignorant, or confused to be clear about my needs. But I needed teachers to teach and prepare me to meet the college requirements in case I chose to go to college.

It was hard to admit to myself that I was given passing grades just to get me out of high school. My passing grades did not reflect my educational learning. What I did learn was that having an accent was a block for higher learning. My accent was something to be embarrassed about; it was not cute like a British accent or alluring like a French accent. And I also learned that Mexican students are not expected to hope for higher education. Shutting down my hopes and essentially telling me to settle for a less intelligent and restricted life-style was a more acceptable way to treat me. Giving up was easier than getting frustrated and confused by my isolated attempts to reach higher goals. I did not want to give up. My hard-working parents were my roots of persistence.

My mother would wait for the summer and winter vacations from school, and as a family we picked field crops or sorted crops in the packing sheds. I didn't mind working because I was contributing toward school clothes, household needs, and sometimes a two-week vacation. My mother, who prepared the family meals before and after she worked alongside us in the fields, would say, "I bring you here to work because we need the money. But understand that if you do not finish school and get a decent paying job, you will have to work like this the rest of your life." My father was in agreement that we should strive to better ourselves. He was raised in Texas during the Great Depression and because there were no jobs his family returned to Mexico, where he worked in the coal mines for twenty years. He married Mom, and four children later they were very settled down, until my aunt encouraged him to bring his family to the United States for a better life.

It was my sister Irma who first reacted against our "better" life in the United States. It was about the middle of the harvest season for picking asparagus. We each carried a big box strapped to our shoulder with a knife in one hand to cut the plant and the other hand to place it in the box. Once filled with asparagus, this box was taken and loaded onto a large bin. Back and forth we went; at noon on this particular day, my sister Irma stopped working and started crying, "I cannot carry this box anymore; it is too heavy for me and my legs hurt." I felt like saying, "So, what's new?" But she looked so distressed I kept my mouth shut. I too ached all over and had to use body ointments and pills to reduce the pains so I could sleep at night. We all worked with the dust and juice of the plant producing a terrible smell that clung to our clothes and stained our hands.

We watched my sister as she removed her hat and the tear-soaked handkerchief from her face that served as a covering against pesticide dust. Her long-sleeved shirt also came off, leaving only her undershirt. She walked toward the car, opened the door, plopped herself inside, and slammed the door shut. Then she rolled down the car window, threw her shoes and socks out, and sat there for the rest of the day as we continued to work. My other sisters and I laughed because we thought her actions were funny. Later that night I approached her in her sullen state. She said, "I feel very humiliated. Look at the way we have to dress in order to protect ourselves from the over-bearing heat and dirt. I feel we are the smallest and poorest creatures in this world."

By the summer of 1968 I knew that my learning in the fields and in high school was not much of a better life in comparison to life in Mexico, but I continued with my hopes working under the hot sun. The heat was not much different when we migrated from the Coachella Valley into the Bakersfield and Fresno fields, where we worked among the long grapevine rows. One day I was securing my facial handkerchief—which helped tone down my skin rash from the pesticide dust—when I heard all this commotion. And guess what? Here come the United Farm Workers (UFW) with their damn picket signs as strikers telling us to join a *"causa justa."* Shit! I hungered for a decent education and prayed for a decent job. Why should I care about the ongoing problems?

Yes, we had slave labor, hard work, low pay, and no health benefits. Yes, we had unsanitary, crowded conditions, one kitchen, one bathroom we shared with several other families, and one room per family to sleep at night. So, who cared? The squalor we lived and worked in was temporary for me. *Adios* to all of this! I was not about to try to improve my working and living conditions when this work and life were not for me in the long term. That year and the following years, every day of my school vacations, I, a strike-breaker without remorse, would drive past the picket lines to go work in the fields. And there they were, every single time and all day long, standing with their ridiculous signs and yelling slogans. I ignored the farm workers because I thought they were fighting for a lost cause. I had no sympathy in my heart.

I also had no inspiration to reach my full learning potential in high school. Anyway, no one cared. I cut corners by taking the easiest required courses, got a high school diploma, got out of Coachella, and moved to Los Angeles, where I enrolled in the Job Corps. There I completed my office training, got an office job, and continued my education at a junior college. I married my high school sweetheart, Ray, and relocated to San Diego, where he had been attending San Diego State University (SDSU), and I enrolled at San Diego City College in 1973. I didn't question how or why, but during this time there were many opportunities for minorities to get into higher education. Finally, my life had improved for the better. I felt protected and so proud walking next to my husband as we explored the sites of his campus on a sunny afternoon.

SDSU was filled with energetic movement. I saw people of all colors, sizes, and shapes. Clearly, some students were from India or countries in Africa, and they wore what looked to me like exotic clothing from their native lands. Then I saw some students wearing blue jeans, military-style shirts, and even army boots. They were dressed in hand-me-down soldiers' clothing while bitterly opposing the war in Vietnam. Everyone on campus seemed to whiz by me, rushing to demonstrations, classes, meetings, and rallies. My head was spinning.

My husband took me to the outdoor Movimiento Estudiantil Chicano de Aztlán (MEChA) kitchen for lunch. The main menu was beans and rice. All the Chicano students seemed to know Ray, but the one that caught my eye was this girl who radiated with energy, and yet seemed so relaxed and friendly. She didn't wear makeup or a bra and wore a loose shirt and pants. She had a walk that dragged side to side, slowing into stops along her path. She talked, laughed, and shook hands with students seated on picnic tables on one side and the whole lunch line up on the other side. When she got to us she greeted Ray and asked, "Who is this?" pointing at me. Ray said, "She is my wife, Hilda. And Hilda this is Delia Ravelo." She struck me as kind of goofy. This girl, Delia, was no competition compared to my well-groomed and serious appearance.

In fact, most of the women looked like hippies and were not what I thought college students should look like. I felt that I was the best-dressed and most well poised lady of the whole bunch. While we waited in line some of the conversation I overheard was about this all-women's group that was going to perform later on at the MEChA meeting. I was shocked to find out that Delia Ravelo was a main connection to the Teatro de las Chicanas. Remember? Ray took me to see that appalling presentation. Now you know where I had come from when I got to their play. What I did not realize at the time was the influence Delia, her *teatro,* and Ray's associations would have on my life. In spite of my first impressions, the essence of my world would change.

Ray happened to become a strong supporter of the UFW and was a member of Teatro Mestizo, another theater group on campus. Some of the Chicanas were also in his *teatro.* I was alone in a big city and gladly went with Ray when we were invited to his friends' parties, where I would come in contact with the women. I think I can be a hard ass but the women in the *teatro* were able to meet me face on and I was able to get past the gossip that targeted these women. They were ordinary people and came from small towns like me.

If I wanted to learn or understand their position on any subject they did not hold back about what they knew to be true. And no matter how loud or bold they acted, underneath was a massive kind heart. I started to like being around them. The second time I saw them perform, their play was about "the working-class struggle." A year had passed since my first shock over their presentation, and they asked me to perform. Can you believe it? I was glad to be asked to join them. Well, imagine how much more shocking it gets! There I was. Yes! Me, in *teatro,* playing the role of a caring UFW striker, demanding better wages and working conditions.

Now, I was acting with remorse, pleading for sympathy and teaching the importance of UFW grape boycott from my stage to a live audience. It was easy to get into the role of a farm worker because of my real-life experience, but this was not enough. I had to read material about the UFW in order to understand my role intellectually. We had study groups to help us grow mentally but what was happening to me was that now I was learning and understanding with the eyes from my heart.

We discussed and related our book knowledge to life's experiences and examples. I was able to understand my struggle for self-identity. One of the books we had to read was *The Woman Question* by Karl Marx. I became stronger and more independent. By the time I played a coal miner from New Mexico in *Salt of the Earth* I felt much more confident about this role and the roles to come.

We became Teatro Laboral in 1975, and the Bakke decision was big news. This was the first big legal case challenging affirmative action. I came to realize that discrimination within the educational system was very real. When I was going to high school I experienced internal doubt and frustration. Understanding that my internal frustration was connected to a system or a world outside of me made me feel less isolated. Learning about my interconnection with the outside world was helpful for me, but now I felt a sense of power in my ability to help others. Figure this: if the outside world can influence me in a negative way then I as a positive individual can influence the outside world in a positive way.

Felicitas Nuñez and Delia Ravelo were usually joint leaders in our study sessions, but they were different in other aspects. Feliz did not have too much patience, but she did put up with our behavior and different levels of political understanding. She knew we had the potential to grow intellectually and always expected us to do our best in performance. She would get frustrated with our lack of commitment when we were late for rehearsal or just wasting time. She pushed us and talked to us over and over until things were done but she never gave up on us.

Delia was more gentle and understanding of our special needs, such as babysitting problems. She would come to our rescue and provide a babysitter or show up to give us a ride for rehearsal or performance. If we had an emotional problem that was not related to *teatro* she was there to listen, counsel, and lend a shoulder to cry on. If we had questions about kitchen curtains, baby formulas, or medicines she would impart her opinion or direct us to a source.

I performed on and off for several years, and by the time I had my children we had become Teatro Raíces. I got to attend two Teatros Nacionales de Aztlán (TENAZ) conferences, one in Los Angeles in 1977, but the most memorable one for me was in San Francisco. It was the 11th International Chicano Latino Teatro Festival, which took place in September of 1981. Delia Ravelo was pregnant and she stayed behind and took care of my two children. The ten of us spread ourselves out trying to cover as many of the conference workshops as possible. As excited as we were, we still got tired and in order to keep up with the next day's busy schedule, we went to bed early. Most of the TENAZ attendants continued to party, and by next morning there were rumors that we were "lesbians." So what?

We were scheduled to perform in the morning at a park, and some of the members were upset about the time and especially the place, because it was not a platform stage. Feliz said, "We came to perform, and it doesn't matter where; we will perform." When we got to the park there were a lot of people from the community. We were glad and then nervous as the audience grew and crowded in front of us. A platform stage would have been nice, but we were no strangers to dirt, grass, or cement; besides, isn't the whole world a stage? I felt we did a wonderful performance and our message was understood. Afterward some women from the park came over and spoke words of encouragement.

This would be my last presentation as Teatro Raíces but not the last connection with my *comadres.*

I completed my Associate Degree and transferred to SDSU in 1978. I recalled how once I felt so protected and proud walking with my husband on a sunny afternoon. But things were very different now. I did not detect an energetic movement in the campus air. There were no peace rallies, political demonstrations, or a collective sense of unity for a better world. Students just seemed to be concerned about getting their degrees and moving on. Scholarships and special programs for minorities were very limited. And only a few programs were available for low-income students or children of migrant workers. I was saddened by the absence of community. And I yearned to see the radiating energy in the youth like I had seen in Delia Ravelo.

I continued with *teatro* and focused on my children.

I became involved with my children's education early in their lives so that they could succeed and become productive adults in life. And also I got to learn so much about the educational system by becoming a member of the Parent Advisory Board. I attended every open house event and every possible school function. It was not easy working full time, but my priority as a parent was to set my children in the right direction. Staying connected to our children's school through our community, I believe, spreads knowledge.

Learning from my experience with my high school counselor gave me the insight to ensure that my children took the proper classes to set them on a college course track. Before my children started high school I went to their counseling appointment and told the counselor, "You are responsible for making sure my child is taking all the right classes that prepare a student to apply and be able to pass the entrance exams." I as a parent had to make sure my children understood and did their homework.

I kept watch on who their teachers and friends were. My husband used to say, "You want to know everything." Do you think I held back and cringed into a corner? No way; I ran with women that believed in the importance of education and developing our intelligence. Knowledge was our most precious asset in the *teatro,* and it continues to be so in my life. Yes, parents need to get involved with their children's education and be aware of everything that affects their lives.

I know that the most important inheritance I will leave my children is the best education I can give them. I tried to establish a positive and open relation with my children, especially my daughter. I emphasized her need to be proud of who she is and for her to understand the richness of her two cultures. We became friends early in her life but I remained the parent at all times. I told her, "I know more than your friends, always ask me anything and what I do not know we will find the answer together." Both my children completed their four-year degrees and continue to learn.

I now address all the children of the world. Understand that you have choices in life. But the freedom to chose also comes with great responsibility. You need to be able to stand on your own two feet in order to help others. You must work to become independent, assertive, and strong. Knowledge and education are the key to bettering yourself. Every human has the potential and capacity to develop, cultivate, and share their intelligence. And as you struggle to better yourself you must also love your every effort and stage of growing rich with knowledge.

My daughter, Krystal, is a high school teacher, and she has told her students that I as her parent know all about her problems, situations, and relationships. Her students find this hard to believe, but it was harder for me to believe and to hear my daughter say, "My mother is a very strong and knowledgeable person. You should try to find that understanding and connection with your own mother. You will be surprised how much they know about life."

I am very grateful for the opportunity to have been part of a group who called themselves "Las Chicanas." I learned something valuable from each *teatro* member. Among other things, I learned about myself, my world, and how in my world to help others. I learned to be open, reasonable, and nurturing. Learning for me has no ending. I am living proof to all teenage Latinas and Mexicanas coming to the United States that, Yes! You can go to college even if you speak English with an accent.

Notes

1. "Low-lifes" or "wires," implying breaking through the border wire fence.

12

Delia Rodriguez

"WHAT THE HELL am I doing here, facing a confused audience and possibly an overcritical drama professor to top it off?" This was the thought that raced pounding through my mind as I was about to perform at the University of California, San Diego (UCSD) in a play titled *No School Tomorrow.* I could not make sense of how I had wound up face to face with fear. Back then, I was much too nervous to be able to organize the reasons that led me to act in a play about education. Now, looking back at this intense moment in Teatro Laboral (originally called Teatro de las Chicanas), I can map the events in my life that connected me to my *teatro* sisters.

My parents had eleven total years of formal education between them. I was raised by my nineteenth-century Mexican father and my Scottish Canadian mother, who was twenty-three years his junior. When we were children, these differences between our parents were the least of our concerns. Our focus was on playing on our wonderful piece of earth. In the springtime my siblings and I wouldn't think twice about tearing off our clothes and running naked in the rain. We would slide in the thick muddy streams that formed along the dirt streets. During the summers we loved playing in the maze of cornfields. We felt so happy and carefree.

We would show up to class with tumbleweeds in our hair, with our clothes rumpled and dirty, and many times barefooted. Regardless of our appearance, we loved our teachers and making new friends. I remember myself in school as that little girl who wanted to be accepted and belong to all the "good groups," but I first noticed in kindergarten that I felt different from my classmates. It was very hurtful to hear other kids criticize our poor smelly rancho and our rural, rustic lifestyle. I began to realize that my parents were also very different from other parents.

Frequently, my mom would say to my dad, "You're so old-fashioned." And he would retort, "*Si yo hubiera sabido que tú no sabías como lavar los trastes, nunca me hubiera casado contigo*" ("I wouldn't have married you if I had known that you didn't know how to wash dishes"). Yet in spite of my parents' shortcomings, I loved them dearly. My mother was good at helping out the non-English speaking parents who needed documents translated, filling out forms and writing letters for them. My father would tell us stories about his experiences in the Mexican Revolution of 1910 as we all sat around the kitchen table drinking coffee. But there were times, especially as I got older, that I did blame my parents for treating me unfairly. At age seven I hated being the primary caretaker of my younger sister and brothers, who depended on me.

My elementary school years had many moments of what I called self-pity parties. I detested being in the kitchen, looking down at my small pink hands rolling out the dough that was then divided into biscuit-size stacks. These would become crooked tortillas resembling geographical maps instead of circular shapes. I tried to make a game of all my chores but still resented being the only one to help with meal preparations. My resentment would build up as I looked out through the murky window and watched my brothers and friends playing joyful outdoor games.

I'll never forget the day when one of my crooked tortillas burst into flames. I tearfully stomped into the bathroom, brutally chopped off all my hair, and put on my brother's clothing. I tore out of the house to dig my feet in the dirt and stretch my arms out to touch the sky. I felt I was kissing the soft white cotton clouds nestled against the setting sun. I felt so carefree again. The other kids didn't recognize me at first and thought I was a new kid on the block. I broke out with a grin and we all laughed out loud. We played until it got dark, and after this I don't remember what my parents said to me.

My father was very religious, with a long list of major sins beginning with "Do not . . ." Included in his list for me was "Do not cut thy hair." According to my father, many of my normal childhood behaviors were inspired by the devil. The only way he knew to ward the devil off was for me to attend church and pray. Repeatedly, he would say, "*Ándale, Delia, alístate para ir a la iglesia, te tenemos que sacar el demonio*" (Hurry up, Delia, get dressed for church, we have to get the devil out of you). In the beginning I would get frightened and for my own sake could not accept his beliefs, but I still went to church. However, I still thought that it was not fair to be a girl. Boys were able to do more fun things and got into less trouble. I wondered why it was easier to be a boy in my family.

My mom had an increasingly hard time caring for us as we got older. But it was harder on my aging dad, who tried to take on more of the responsibilities. He had very long workdays that would start with milking several cows by hand. After this he sold milk, eggs, and his homemade cheese to regular customers in the neighborhood before he took the bus to work in the fish cannery.

No matter what was happening at home, I kept trying to do my best at school. I thought that everyone learned and understood school concepts like me. I was surprised and encouraged when my friends would make comments such as "*Eres muy viva,*" or "You are very smart." I was wonderfully shocked by the scholarship award I received for my sixth-grade graduation. But although I felt my school situation was improving, my life at home was falling apart.

My aging father became ill and was unable to help my mom as well as protect and manage our family. My brother and I were out in the streets at all times. At age twelve I became a victim of a sexual assault and my grades at school plummeted. My eldest brother, due to drug-related problems, was being detained by the California Youth Authority. Shortly after, the courts placed my three siblings and me under foster care. Fortunately, our foster parents provided a stable environment and drove us to see our parents every weekend.

In this new home I did come to realize that my parents had done the best they could. But like most adolescents around me, I continued to be very immature and somewhat rebellious during my high school years. I ended up in continuation school and completed my General Education Diploma. I was again surprised in 1966 when I won a scholarship to help out with my college expenses. I was counseled into the field of cosmetology and managed to finish an Associate of Arts degree at a junior college. I transferred to San Diego State College and in three months was recruited to UC San Diego for the spring quarter of 1969. My plan was to go to college and get a degree in who knows what.

Two spouses, three kids, and eleven years later, I finally graduated with a Bachelor of Arts and a California Teaching Credential. Afterward I thought it would have been easier to get my degree and establish a career before having children, although earning diplomas along with all of life's other experiences had given me a sense of maturity.

After graduation I joined a women's theater known as Teatro Laboral. This group was soliciting new ideas and new members, including a couple of males to spice up the show. I was well acquainted with these women who supported my stand for higher education for all.

Together we wrote the play *No School Tomorrow,* which was about Allan Bakke. He was an Anglo student who claimed "reverse discrimination" when he was first denied acceptance to medical school. The Bakke case had started around 1975, and by the time I graduated as a teacher it was going strong. This case on behalf of one white student reached the Supreme Court. In Allan Bakke's case it was resolved that he was a victim of reverse discrimination. In my case, I was accepted to the university that granted me equal opportunity through affirmative action. (Affirmative action was dismantled in California in 1996.)

Today there has been no resolution about what is called affirmative action and intense public debate continues on reverse discrimination. The mere existence of "reverse discrimination" and "affirmative action" means that education is not intended to be available to all. The Bakke lawsuit devalued an important solution to a long history of institutionalized discrimination against students of color and families with meager formal education.

It seemed so unfair to me because I was one of those deprived students who were able to get into a university through the educational opportunity programs. At that time, I was certain that college opportunities were at risk for many students with a background similar to mine. I felt a responsibility and a strong connection to all promising college students and graduates who had a passionate desire to help others. *Teatro* was a great way for me to reinforce my beliefs and possibly my acting skills.

I had loads to learn about *teatro,* yet I felt worthy and accepted in the group. When I didn't have a babysitter, I would pile the playpen, the toys, and my three kids into my Ford Pinto. We were set for an evening of training and practice. Rehearsals were fun and lively, making me think that it would be easy to jump right in and act. We would meet at Delia Ravelo's house on Friday evenings and do creative expression through mime. Others would try to guess what our body language was communicating. We worked and socialized. This was extremely nurturing for my spirit.

We also practiced and had training workshops at the Centro Cultural de la

Raza. We did group bonding activities and voice training. In one session I was lying on the floor. Everyone formed a circle and kneeled around me, looking into my eyes and asking personal questions. I thought it was fun and I felt very comfortable. Some performers said that I looked scared and insecure. Unfortunately that tidbit of observation had more truth than I cared to admit.

Even though I face serious challenges trying to carry a tune, I was actually complimented on how good my voice sounded while singing *"De Colores"*. I could sing very well when I bent over and held my ankles with my hands, with my head hanging between my legs facing the audiences. A very strange and embarrassing position. But, I thought, I've got the hang of this. Piece of cake!

Still, I was in for a rude awakening. I quickly found out that an actor's job isn't as easy as it looks. I required a written script and many rehearsals to get into the role of Bakke. Unfortunately, on very short notice, especially for me, we were asked to perform for a few community events. We quickly wrote the play, assigned roles, and practiced a few times. It really wasn't a script. It was an outline, consisting of brief statements for each act. The actors were expected to improvise and convert the main ideas into a spontaneous dialogue that I never wrote down. It was innovative and inventive, but hadn't been retold enough to stick to a specific story line. We added embellishments and versions to match our audience. Since there was no real script, I was not able to practice any lines over and over again to feel secure. Furthermore, we didn't have enough time on our hands to rehearse and concretize the play. What was I thinking? That it would all come together by magic.

So, I panicked when I was onstage playing the role of Bakke. I was having a hard time formulating my imaginary lines. All I could focus on were my doubts about being able to act. But I knew I had to hide these feelings and get them under control. By the time I felt it was coming together, I was practically depleted of energy and my mind was tired. Oh no, we were not done yet—it was time for the dancing part to "Staying Alive" by the Bee Gees, and this is where I lost it. "Get a little in front of me," I whispered to Maria LiMandre, who was the choreographer. Desperately looking at her through the corner of my eye, I followed her steps. We all managed to pull it off through our support system of hit-and-miss improvisations.

The audience at UCSD was confused and responded with a low hum toward the end of our performance. We weren't sure whether they thought our skit was good or bad. We received many comments like, "Your *teatro* is full of energy," and this tended to make us laugh. As a group, we primarily wanted to get our message across, but a decent performance would have been nice too.

After my several failing star performances, I hesitated to continue polishing up my *teatro* skills. Instead, I polished my educational teaching skills and held on to my hopes about education.

My vision was that once students were accepted to a university, almost all would work very hard to achieve success and graduate. Of course, all graduates would then earn an honest living. No one would be unemployed, and no one would need to turn to crime. Therefore educating all would create responsible citizens. Thus, social and political issues could be resolved through dialogue instead of war. This vision was not forgotten but set aside as I got busier taking care of my family.

I felt the years pass quickly as I followed my husband around the globe. To join him, I moved with my three children to Guadalajara, Mexico. Meanwhile I kept flying back and forth to San Diego, to finish a Master's degree at UCSD. After Guadalajara we hopscotched from San Diego, to New Orleans, back to San Diego, and then to Oregon.

While in Oregon, my younger son became severely depressed and was hospitalized. I thought that I must have done something wrong somehow and that I was responsible. As a mother I felt extremely guilty.

Two months later, just when I thought I could not endure another bit of bad news, I was diagnosed with breast cancer. I broke down and didn't know what to do. I was afraid and felt neglected by my husband. I thought I was going to die. But I couldn't die because I still needed to unpack two hundred boxes. I stumbled about with my disease; the relationship with my spouse kept declining and my outlook on life got dimmer.

After my third round of chemotherapy and a final separation from my spouse, I moved back to San Diego. I could not afford to break the lease on my house and was left without a home. I managed to rotate my stays with family and friends. Meanwhile, my immune system was very compromised; I could barely move. The highlight of every day was pulling myself up from the couch, taking a shower, putting on clean clothes, and then collapsing from exhaustion.

I was wasting away and fumes from my flesh were the smell of decaying cells. I was weak and depressed. I didn't want to believe or admit out loud that my marriage was doomed. But I felt that my chances for recovery would be better if I freed the weight of this painful empty relationship from my chest. I did not want to get a divorce; however, I wanted to live.

Many days I lay on the couch at my aunt's house, trying to find the energy and spirit within my body to focus on healing myself. I had no hair anywhere on my body, but this was the least of my concerns. Then the phone rang and interrupted my self-pity party. The voice on the other end said "Hi, Delia. This is Felicitas, I heard from Delia Ravelo who heard from our friend Remigio Gonzales that you have breast cancer. Well, I've had it too."

Just at the right moment! What an inspiring conversation! Who would have thought these few words would lead to renewed friendships and a strong support system that I so badly needed. Delia Ravelo Reyes and Felicitas Nuñez were like my guardian angels. We would talk frequently on the phone and when Felicitas came into town, the three of us would meet for lunch or dinner. We attended the reading of a play, *La Lupe,* written by Evelyn Cruz, who had been in the *teatro.* What a rejuvenation! This comeback performance was very impressive. After the reading, Delia formally introduced me to Evelyn. We spoke briefly and I sensed that we belonged to the same family.

Delia Ravelo invited me into her home and heart. She would share her creations and imagination. She painted on glass, worked with broken tile, and decorated birdhouses. She would say, "I have a voracious appetite for literature." I was most impressed by watching Delia work in her garden, displaying its soil under every fingernail. She would tour me around the yard in her muddy Birkenstock sandals, marveling over the miracles that sprouted from the rich earth.

Felicitas pointed out ways to restore and support my health beyond those of conventional medicine. I had read Dr. Susan Love's *The Breast Book,* and I was a spout of information on current views of cancer treatment. I confessed that I was reading a lot because I was afraid to close my eyes for fear that I would die in my sleep. Felicitas gave me a copy of Bernie Segal's *Love, Medicine, and Miracles* to ease my fear, followed by other self-help books such as Elaine Nussbaum's *Recovery From Cancer,* which focused more on macrobiotic foods such as organic vegetables and whole grains.

Delia and Felicitas had gotten into Bee Venom Therapy (BVT) in addition to other nonconventional healing methods. They had the literature to explain this phenomenon. I could accept chemotherapy as a poison going into my body with all the side effects but not this bit of poison. They suggested stinging the wart on my thumb. I retorted "*¡Están locas!*"[1]—I'm not putting any killer bees on me! One evening Delia and Felicitas came to visit me with a jar of bees; by then I had an apartment, a rubber boob, and a wig of my own. I was also feeling stronger, had started working, and had made up my mind to finalize my divorce after twenty-five years of marriage. I knew these two women would not criticize or put me down. Instead they distracted me.

Felicitas asked me to put some bee stings around the one-inch circumference of a blue lump she had on her right lower back. I was able to place about five bee stings around her lump. Then I got the courage to say, "Put one here," on a weird lump between my armpit and remaining breast. I got a feel for BVT and used it on my wart to decrease its size and to alleviate the pain of a hairline fracture on my arm, and I even put one on the top of my head to stimulate my thinking. This was painful, but I laughed as I ran around the house trying not to feel the sting.

Soon after that Kathy Requejo, another *teatro* sister, called me out of the blue; we connected immediately. While I was on medical leave from work, she stayed with me on several occasions. Together we attended the Adelante Mujer conference for young adolescents and went to the workshop led by Delia Ravelo and Felicitas. They also got us together with our friend Remigio and we attended the Latino film festival, where we took pictures with actor Edward James Olmos. I remember expressing my dissatisfaction later about the lame roles that women played.

I was determined to write a letter criticizing the stereotypical roles for women as mothers, virgins, and prostitutes. But my *teatro* sisters pointed out that I really needed to write plays with intelligent and proactive roles for women. In other words, "Do not whine. Act!" I understood where my *comadres* were coming from. We can be very direct.

During this visit Kathy listened to me talk in depth about my emotional weaknesses and my physical condition. I started to regain my confidence and self-esteem. We also shared many things about our personal life. Jokingly, we baptized my rubber boob Cheech and my remaining breast Chong. It was amazing how this gummy substance shaped into a breast could feel so real yet be so fricken heavy. Wow! I had graduated from being afraid about breast cancer to being able to poke fun at my big huge falsie.

A few months later I got a serious call from Felicitas to inform me that Delia Ravelo was very sick in the hospital, diagnosed with stage IV ovarian cancer, and not expected to live long. To everyone's amazement, Delia bounced back on a very strict macrobiotic diet prescribed by Mina Dobic, who wrote *Recover from Cancer.* When Delia had first started her chemotherapy we had a small dinner in her honor; Gloria Escalera, Guadalupe Beltran, and Evelyn Cruz were present. Felicitas and I had already decided we were going to shave the rest of Delia's balding head and then both of us would follow by shaving each other's hair off. We had been reading how to show support for loved ones on chemotherapy. Gloria and Lupe were traumatized, in disbelief at our bald bold image. Delia and Evelyn cried over our brave bold love.

This time around I didn't hide my baldness; I demonstrated my support with pride.

I feel a very strong spiritual bond that keeps me connected to my *teatro comadres* even when years pass without contact. Kathy reconnected with me when I was going through my recovery. Perhaps our reunion gave Kathy some sense of how to deal with her own diagnosis several years later.

My twenty-one year journey toward an M.A. (Master of Arts degree) was more than motion toward a goal of scholastic achievement. It was a process of placing great value in all my life's education. I remain hopeful that the time will come when our three branches of government will make higher education a social right for everyone.

My involvement in the *teatro* as an actor was very short. But for me my association with the *teatro* continues to be a real education. I am blessed because my *teatro* family ties are eternal.

Kathy went through recovery and joined us for Delia's memorial service. Delia Ravelo Reyes' humanitarianism, like billions of earthly stars, lives forever in our hopes and dreams. She was with us for another twenty months after her grave diagnosis. But before she became a heavenly star on November 26, 2002, she had made a trip to Europe and came back speaking French. She made friends with the owner of a restaurant named "The Anarchist," and talked about a plan to return one day to France with the *teatro* group to do a presentation on world solidarity. Hopefully, someday we will make this trip in Delia Ravelo's honor.

Notes

1. They're crazy!

13

Guadalupe Beltran

From Chicana to Woman

There she is, that little Mexican girl running after her brothers, wanting to belong.
There's that Chicana girl, chanting "Brown Power."
There's that Chicana in *teatroz,* expressing her political views.
There's that Chicana with a family of her own.
There she is, the Mexican Chicana Woman:
Who at the age of six was molested by a neighbor.
Who at the age of six and a half learned to say no.
Who at the age of seven started working in the fields.
Who at the age of eight was left in a work field because there were too many in the family to keep track of.
Who at the age of fourteen had such low self-esteem that she resorted to fighting just to belong and to get approval from her father.
Who at the age of sixteen would cut classes to go drinking and smoking just to feel good.
Who at the age of seventeen decided to quit school.

Who at the age of eighteen realized she had made a mistake and joined
HEP to get her GED.
She, the only one in a family of nine who left home for an education
Instead of for marriage.
She who joined *teatro* to express her political views.
She who now looks back at her time with teatro and realizes that she
Learned more than what she put in.
She who learned that life is a *teatro.*
Teatro taught me to act out feelings. Real life taught me to hide feelings.
Teatro taught me to express honesty. In real life we learn to lie with a smile.
Teatro taught me to face the truth. In real life we learn to bullshit with a
straight face.
And just as in *teatro* we learned that
"THE SHOW MUST GO ON"; so LIFE MUST GO ON.

On the night I am born a male doctor attends my mother at our home. My mother has already given birth to José Angel, Lázaro, Juanita, Julian, Antonio, and Luis. Midwives brought them into this world. You can imagine my mother's shame in having to open her legs to a man other than my father. The young doctor gets upset and yells at my mother for not wanting to open her legs for him. Immediately my father puts a stop to the doctor's yelling. The young doctor is forced to be patient with my mother. For the first time, *cuando mi madre da luz*[1] her baby is held by a man, and a tradition has just been broken! My brothers, Alfredo and Juan Jr., are born later in this new fashion.

Five years later, there I am, the little Mexican girl running after her brothers. "Hey, Luis, Freddy, wait for me. Come on, I want to play too." Julian and Tony are too old to play with me and my fifteen-year-old sister hates me. I hear my Aunt Paula yelling out to me, *"Allá vas, Juana Gallo, descalza come siempre, córrele pronto, alcánzalos."*[2] "I'm not Juana, *tía*. Juana is my sister. I'm Lupe." Why does Tía Paula call me Juana Gallo, Mother? "It's a compliment, *m'ija*. Juana Gallos were what the women were called who fought in the Mexican Revolution side by side with the men." So I continue to run barefoot and free.

But I don't want new shoes. "You have to have new shoes, Lupe; you can't continue running barefoot," my mother tells me. I reply, "Mom, do I have to wear my new shoes? They hurt my feet, especially my left foot." "*M'ija,* your left foot hurts because you had polio when you were over a year old. You suddenly stopped walking. I wanted to take you to a doctor but your father said no, that you were just being difficult. That's when I noticed your left foot was curling up and both your feet did not seem to be growing. So I started massaging your feet and praying a lot. I prayed and massaged and prayed and massaged till one day you started walking again. But the damage had been done; your feet were deformed and your left foot never caught up in size with the right foot. But, *m'ija,* you could walk again." I tell her, "But I can't walk well with shoes, *Mamá,* and I can't run." The shoes have killed a little more of my spirit! I hear my father tell mother, "No, I can't take her to a specialist; we don't have the money." I understand, Father; I think I understand.

My sixth birthday has come and gone and no one has bought me a present. My father's boss, who is the foreman in the fields and our neighbor, gives me a hug and kisses me on the cheek. He winks at me and makes me feel special. He must like me, as he likes his daughters who are my sister's age. Oh, the next day, he gives me a quarter and kisses me on the lips. Now I know he likes me.

Everyone is working in the fields. My father's foreman leads me to the shed. He touches me down there. I have no special feeling. Now he wants me to touch him. He pulls something out of his pants and he wants me to kiss it. Oh, not again; he's giving me signals with his eyes. His eyes tell me to meet him in the shed. Doesn't my mother or father see this? They are too busy talking. I don't want to go. He tells me he does not want to tell my father that I have been a bad girl, so I go with him to the shed. He puts his thing in my mouth and touches me down there but I must obey; he is the adult. I feel very bad, I am a bad girl. I don't want to be spanked. What can I do? I pee. He gets angry and yells at me, tells me to go home. And the next day he is giving me signals again. I turn away; if I don't see him he can't give me signals. For two weeks he gives me signals. I turn away. It works because he leaves me alone.

Oh joy, we have moved to Gilroy. My father's foreman has come to visit. He and his wife have a little girl with them, who is not their daughter. I see him giving her signals and she goes outside. I follow her. "Wait!" I tell her, "You don't have to do what he says. You don't have to see him when he gives you signals, just look away." We go back inside the house to play with my dolls. They are really half-dolls because my brothers have ripped the heads off the dolls. They think it's funny. I'm thinking I'm going to hit one or all of them if they come back into the room. But for now I just want to play because I'm to start working in the fields.

I start working at the age of seven. I remember clearly the day because my mother and I planned for days before it happens. My mother used to buy lard from the store. This lard came in a container that was actually a small tin bucket with a lid. These buckets were red in color and came in different sizes. My mother buys the second-to-the-smallest size and tells me that when she finishes using the lard I will have my very own bucket to use on my first day of work. I am going to pick prunes and I can't wait. The day finally arrives, and my mother washes the red bucket and hands it to me. I hold that red bucket as if it is an Easter egg basket and I am going to my very first Easter egg hunt.

It is at this time that we have moved from San Jose to Gilroy. We still drive to San Martin to work in a field there. I don't know our new address. I just know that we live in Gilroy. One day my family takes three cars to work. We were nine children and two parents. One of my brothers is already married with two or three children of his own. On this one day I accidentally poke my eye with a tree branch and my mother tells me to go lie down and rest. When I awake we are ready to go home. "Mom, I forgot my sweater, I'll be right back." I rush into the field to get my sweater. When I return everyone has left, and I cry. A man near by notices me and yells, "Are you lost, little girl? I'll help you." I am very frightened and I walk away from him. I start walking home. I follow the highway and walk and walk and walk and cry and cry and cry. While crossing a driveway I fall down and at that moment a car pulls up, a man gets out and asks if I need help. I don't answer him. I get up and continue to walk.

A woman gets out of the car and says, "*Niña, no llores* [Do not cry, child]. I am a mother and I have children, let me help you." I rush into her arms and start sobbing. I tell her, "I don't know where I live. I know the town is Gilroy, but we just moved there and I don't know the address." This couple takes me to the San Martin police station. The policemen buy me an ice cream cone. I tell them, "If you follow the railroad tracks I can lead you to my house." Two policemen are assigned to take me home. They light the railroad tracks with their strong searchlights and I say to them, there, there follow that street, turn here, here is my house! My parents don't notice that I am missing until a half an hour before I arrive with the police. Everyone thought I was in the other car. My parents are relieved that I am home. How can I blame my mother? She and my older sister get up at four-thirty in the morning to make breakfast, get our lunch ready for the day, work right beside us in the field, and then come home to make dinner.

Four months into the school year, I should be in the first grade but they put me into the second grade because of my age. I'm having trouble understanding the lessons. The teacher is upset with me again. The boy who sits behind me calls me stupid. I work extra hard. There is no one at home to help me with my homework. Both my parents, who were born in Texas, do not speak English and did not go to school like me. Oh, what joy; I passed the second grade!

The boy who sat behind me does not pass. I don't call him stupid; I just smile at him while I am passing by his desk.

In the eighth grade I make a new friend; her name is Maria. She has older sisters but no one to study with. Like me. She and I become close friends. She is being picked on by other girls and I defend her. This is my first big fight. Oh, Father is proud of me. All he wants to know is if I won the fight. I did. My friend Maria can't play with me anymore because her parents don't believe in fighting. Up until this time I was a student who enjoyed studying with my friend Maria to get good grades. I never got into trouble with the teachers. After my first fight I make a new friend, Yolanda. She admires me for standing up for Maria. This new friend is a *chola,* a street-wise girl. She introduces me to playing hooky, cruising, and drinking. Through her I meet other *cholas.* I fall behind in my schoolwork, but am still able to pass the eighth grade and enter high school.

My first year in high school—what a thrill and yet scary. I now have ten *chola* friends and we hang out together. No one loves us. I have seven brothers and my sister is married. I can't rely on anyone except my friends. They are my family. I am now a *chola.* My father is proud of me. I can fight just like my brothers. He doesn't know I cut school to go with my friends cruising, drinking, and listening to oldies on the radio. And if I'm not doing this I'm in the library reading fairy tales and make-believe stories, because these stories are more interesting than my life.

One day, my older brother, Luis, has something interesting to tell me, "Hey sis, come with me, there is a meeting and everyone is invited. Have you heard of the Brown Berets? Yes, you can come. The group is for men and women. They want to help young people get out of drugs and stay in school, or I think that's what it is about."

It really isn't the Brown Berets; it is a Mexican teacher from the city college. He has a speaker who was a member of the Brown Berets. I hear the speaker say, "We are not treated equal. We have to respect ourselves and see ourselves as equals. We need to educate and organize ourselves. We are asking people to start a chapter in our town." We start a chapter and do activities. First we have a successful car wash and a community dance to raise funds and participate in a parade. We put together a float that reflects the pride of ruling indigenous warriors. This is the very first time I see the Aztecs as a very powerful race. Because of the Brown Berets I learn of our true historical culture and roots. Up until this time I was invisible in our educational system.

I decide to quit high school at age seventeen since graduation for me is not in sight. I do not want to be embarrassed because I am tough. Most of my *chola* friends are using drugs and are getting pregnant. I decide that this way of life is not for me. I had heard of a program called HEP (High School Equivalency Program). It is a new program for children of migrant workers and it offers a

GED (General Education Diploma). Of course my parents refuse to let me go. I would be by myself, living in a dormitory, within a college atmosphere that would be a piece of heaven for me. It takes the favorable opinion of José Angel, my oldest brother, for my parents to let me go.

The decision to go to Stockton University for my GED is very hard for me. The night before I leave for Stockton I get very drunk. I break up with my boyfriend because he does not want me to leave. He is a tall, dark-haired handsome man who plays the drums in a band. His drumsticks still beat at my heart. On the day of my departure I get on the bus with a very bad hangover. My head is being hammered and my stomach is hot and dry with wrenching acid. Yet I am feeling very scared about being on my own. I sit at the back of the bus, covering myself in a blanket of fear. An hour into the trip a young friendly boy starts a conversation with me. His name is Philip, and guess what? He is also going for the HEP program and he offers me weed on our arrival in Stockton.

The first three months I do nothing but party. Oh, we go to classes but don't really see the importance of the program. One day I wake up and say to my self, "What am I doing? Did I forget why I really came here?" Yes, I have forgotten. I decide to get back on track, and in one month I have my General Education Diploma (GED). I am the only child of nine who even got a GED. I go back home feeling very proud. The next week I am back working in the fields, dating the same old boyfriend. Nothing has changed.

A few weeks later I hear about College-Aimed Migrant Program (CAMP), another program for the children of migrant workers. This program helps me get into college and apply for financial aid and grants. This time I do not ask my parents for permission to go to college. I tell them, "I am going to college!"

I arrive at San Diego State University (SDSU) in 1973. I know nothing about college. Hell, I don't even know how to study college material. Well, it's party time all over again. There are classes at SDSU I have never heard about: political classes, women's rights, migrants' rights, minority rights. One day I see a play at SDSU performed by an all-woman group. Two women I have been hearing about, Felicitas Nuñez and Delia Ravelo, perform the main characters. These two women are very involved in politics. Women's rights are a big issue to them. At this time this street theater group is called Teatro de las Chicanas.

The women in this *teatro* are very much feminists, they believe in equality for both men and women. They are very vocal at MEChA meetings. They aren't the meek type of women I am used to seeing on television shows, like the *Leave It to Beaver* mother, or the *chola* type of women who seldom stand up to their men. This *teatro* group is desperate for members. I take this opportunity and join. First, to prove that I can act. Second, to prove that I can be as knowledgeable as any one of the *teatro* members. Of course I am wrong. This *teatro* is more than I expected. For me it is beautiful; I learn so much about politics and subjects that a regular college class cannot teach me. I learn about issues related to migrant workers, welfare, unemployment, and the roots of what is to eventually become the civil war in El Salvador. My mind is a sponge and there is no better place than *teatro* to absorb so much information.

As a woman I don't regret anything in my life.
As a woman I now enjoy life in spite of everything I've gone through.
Teatro was a stepping stone to where I am now.
As young girls we learn to mistrust men.
As young Chicanas we learn even to hate men.
As women we have learned to live with men and even teach them.
Teach them by teaching our young men and women to respect each other
As human beings. I have taught my two sons these lessons.
I am this woman who is ever so grateful for meeting my husband.
My husband who encouraged me to join *teatro*. He who has helped me
Outgrow my childhood. He who has always been there for me and my sons.
This woman will never forget her stepping stones through *teatro*.

In the beginning of my *teatro* years I played small parts, sometimes three or four different characters, because we didn't have enough members for all the roles. All the roles were important to the play. Each character had to be different and had to be believable. In my later years in the *teatro* I played main characters like Rudy in *So Ruff, So Tuff*. This is a play about two young high school students who find out the importance of staying in school. I played the role of the brother and my sister was Gloria Escalera. I played Archie in *Archie Bunker Goes to El Salvador*, and Gloria played the daughter "Gloria." I was also Enriqueta Tejeda in *E.T.—The Alien*. The play is about a young Latina woman who is seduced into coming to the United States by a coyote, played by Felicitas Nuñez. A *coyote* is an exploiter of unsuspecting immigrants called *pollos*, or "chicks." The *coyote* takes the money of immigrants to bring them across the border to the United States.

Felicitas and Delia Ravelo were in the forefront of the *teatro*. I felt intimidated when I first met them. They scared me. Me, a girl who would stand up to any *chola* and throw the first punch. Delia was more friendly than Felicitas, but both were very demanding. What scared me was the intelligence these women possessed. I didn't know how to fight this type of battle. I had to learn the rules first. Yes, I overcame my shyness and pretended to know what I was doing, knowing that one day I would learn so much from these two women. And these two women were not the only ones in *teatro* who contributed their time and efforts. I also learned a lot from other *teatro* members who came and stayed to the very end of the *teatro*. There were several girls who started with Felicitas and Delia who I never met, but thanks to them *teatro* was possible.

Being in *teatro* was not easy, especially in the later years when most of us were married and had children. We traveled with our children when we could not find babysitters.

The Teatro de las Chicanas was renamed when we became more politically involved and we realized that the name had to be changed so it would reflect our political views to the community. We were getting more involved with working-class issues and needed a name that they could relate to. We came up with the name Teatro Laboral. We performed for migrant workers, community groups, and our friends. Most of us got married and had our children, yet we still believed in the cause and continued in *teatro* activities.

Between 1977 and 1979 I lost track of the *teatro* women. I had moved to Salinas along the central coast of California, and had my first child in 1978. I returned to San Diego in 1979. When I returned Felicitas was restarting *teatro*. This time we decided to change the name to Teatro Raíces. Most of us in *teatro* came from migrant families and we now had children of our own; I was eight months pregnant when I played Archie for the last time, and I am proud to say that the silhouette on one of our flyers is me. I was about four or five months pregnant and Felicitas drew my silhouette; I am kneeling on one knee and have one arm held high, my hands and feet are roots, and I am pregnant. Teatro Raíces now targeted a younger generation, high school students and their parents. Too many teenagers were becoming parents and going on welfare. We felt the need to educate them on the importance of continuing their education. There were still issues of unemployment, immigration, education, welfare, and El Salvador. We were performing at high schools, colleges, homes, and once at a nightclub.

Then Teatro Raíces was dissolved. I became a medical assistant and was able to find a job that allowed me to spend time with my two sons.

I know that the social and political journey that I started in 1972 has not come to an end yet. More than thirty years have gone by and all the girls from *teatro* have taken different paths. But those paths have all come together at a corner and we are all getting reacquainted. We have lost some friends along the way, but we will catch up with them at another corner when the time comes.

I have memories of my past that have served as stepping stones to my future. Within these memories, I have been able to confront my past. I was able to speak to my mother about the molestation before she passed away. I had surgery on my left foot and I now wear more comfortable shoes. I have a job that I enjoy very much, and I use a lot of my *teatro* skills in this job. When I compare this job with my very first job at age seven, all I see is that little Mexican girl skipping to work with her little red bucket, happy as can be. My barefoot spirit has been returned to me. I am now ready to start a new chapter in my life. I hope that the ending of my next chapter is as good as, or even better than, my first.

Notes

1. When my mother gives birth.
2. There goes Juana Gallo, barefooted as always, run quick, catch up to them.

14

Maria Juarez

I WAS BORN in Cuba so I became known as *la Cubanita*. My mother, who remains in Cuba, was overwhelmed by the care of her children who were my younger stepbrothers and sisters. She had remarried but was so poor that my grandparents had to adopt both my brother and myself. My grandparents did the best they could to raise me. My father, who was already living in the United States, offered to bring me at age seventeen to a country where I could finish my education and choose a different kind of life.

When I left Cuba I was very proud of the people because they were also struggling to make a better life for themselves. I had experienced the harsh regime of Fulgencio Bautista. The economy was at a very low standard for the majority of the people, and many were starving. It was impossible to obtain any kind of education, to learn a trade, or to earn a professional career. There were mainly two kinds of people. There were the few who were educated and owned most of the land. Then there was the majority, who were illiterate, who owned only their labor, to sell at a cheap price in order to eat. Fortunately, for the majority change was beginning when I left.

Today Cuba has a different government. Prostitution, drugs, and the high rate of poverty have significantly lessened. Cuba could progress even more if the embargo that the United States has imposed on this island were lifted. This way people could trade freely with other countries. Instead, it has become an imprisoned country "frozen in time." And in spite of this embargo the people have maintained a great state of physical health with their rationed food and have managed with their limited resources.

I had an opportunity to leave the past behind, but I still think of my family back in Cuba. I don't think I will ever see my Cuban family again because of imposed restrictions. Even so, I believe people should have the freedom to move around and go beyond the boundaries of their country. I had the chance to travel, learn, develop, and be nourished outside of La Habana. When I first came to the North American continent its cities seemed so different, but what impressed me the most was the vast expanse of land everywhere. I landed at San Diego State University (SDSU) in the early 1970s, where I enrolled in the High School Equivalency Program (HEP) and got my General Education Diploma (GED). I met other students who were the sons and daughters of farm workers. I related to their world because I was a field worker who had harvested crops on the land of both Cuba and California.

Farm workers and their children had much in common with my Cuban roots, because they also wanted fulfilling lives. It was easy for me to sympathize with the United Farm Workers (UFW). Their grape boycott had a positive influence by improving fair labor practice. I thought that the UFW gave the Mexican American students at SDSU a great sense of pride. There was so much excitement on the campus of SDSU, but what most attracted me was a very outspoken all-female group called Teatro de las Chicanas. Speaking my mind was not my idea of being attractive or attracting the opposite sex, but still they seemed to attract a lot of attention. Delia Ravelo from this group befriended me first. I got to meet some of the women who later became my bridesmaids when I got married.

I married the son of farm workers and he did not oppose my becoming involved with this theater group. While pregnant, I attended the Teatros Nacionales de Aztlán (TENAZ) conference in Texas in 1975, and the *teatro* around this time had changed its name to Teatro Laboral. The women were patient and encouraged me to continue improving my English, not just to be vocal but to develop political understanding. I never saw myself as a professional actor, but I agreed with the *teatro*'s goal of making our world a better place to live in for everyone. Education is what the *teatro* meant to me. Our agreement to use the *teatro* to express ourselves became very important to me.

Eventually, the *teatro* changed its name to Teatro Raíces. By this time I had two children, was working full-time, had a marriage in crisis, and was completing my Bachelor's degree at SDSU. Being in the *teatro* helped to stabilize the storm inside me. I was able to release tension by learning new body movements, doing Mexican dancing, singing, and expressing myself. The *teatro* was all about action, learning different concepts, and being in the experience of life. There was not much time to sit and cry or feel sorry for myself. Besides, my problems were nothing compared to other people who were starving for food. The tragic history of people all over the world made me realize how lucky I was. As a *teatro* we couldn't fix the world's problems, but doing what we could gave me some consolation.

I was able to face my painful marital crisis. I always wanted the right man for my children. It just did not work out, and I worried about the future of my son and daughter. I even tried putting on a false appearance of a happy wife and mother. But my dignity was at stake, and I filed for divorce. This was not the end of my pain because within the *teatro* I highly suspected that one of the members had something to do with my husband. I felt betrayed, but still saw that the *teatro* needed me to perform. This was very hard for me. I was able to overcome my emotional turmoil for the purpose of our *teatro*. More important, because of the *teatro*'s determination to make a difference in the larger scheme of things, I became stronger.

I also learned from the *teatro* that plans can fail, but we would always try to work out a different way. This caused a lot of tension, but also brought a lot of laughter. I would even forget my personal problems at times. But what the *teatro* taught me was to be responsible for my actions and my beliefs. I had believed and planned for a lifetime marriage, which made it harder for me to deal with my life as a single mother. But I brought two human beings into the world and they needed me to accept responsibility for my actions.

I was left with the whole responsibility of raising my children when my marriage failed. I did not have the wish or option to have my children raised by anyone else. If a marriage or a relationship fails, in most cases women keep their children. This is why it is so important for women to know from the beginning that having children is a serious commitment. Relationships can change for the better or for the worst, but children must always be cared for and loved.

My Cuban roots, my new country, and my life are who I am today. *Teatro*, and especially Delia Ravelo, was there to help me adapt. I have also learned that whether being outspoken is attractive or not, I need to speak for my rights. Speaking for human rights is necessary in order to have and keep on having a better way of life for our children, the future of our country, and the world we live in.

15

Gloria Escalera

TEATRO PLAYED A major role in my life. Before having to play different roles onstage, I could not separate myself from the roles in my life. Before this self-awareness my life was like that of many Latinas or other young women who feel isolated and stuck in a certain location and way of life. I was born in the desert town of Brawley, California.

I come from Mexican heritage. My paternal grandparents came to this land when there was barely a border dividing the United States from Mexico, our motherland. We were Mexico's children. We are natives of this soil now known as the Southwest. My grandfather was a shoemaker for the U.S. soldiers and my grandmother a cook for the railroad workers. They raised six children. My maternal grandparents came from Texas. My grandfather died of tuberculosis at the age of thirty and my grandmother raised six children on her own. I recall that she was fluent in both English and Spanish. She impressed me as being a very independent woman.

My parents were united in their common background of migratory labor. In the winter months they worked in the seasonal crop fields of the Imperial Valley of California. In the summer they went north to pick grapes in the Fresno area. It would have been different if my father's inheritance of a few acres of land had not been lost to Bank of America. Eventually, a pesticide company employed my father. He would come home reeking of sulfuric acid, which he cooked nine months out of the year. It seemed to cook into his skin as well. After this my parents would take their six children to pick grapes when we were out of school during the summer.

The main employment in Brawley for Mexicans was, and still is, working in agriculture. Workers do not have a say in what crop is to be grown and cannot suggest markets or prices, determine the safety of pesticides or fertilizers that are used, or negotiate fair wages and benefits. Workers mainly plant, pick, sort, package, and store the harvest for further transport. All our families—aunts, uncles, and cousins—worked for the landowning farmers in one way or another. The alternative extreme to having a job in the fields is unemployment and welfare. Brawley's agriculturists required Mexicans with strong bodies. They did not require Mexicans with strong, developed minds.

Most working families did not prioritize going to school and developing the minds of their children. Needless to say, education was not even considered for the future of most of the population in our small town. We were just grateful to at least graduate from junior high. The joke was, "Hey, you didn't even graduate from Barbara Worth Jr. High, so shut up." However, my parents were different and they were well aware of the value of a good education. They knew education gave you a better life.

They scrimped together enough money to send the six of us to Catholic school, but my three brothers were kicked out right away because they were too rowdy. The majority of the school population was made up of Anglos who were the children of farm owners or businessmen in the community. It was here on my first school day starting the first grade that I had my first racist encounter. I remember looking up at the stairs and a nun was standing at the top. She looked so tall and white; I was afraid to go up the stairs and started crying because my mother had left. I climbed up the stairs and upon my reaching the nun she yanked my arm hard and told me to be quiet. I cried even louder and she took me to an office away from the other students and told me she was going to wash out my mouth with soap. After this I learned to be quiet. I felt more threatened than calmed by that "holy" nun.

School was very traumatic. Some of the students treated us Mexicans like we had a disease. They would make remarks like, "You have cooties," and then not drink from the public fountain after we had used it. We had to put our tuition in a bright orange envelope, which meant we got a school discount because we were the token poor Mexicans. At lunch we tried to hide our *tacos* in big brown bags instead of the nice shiny lunch boxes that most of the white students had. The Anglo students would report us to the nuns if we spoke Spanish. It was not allowed, and if we were caught speaking Spanish we were punished. I turned into a terrible student and always ended up in the office getting paddled. All my friends and family went to Hidalgo School on the east side, the Mexican side. I felt alone and hated by these strangers on the west side of town.

I miraculously endured eight years at that school without being expelled. When a holy nun tells you, "You're going to burn in hell because of your evil ways," you've passed the test of being a rebel. Along with learning how to rebel, I learned to love reading. Literature was my favorite subject: Edgar Allen Poe, Emily Dickinson, and the Nancy Drew mysteries. Reading was an escape. I would fantasize that my family was a portrait of *Little Women*. The nuns educated me well, but I also learned to internalize the racism and hate myself. At this time I did not know about the working-class struggle or how economics played into our daily lives. Mexicans were invisible in my history books. We had no heroes or role models.

I graduated from a Catholic school where I was an invincible rebel and went to a public high school, where I became a notorious rebel bent on a mission of going up against all authority in my life. I took the role of teaching everyone a lesson. I gravitated to other rebellious friends and found I wasn't alone in these feelings. Gang life provided me with acceptance and belonging. This caused my mother much grief because she was helpless in saving me from me. The scars of dealing with a racist education and domestic violence finally surfaced, turning into internal turmoil and raging anger.

Heavenly bliss for a Brawley girl was to get married, have babies, and have a husband with a job, if she was really lucky. Naturally, this doesn't exactly happen this way when every obstacle in your pursuit of happiness is working against you. In my case, a shotgun marriage was arranged so that my Catholic parents could cope with the shame of my pregnancy at the age of fifteen.

I try not to remember my wedding day at the courthouse forty years ago. My mother, standing next to us, was very quiet and sad. She knew my fate, and my father was so angry that he stayed home. The judge scolded us for being so irresponsible, and for me being pregnant at such a young age. He made us feel like the losers that we already knew we were. At first I wasn't so sure that the dress I bought for the solemn occasion was too drastic. But when the judge pronounced us man and wife I knew I had consciously made the right choice in wearing a tight black dress for the wedding. Even though I was only fifteen years old I sensed that this was my funeral. This was not the beginning but the end of my young life.

Subconsciously I knew I had to struggle in life, just like our mothers and the generations before us. Barely surviving on welfare, I went back to high school and tried to finish but failed again by getting pregnant. I decided to try cosmetology and went to the community college, where I took the General Education Diploma test required for the course. I was suspicious when the teacher shook my hand. He handed me the test paper and said I had scored a 99 percent, which was higher than most high school students. Imagine how surprised I was since I had ditched classes most of the time. I wished I could go to college, but by then I had two children and a husband to support. I worked as a hair stylist for a while but it barely paid the rent.

We moved to Los Angeles to get better jobs and get away from drugs. And we did do that. We were only in our teens and we had family responsibilities. We partied on weekends and had no money left for the rest of the week. Our relationship went downhill fast, and I ended up in an apartment alone and broke. My kids and I, minus a husband, drove back to Brawley defeated, in an old Ford with bald tires and our meager belongings piled in the back seat. So much for life in the big city. I moved back in with my parents and I started attending Imperial Valley College.

Going back to school and having my parents help made me feel like a new person. I wanted to do something with my life but didn't know what. I had no direction. I felt strange in school and some of the students seemed so childish. The big city had knocked me around and matured me. I took some business classes, which were boring, and then dropped out. Afterward I joined a program called WIN that paid me to go back to school and provided on-the-job training. I ended up working with the principal in the office at Brawley Union High School. Luckily, my last name was different and this is probably why they didn't remember expelling me years earlier.

Life got better when I met a nice guy who cared about me and we were able to set up a stable home environment for my two girls. Everything was going well; we both had jobs close to home and the support of an extended family around us. It made us look forward to our future together, until disaster struck. Within a matter of days my eldest daughter became seriously ill. By the time the ambulance came to take her to the hospital she had developed encephalitis from taking aspirin. She was diagnosed with Reye's Syndrome and was in a coma for months in the intensive care unit. It was a daily nightmare not knowing if she would wake up. I really didn't care about losing my job or anything else by then. Just trying not to lose my mind was enough. I ended up moving to San Diego and renting a place near Children's Hospital. I was back on welfare and pregnant again.

My son's birth came at a bad time, when my daughter was still in the hospital. I felt so guilty bringing another child into the world. We should have celebrated his arrival, but instead I worried about my sanity and questioned my ability to handle any more of life's tragedies. I was barely in my twenties when this happened. My son spent the first year of his life in a baby carrier, from nine in the morning until five in the evening, at the hospital while I helped with my daughter's care. Months later when we brought her home, my children learned that because of their sister's disabilities, she came first. My son has always been an easygoing, adaptable child. But it was more difficult for my younger daughter, Michele, and she became resentful.

It took a couple of years to return to some semblance of a normal life. During this time, I got a legal divorce from my first husband and managed to start a new life. We bought a home, and I played the role of homemaker and wife, sending my new husband off to work. I played the role of mother sending my children off to school and the role of nurse caring for my eldest daughter. At my part-time job, before and after my role as a teacher's aide I also volunteered in other school and community projects. These were my roles and the way I coped with life.

I never thought of playing other roles until *teatro* came into my life. Felicitas, whom I knew as Phyllis, was a long-time friend from Catholic school who came and visited me in National City. She was the only friend I knew who had not gotten pregnant and who had left the *barrio* to go to college. She had kept in contact with me throughout the years. During one of those visits she mentioned being involved in fundraising activities, organizing *teatro* performances, and especially emphasizing social and political awareness. I was invited to attend one of their fundraising performances.

It was so exciting to watch the *teatro* group perform. I was amazed at their confidence and knowledge. Most of the women in this group had participated in the Chicano Movement at San Diego State University (SDSU) and it was interesting to hear stories about the Young Lords, César Chávez, the Black Panthers, and other theater groups. I joined their study group and began reading political newspapers and becoming aware of world injustices. I knew about injustices already; I had lived them but I never had the tools to understand them. Well, *teatro* had a way of teaching me. I had to overcome my insecurities of acting out roles on a stage. And if these theatrical roles could serve to make an audience understand a message, then I wanted to be a part of this group. I believed we could make a difference, and so I joined Teatro Raíces.

Being a newcomer to the *teatro* was not easy. There were jealousies among us and competition about who got which role. We overcame our ego trips by understanding the political issue the play was addressing, or by just laughing hysterically. It was strange when a "she" played the role of my loving boyfriend or I acted as a loving daughter to my father who was played by a woman. One rehearsal the others don't let me forget was when I played the role of Archie Bunker's daughter, Gloria. My cynical, beloved father was dying in my arms while I was uncomfortably holding him and trying to squeeze out some tears as I kneeled over him. At the time Archie was played by Guadalupe Beltran, who was being smothered by my protruding breasts and exposed cleavage. I was unaware that my shirt top had popped open. I was seriously into the role and moment, until everyone at rehearsal burst into laughter. My self-induced spell was shattered.

I got used to dealing with my indignation by separating myself from the role I was playing and finding humor in it. Hysteria was softened by an interconnected wit that was shared by this all-woman group playing both gender roles. I never realized until now that being with this *teatro* was a great release from my everyday role-playing as mother and wife. *Teatro* was an escape; I felt important and part of a group, especially when it came to writing the scripts. At first I would wonder why Delia and Phyllis wanted our input into the dialogue. I guess because they wanted us to not only learn our lines but also understand how this contributed to the whole play or skit. Later on I liked having input in the writing process because my suggestions were valued and sometimes used in the scripts. It was truly a collective effort.

We performed everywhere and anywhere in order to educate our audience. We wanted to reach everyone and even performed at "Macho's," a popular nightclub, in March 1982. There we performed our play titled *E.T.—The Alien*, where I played the role of a snotty valley teen girl who has a vacant brain and heart. The nightclub audience was tolerant and would have preferred to party, but we still performed. Once we performed in front of a mercilessly heckling audience at University of California, San Diego. They could have been labeled right-wing students. And we could have been labeled left-wing "want-to-be-actors" in flight. We had done a play on Rockefeller to expose the practice of union busting among workers. We quickly took off after our performance, with a fully exposed mind and a big jumping heart at our throats.

In April 1983 we performed *Challenge to Learn* at Sweetwater High School, and were not asked to come back. I was working as an aide at the high school and had told the students and staff that I was "Rosie," who was a *chola* in the play. It dealt with issues of drugs, sex, racism, and ignorance. The staff was surprised and the play was seen as too controversial for high school students. Then we performed the same play for the SDSU high school recruiting conference and it got a great round of applause. We performed *Archie Bunker Goes to El Salvador* for a Veterans of Foreign Wars audience. This was an antiwar play against U.S. involvement in that country and did not go over too well with those veterans. But, surprisingly, some of them were not too antagonistic. They stayed around after our performance and gave us their honest opinions.

Much of our material was controversial, and it hit home for the majority of our working-class audience. This was our goal; they were the audience we wanted to wake up and share our knowledge with. People would come up to us and thank us for the message of unity and *"El pueblo unido jamás será vencido"*—the people united shall never be defeated. I was amazed that they would come and thank us for being there for them, saying that we had lifted a weight off their shoulders, and that they were willing to take action. I came to see that we are enslaved when we blame ourselves for our condition in life. We are freed when we come to realize that it's a class struggle.

In the *teatro* we traveled to different cities to perform. We went to other college campuses and to Chicano conferences. We met professional *teatros* from other countries at the TENAZ conference in San Francisco in 1981. There were political groups from Mexico and Chile. We would meet and discuss different political issues that everyone was raising. It was exciting and educational to discuss issues that dealt with human rights, women in the workforce, abortion, and antiwar stands and to be listened to. WIT, Women in Teatro, was a statewide organization that arose to ensure that the women's voices were being heard. Leticia, Phyllis, and I from Teatro Raíces had the privilege of attending one of their meetings in Yosemite in 1980.

After Teatro Raíces stopped performing, I felt I needed to stay active politically. Luckily, Delia Ravelo mentioned my name and I ended up joining Teatro Mestizo, another theater group in San Diego. We performed a play called *Soldado Razo*. The play portrayed Chicanos going off to war; this role was my last performance, but in real life it was just beginning.

I stopped *teatro* role-playing and dived into real-life issues affecting our working-class lives. I got involved in local community issues and started speaking out—without a script. At work I became a union representative for the Service Employees International Union and defended co-workers and our union contract. I marched to the U.S./Mexico border and picketed against Immigration and Naturalization Service racist policies. My shyness and insecurities went out the window. I gave a speech at San Diego City College in defense of the undocumented workers who were being run over while crossing the freeways. MEChA was surprised, because they had expected me to do a song and dance for Cinco de Mayo.

Instead I spoke up in defense of the undocumented workers who were being killed crossing the border. It was like being on a mission. I would get up at 4 A.M. to distribute flyers to shipyard workers at National Steel and Shipbuilding Company (NASSCO) before going to work. I organized and marched against the Persian Gulf War in a pro-military city. I was part of several Chicano organizations whose members were very *macho* (male-centric), but I learned to work with them so that my voice could be heard regarding police brutality. All of my activism came from the training and power that the *teatro* women infused in me.

When I look back on my life's journey, I see that it has been a long struggle of constant change that was both good and bad. Along the road I educated myself both in school and out in the streets. Studying about my Mexican culture gave me pride in my heritage and relieved my inner self-hatred. Accomplishments of service to my community have been rewarding. I've come a long way in finding out who I am. I have allowed myself to let go of past mistakes and of remorse; most painfully, I have laid my thirty-year-old daughter to rest. I've learned to never get too comfortable, because chaos erupts as soon as you do. I've had many experiences good and bad in this intertwining journey. I can honestly say that almost every issue that *teatro* addressed has touched my life. I have come to understand that my right to practice freedom of speech derives from the very foundation of this country and from all the progressive movements in the world intended to better humanity. Optimistically speaking, women have more power over the choices of roles in their lives.

The struggle for positive change continues, especially in regard to education. Working in San Diego's South Bay, every day I meet people who attend school despite many obstacles. They attend school while lacking childcare for their children, having financial difficulties, fighting drug dependency, dealing with domestic violence, and facing unemployment, to name a few. They are striving for a better life and a secure future for themselves and their families. In their daily lives they deal with many of the same problems that I continue to try to overcome.

I owe much to the people in *teatro* who supported me and believed that *I* could play a positive and active role in changing the direction of *my* life.

16

Evelyn Cruz

UNDENIABLY, THE YEARS I spent with Teatro Raíces continue to influence my work today as a playwright. Many of the themes addressed in our theater were driven by an examination of class inequality, racism, and sexism from a primarily Marxist perspective. This sobering perspective was counterbalanced by the spiritual element of collectively writing and performing scripts with an all-woman theater group. I met the women of Teatro Raíces when I was twenty-one years old and a single mother of two children. I was introduced by my boyfriend, Saul, who later became my husband. The fact that we had no actual theater arts training was of secondary importance, for in our collective mind's-heart the real work was the political content that could raise awareness of an issue and then spur the audience to action. More important, it provided an immediate way to give back to the communities that we loved. The creation of these types of theater, be they agitprop, street theater, or guerrilla theater, continues to open up the world for its participants by making the arts accessible to everyone.

All we needed was our strong work ethic and the desire to speak out against injustice. We performed with minimal props, and everyone contributed costume pieces. We had no lighting designers, stage managers, or official director.

We typed our own scripts on typewriters without dramaturges and performed anywhere we were invited, from universities to rallies to someone's private backyard. Although we didn't know it at the time, we were creating works that followed in the traditions of other theater artists, such as Augusto Boal and his work with Theatre of the Oppressed and Luis Valdez's Teatro Campesino.

True to our form, we had enough slice-of-life experiences within the makeup of the group to enhance the dramatic storytelling. For example, at one of our writing sessions Feliz proposed including a scene about a woman who was so hungry she had to hunt down rats in the fields to feed to her children. In my mind that sounded too unbelievable, even disgusting. I raised an objection to that contribution. I remember saying "Nobody will ever believe that." Feliz answered that it was true and that it had happened. As a child, her mother had been fed a rat by a neighbor who hunted them for her family. I remember no one spoke for a long time. I asked then, and I still ask now, how does anyone survive that? At the time Feliz responded, quite matter-of-factly, that the neighbor had made the decision to cross the border illegally when she had no other means of feeding her children. Needless to say, we included the scene. No amount of statistics or droning lectures can carry quite the same impact of live performance. That essential human element, in the form of a breathing theatrical piece of art, is best realized in these transformative spiritual moments. It is truly when we can connect with others. Although Feliz's story is rooted in a migrant farm worker's experience, it is not far from my own experience growing up in the Bronx and being raised by a single mother of eight children.

Although my mother was constantly working, it was always a struggle for her to provide for us. I recall coming home from school one day in the third grade and being surprised that my mother was actually at home and cooking! She was frying plantain bananas in our tiny, sparse, but brilliantly clean kitchen. I remember how disconcerting it felt to come home to my mother and the delicious smell of *sofrito* simmering and *platanos* frying. I watched as my mother, deep in thought, carefully speared the golden *platanos* and flipped them upside down to brown the other side. Afterward she would lift each piece and tap the oil from it onto the inside of the frying pan, and then lay the *platano* on a napkin-lined plate for draining. Although I was in heaven there was something uneasy about the whole scene. I remember thinking how beautiful my mother looked that day. *Mamí* had this beautiful long, black, thick, curly hair that hung in one long braid down her back and below her waist. "Mamí, what are you doing here?" She let me hug her and I buried my head in her waist. I took comfort in the smell of her perfume. She didn't hug me back, but stayed focused on the frying pan. "Why are you surprised? Don't I live here

Teresa Oyos at a Cinco de Mayo celebration, San Diego State College (1971). Courtesy of Teresa Oyos.

Emma Castillo (*left*) and Peggy Garcia performing in *Chicana Goes to College*, San Diego State College (1971). Courtesy of Felicitas Nuñez.

Lupe Perez (*left*) and Patty Quiroz performing in *Chicana Goes to College*, San Diego State College (1971). Courtesy of Felicitas Nuñez.

A Third World Dance is performed for the Seminario de Chicanas, San Diego State College (1971). The dancers are (*left–right*) Socorro Rascon, Clarissa Torres, and Teresa Oyos. Courtesy of Felicitas Nuñez.

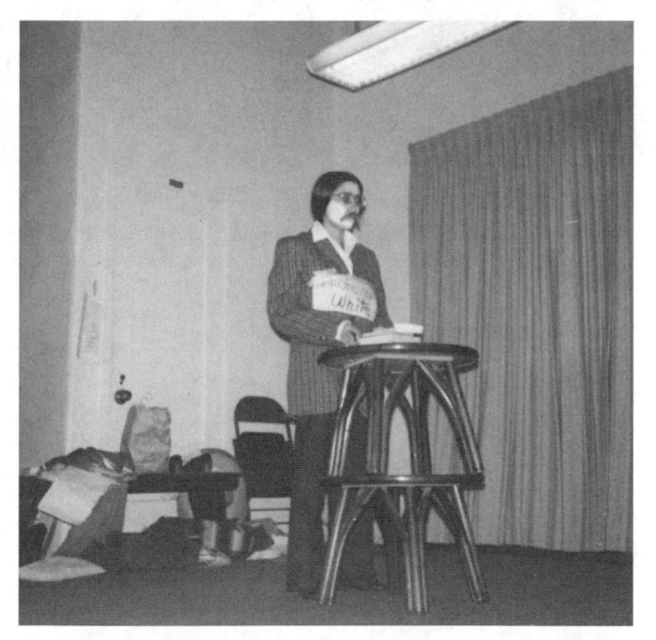

Gloria Barlett performing the role of an Anglo professor in *Chicana Goes to College,* San Diego State College (1971). Courtesy of Felicitas Nuñez.

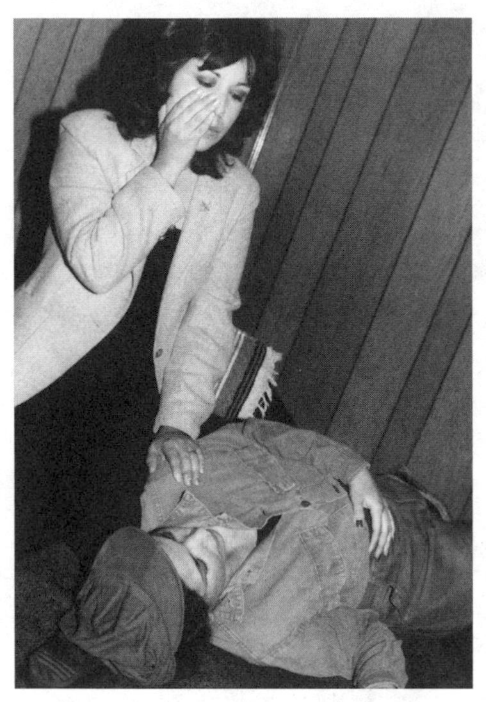

Teatro Raíces (1981). Gloria, played by Gloria Escalera, cries over her father, Archie, played by Guadalupe Beltran, in *Archie Bunker Goes to El Salvador*. Courtesy of Felicitas Nuñez.

Teatro Raíces (1981). Maria Juarez playing the role of a revolutionary's mother in *Archie Bunker Goes to El Salvador*. Courtesy of Felicitas Nuñez.

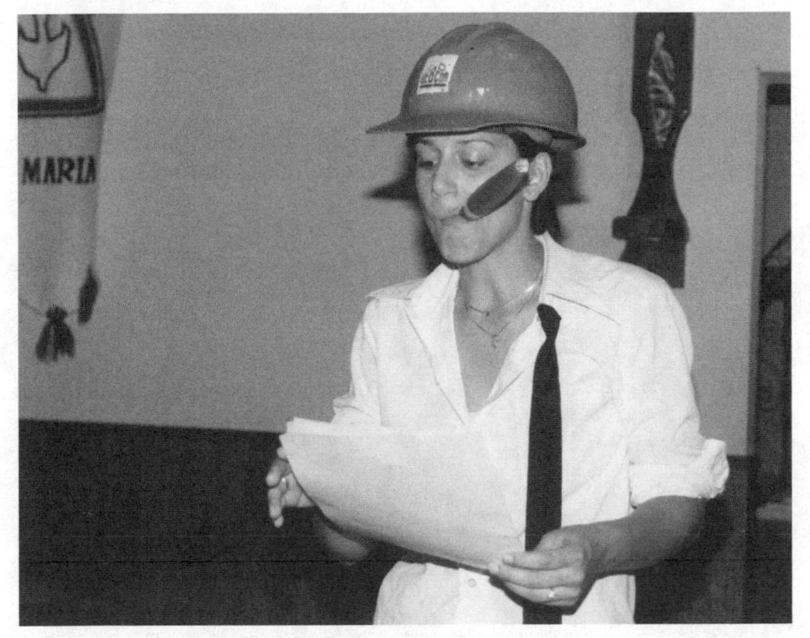

Teatro Raíces (1982). Evelyn Cruz performing in *So Ruff, So Tuff.* Courtesy of Felicitas Nuñez.

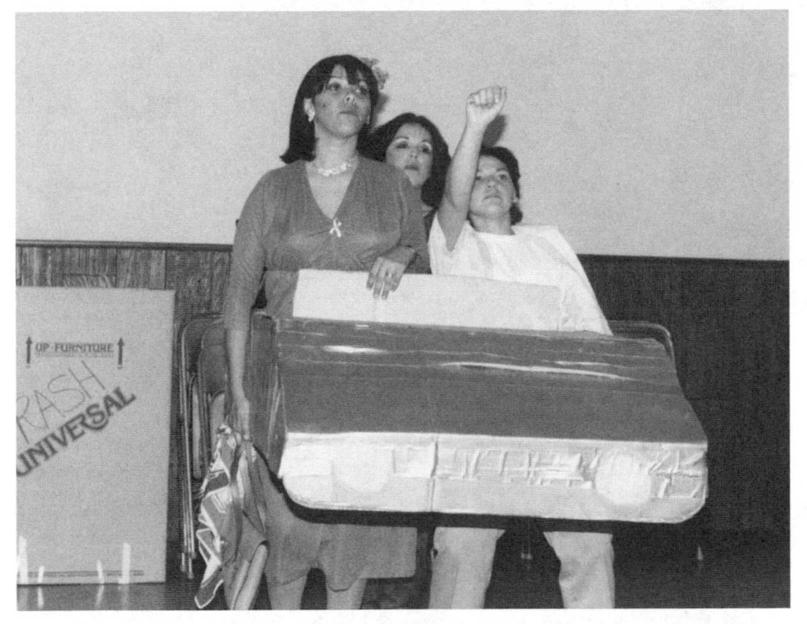

Teatro Raíces performing *So Ruff, So Tuff* (May 1982). *Left–right:* Delia Ravelo, Gloria Escalera (*back*), and Guadalupe Beltran. Courtesy of Felicitas Nuñez.

Teatro Raíces (1980). *Front, left–right:* Gloria Escalera, Delia Ravelo, Guadalupe Beltran, Maria Juarez; *back, left–right:* Becky Nuñez, Kerry, and Felicitas Nuñez. Courtesy of Felicitas Nuñez.

Teatro Laboral members performing at a park, San Ysidro, California (1975). At the microphone is Kathy Requejo. Behind her are (*left–right*) Clara Cuevas, Irma Mendia, and Felicitas Nuñez. Courtesy of Felicitas Nuñez.

Teatro Laboral members, San Ysidro, California (1975). *Left–right:* Margarita Carrillo, Clara Cuevas, Irma Mendilla, and Felicitas Nuñez. Courtesy of Felicitas Nuñez.

Irene Urista, Peggy Garcia, and Felicitas Nuñez attending the Indo-Chinese Women's Conference, Vancouver, Canada (April, 1971). Courtesy of Felicitas Nuñez.

too?" My mother had never taken a day off of work, never before and never since that day. It was all too strange, and something about her tone of voice, even to my seven-year-old mind, let me know not to ask anything else. My two sisters and I went to our room, where we settled down with homework. Later that evening, we all washed our hands and sat down with our stepfather for dinner. The food was exceptionally plentiful, due in no small way to our stepfather, but there was an unmistakable thickness in the air as we ate in silence. Years later I would find out that the evening was a turning point for the lives of me and my sisters. Ironically, that quiet evening marked the breaking of a silence, a silence that had allowed our stepfather to sexually abuse one of my sisters for too long.

In one of my plays, titled *Winter Heat, Summer Snow*, the protagonist is a woman who has had to steal food in order to feed her children until a man comes into her life. My play opens with the following scene.

(*The stage is basically dark because a family is sleeping. In the living room there is a sofa sleeper with the bed drawn and a man and woman are asleep. The house is sparingly furnished, rather meager. There is one light bulb with a chord that leads out over the door SR, where it can steal electricity from the hallway. The silence and darkness are broken by a loud banging on the door.*)

BILL COLLECTOR: (*Banging furiously on the door.*) Milagros! Milagros! I know you're in there! Open up this door. I know you're in there! I said open up the door. Now! I just want the money you owe us, that's all. Just give me the money and I'll go away. Otherwise I'll wake up the entire building. I know you can hear me. You lazy Spanish bitch. Why don't you go back where you came from? Huh? All of you. Bastards. . . . Open up, I said!!

(*During this tirade Linda and Nina have come into the living room, startled. Millie and Eddie are trying to calm them, but also trying to keep quiet so that the bill collector can't hear them. Eddie puts on pants under the blanket.*)

EDDIE: It's okay. It's nothing. Shsssh. Just be real quiet.
NINA: (*Scared.*) Who's at the door?
EDDIE: Some crazy man. Don't worry. He can't get in. (*Forces a small laugh.*)
LINDA: But why is he banging like that?
EDDIE: *¡Por que está loco!* He'll get tired in a minute and go away.
BILL COLLECTOR: Milagros! Milagros! Pay up or I'll wake up the whole goddamn building! I'll break this door down. (*Continues banging.*)
NINA: (*Scared.*) Mamí?

MILLIE: Shssssh! Keep your voice down. Go back to bed and try to ignore him. (*With feigned reassurance.*) It's okay.

(*Nina is reluctant to go, looks for reassurance.*)

LINDA: I'll take care of you. Come on, Nina. It'll be all right. Nobody's gonna mess with you. I'm right here.

(*Linda leads Nina out. Meanwhile the banging has gotten less frenzied. And it sounds as if the door is given one last kick. It appears the bill collector has given up and gone away. Because it is so cold, Millie gets dressed under her nightgown.*)

MILLIE: Sounds like he's finally given up.
EDDIE: *¡Que maricón!* One of these days . . .
MILLIE: Forget him.
EDDIE: I don't know how you can take that.
MILLIE: Have I had a choice?
EDDIE: You've got one now. Just once. Let me at him just once.

(*Eddie goes to the window.*)

MILLIE: Why? It's not worth it.
EDDIE, *DISGUSTED:* Look at him down there.
MILLIE: Just be glad he is gone.
EDDIE: I don't know how some people live with themselves. Knowing what kind of job he does everyday. I'd rather shovel snow in below zero weather than do that.

(*Eddie goes to check the wiring on the light bulb and brings light into the room.*)

MILLIE: Who cares?
EDDIE: I do.
MILLIE: He'll get his.
EDDIE: Hey, what are you doing?
MILLIE: What does it look like?
EDDIE: Why? It's not even four yet?
MILLIE: So?
EDDIE: So stay in bed.
MILLIE: We have to get going in another hour anyway.
EDDIE: (*Suggestively.*) A whole hour. To ourselves?
MILLIE: A whole hour, three children, and—
EDDIE: Have I ever told you how beautiful you are at this hour of the morning? I love you, *negrita*.

MILLIE: I am freezing cold. I don't know why you ever agreed to be the Super of this building. It's not worth it. You already have a job.

EDDIE: If you call that a job. (*Beat.*) Let me show you how to keep warm.

MILLIE: You can't steal me so cheaply. (*Indicates light bulb.*) Why didn't I marry Con Edison?

EDDIE: What does Con Edison have that I don't have?

MILLIE: Electricity! Heat?

EDDIE: I've got plenty for both of us.

MILLIE: That's not the kind that I need right now. (*Millie has finished dressing.*) Look, I have to go get some bread and milk. There's still some milk on the fire escape, but it's not enough.

EDDIE: I know what you're up to, Millie.

MILLIE: What's that?

EDDIE: You know what.

MILLIE: And?

EDDIE: I really don't want you to do that. You have a husband now.

MILLIE: It's no big deal.

EDDIE: For me it is. How do you think it makes me feel. I'm the man here.

MILLIE: Why are you trying to make me feel bad about this?

EDDIE: Oh, that's just great.

MILLIE: (*Pause.*) Look, I used to feel bad about it, but not anymore. I actually went to see a priest once and confessed it. Can you imagine? Do you know what he said? He said, "Millie, how much money do you earn at the factory?" I told him. And he said, "I won't give you absolution from this (*pause*) because that's not a sin." That's a true story!

EDDIE: Now that's what I call a priest.

MILLIE: Yeah, except that he's also the same priest who told me that I'm living in sin, because I've had too many men in my life.

EDDIE: You call them *men*? Look, I can provide for all of us—and I want to! You don't need to steal bread and milk. I love you.

MILLIE: Well, sometimes love is not enough. Is it?

EDDIE: Just tell me where to go. Tell me, Millie. 'Cause I'm not letting you out of here.

MILLIE: Bonilla's *bodega*. The bread is delivered at three, but he never gets there before four. They hang the bread on hooks in front of his store. He'll never miss a loaf.

EDDIE: You know, man does not live by bread alone. Stay warm until I get back.

MILLIE: And don't take any milk from this building. Go to the Grand Concourse.

EDDIE: Why is that?

MILLIE: Because they're all Jewish over there. They can spare a bottle of milk without hurting.

EDDIE: Have some coffee ready for me. I'll be back before the water boils.

(*Eddie exits.*)

MILLIE: *Que Dios te bendiga.* (*Closes up the sofa bed.*)

(*Enter Linda.*)

MILLIE: What are you doing up so early?

LINDA: It's too cold.

MILLIE: Put some warmer clothes on.

LINDA: I can't sleep.

(*SOUND: Radiator clanging. Millie practically yells at the radiator.*)

MILLIE: We hear you already! We're all cold!

(*Takes clothes that have been draped on the radiator to dry overnight and sorts and folds them.*)

LINDA: Do you want me to wake up Manny?

MILLIE: For what?

LINDA: To heat up the building.

MILLIE: Let your brother sleep. They can wait a little longer.

LINDA: Sure.

MILLIE: I'm going to leave your clothes right here. You can put them away later. Your socks got a little burned from the steam.

LINDA: God! I hate when that happens. (*Walks to the window.*)

MILLIE: I've told you a million times, put a towel under the clothes before you lay them down on the steam.

LINDA: God, look. It snowed last night. I want to eat it. It looks like one giant *piragua*. Look at it. (*Crosses to window.*)

MILLIE: Isn't it beautiful? The whole street has disappeared. You can't see anything else. When I was a kid I used to walk in Central Park in the winter, when the water dripping off the tree branches would freeze in midair. They looked like crystals just hanging there. It made the whole tree look as if it were made of glass. For me it was the most incredible thing to see. I was so young and really hated winter, so different from Puerto Rico, but the snow made up for it. To see nothing but crystal and powder everywhere makes you feel rich somehow. It's like some kind of miracle.

God waves his hand and covers everything up with a fluffy white blanket. There's no dirt, no garbage, nothing old or ugly. Just pure white untouched snow. We needed a good snowstorm.

(*End of scene*)

The reality of losing a man's much-needed income is taking shape just as much as the harshness of a New York winter, which is looming right outside Millie's window. The hope for change, however, will not be realized by a covering up of the circumstances that conspire to oppress. Rather, it is in the painful addressing of those issues by connecting the energies of people in an artform that by its very nature is spiritual. The theater nurtured by Teatro Raíces did just that, by bravely facing the past, yet working in the present and looking to the future with all the brilliance of that much-needed snowstorm.

17

Felicitas Nuñez

DELIA RAVELO AND I first met in the summer of 1970 at San Diego State University (SDSU). Our field of awareness was spectacular, animated by Chicana students ripening into their potential worth and power. We came upon *teatro* as a way to discover ourselves and connect with our surroundings. Our street theater became a cradle that rocked us on the rivers of the world. It became a training ground for the individual to further strengthen self-worth and self-power. This awakened in me a means and a desire to support the voice of younger women who for the first time were apart from their family. The outcome of their development would be our joint evolution, and my personal empowerment.

I learned from my mother to use my hands to work, direct, and guide. My mother's hands blessed everything she touched, including me. My hands redirected the young Chicanos and Chicanas from the restrictions of religion and the confines of culture to the wonders of education and experience of our world. My hands carried the Grape Boycott picket sign of the United Farm Workers (UFW). My hands became accustomed to forming a fist, the symbol of power and self-determination. My changes within were reflected outward.

My mother cried when she recognized my transformation after a visit home from college. All I could do was embrace her, using my hands to stroke her silvery crown. When I first left home, my hands were bigger than my mother's hands, except hers had been made hard and strong. Her hands had wiped away countless tears. Her hands had sewn clothes for her children, defended, disciplined, and labored to ensure the survival of her nine offspring, including me, the second youngest. I left home in the summer of 1968 to go to an unknown college in San Diego. I didn't know then, but of all the treasurers in the world, none would compare to the nurturing mother-love hidden in my heart. I, more excited than fearful of the unknown, unexpectedly ventured into an inspiring, wondrous world.

I was inspired: by Rosa Parks, who ignited the nation's March for Civil Rights, by Dolores Huerta, who was a leader and cofounder of the UFW, and by Jane Fonda, who gave voice to the Women's Movement opposing the Vietnam War. These were examples of self-made women symbolically walking in their own red handmade shoes. Symbolically, I yearned to make my red shoes with my own hands and walk with the dignity of a self-made woman. My insight and involvement in the Chicano Movement became a genuine link to all struggles for human rights.

I made an attempt to restrain my boldness for self-protection, yet like everyone else I was receptive and virginal in many ways, including being in a social organization like the Mexican American Youth Association (MAYA). In the fall of 1968, for the first time in a college setting, I became a member of MAYA, which later became the El Movimiento Estudiantil Chicano de Aztlán (the Chicano Student Movement of Aztlán, or MEChA). I wanted to give back to society in some way after realizing that countless others had sacrificed their lives so that I could have a chance to better myself. I volunteered to recruit and encourage young Chicanos to obtain a higher education under the guidance of the Educational Opportunity Program (EOP). I identified with and supported the farm workers in their struggle for labor rights. I strongly believed and encouraged freedom of speech for all people. I also proudly chanted, "Chicana Power," which meant liberty, equality, and freedom to learn and grow in my humanity as a woman.

I could not help but take note of the strong women's movement on the college campus and became aware of books like *The Origin of the Family, Private Property, and the State* by Friedrich Engels. This book provided a very welcome understanding for me of all women's universal history and helped me to objectively understand my personal feelings of embarrassment, confusion, and resentment over being female. These negative feelings were connected in many ways to my experiences in a male-supremacist society. But mainly I had allowed myself to feel belittled, and when I did struggle against feeling belittled, I felt guilty or insane. It was such a relief to learn that it was sane to question my place, and it was normal to want change, to eliminate stereotyping. I learned that even privileged white women within a male-supremacist society were also stereotyped as the "weaker vessel."

For the first time I could make choices with less guilt, and I did not have to accept any commercials, movies, religion, literature, or political or cultural beliefs that degraded women. Learning diminished isolated feelings and connected me to my culture and my universe in a new and expansive way. Yes, but I was learning from Engels, who was a white male and, to the horror of every restricted religious and limited cultist, a Communist! However, my understanding of universal love made the compassionate Jesus Christ an exceptional communist. I could not say this out loud without being condemned. But I was still condemned as a student of action.

I learned from those opposed to my actions that anyone who believed that higher education was a social right, or anyone who supported the UFW Grape Boycott, or anyone who spoke out against the Vietnam War would be slandered as a communist. My curious nature led me to wander, and I was met with moral and political smears. Yet it was like discovering a deeper layer of myself. Learning about matrilineal origins and communal ownership of land within primitive communism was like biting the forbidden apple of knowledge. I had a deeper understanding of my being in this world and of the human race born of women.

My yearning for understanding, universal knowledge, and equality also invited the disapproval of the overloaded testosterone males in the Chicano Movement. However, I was not alone, because the yearning to be a self-made woman was shared by most of the females who started out like me. If we were cultural or religious, we wanted to take the best of both backgrounds that could connect us to the outer world as self-made women. I felt consumed and yet nourished by the generous energy of women with a desire to learn, to go beyond their borders, and to reach the heights of their own humanity. I found strength in las Chicanas; we regrouped with the sole purpose of revisiting our maternal roots and the fertile ashes of our history. Then we planned a Seminario de Chicanas for just our mothers that involved talking, singing, dancing, and acting using *teatro!*

"I want to write," said Delia Ravelo. I asked, "Don't you want to act for the mothers at our seminar?" "No, because I am an orphan and it saddens me." We were grateful for Delia's writing and moved on. "I would love to act but

I have no real training," said Peggy Garcia. I said, "We can do it!" We were a part of a larger group of las Chicanas. I saw the magic of working hands belonging to "Maidens" like me in full bloom and "Maidens" starting to bloom. We prepared our props, fluffed costumes, rehearsed our lines, and prepared speeches; the guitar was tuned and the dances choreographed. Others behind the scenes designed the programs, acted as ushers, managed the props, arranged the setting, cooked manna, and blessed our sacred space. We came up with three scenes for our play called *Chicana Goes to College*. Peggy and I volunteered for two of the three main male roles.

"I'll do the third," said Gloria Bartlett. "I will need some props to go with my parts." It turned out that Gloria was very picky about her role. Her mustache had to be real hair and not painted on with mascara. Her shirt had to be clean and ironed, and she had to have white facial makeup. We thought her blue eyes and glued-on mustache were good enough to help her pass as a white male, but we got her the white paste. Then there were Patty Quiroz and Olga Navarro, both thin, small-boned, with soft voices, almost invisible except in the limelight of the stage. Both played female parts; it was easier to fill female roles even at the last minute. Initially, all the actors had their own names marked on a sign pinned to the chest. If the actor changed, the name changed. At least three among us saw *teatro* as a high priority.

Anyone who came whenever they could was welcomed. Teresa Oyos, one of the dancers at the seminar, occasionally helped us out with the *teatro*. She had hazel eyes, tanned lemon skin, and hair that flowed below her waist in bright sun streaks. Peggy referred to Teresa as Lady Godiva. Emma Castillo had skin the color of wheat bread, coal-black hair, and a beauty mark on her cheek. Maria Roman had skin like a snow-white rose, with nappy hair highlighted by indigo blue. Lupe Perez, who wanted to act from the beginning, had a nasal-sounding voice and danced with a rigid bounce. Maria Rosa filled our parties with laughter and delight. She was a doll: petite, cute nose, cranberry lips, big eyes, and wavy hair. Onstage she could raise her voice way above everybody's height. And off-stage she could drink like a sailor and swear like a truck driver. This "Maiden" was best described as an *Adelita* doll (women who fought in the Mexican Revolution of 1910) ready to act at the drop of a *sombrero*.

The day of the seminar came in the spring of 1971; Peggy and I managed to get our mothers to see us do *teatro*. We were nervous, because our roles mocking the male ego could destroy any tiny speck of the darling-daughter image our mothers did have of us. We were having fun, but at the same time we were worried about the trauma to our mothers in witnessing our raw, naked stand against male supremacy. Our darling traditional mothers somehow managed to laugh with our performance, and still my mother tugged my arm with her strong hand and said, *"Como eres bocona"* (You have a big mouth). Then she broke into a smile, and I swelled with pride; this was my moment, yet to be expanded still more by the whole seminar. We listened to Viviana Zermeño lead the panel discussion on *La Mujer* in "Herstory." Armida Valencia directed the women's third-world dance, and Olivia Reynolds played the guitar and sang her own songs. Among las Chicanas, the silent, gentle, and intelligent Marta Tapia became mistress of ceremonies for our mothers.

I thought this was a one-time performance by an all-women group, so I continued on with my life roles at SDSU. Then during one of our MEChA planning committees, we wanted a *teatro* to perform for our High School Recruiting Student Conference and decided on Teatro de la Esperanza. Then someone asked, "Why don't we do the *seminario* play for the students?" But our play was intended for women and we as students could only hire outside groups. "Yea, but we can do it for free and call ourselves El Teatro de las Viejas Broncas [Wild Women Theater]." "Why not? Our message does direct the youth into higher education." Yes, thought I, and we will parade in our red handmade shoes.

This time Delia Ravelo was in the forefront as a writer and actor; Peggy Garcia was exhilarated; and I danced in my red homemade shoes. We were more prepared to recruit, replace, and retain women for our play *Chicana Goes to College*. The auditorium was filled with hundreds of noisy, rowdy, pimpled, and baby-faced high school students. I went first onstage, introduced us briefly, and looked to my right, and seeing the frozen actors sent me into a cold sweat. "Come on!" "They don't want to," loudly whispered Delia while Peggy, shrugging her shoulders, said, "They are afraid." I looked at them and said, "Of course we are afraid, but what have we got to lose, our virginity?" To my relief, the women actors broke out in a roar of hysterics. Adolescent excitement, laughter, and applause accompanied our performance to its end. We did not compare in sophistication and technique to Teatro de la Esperanza, but I could envision our red handmade shoes gleaming. Most important we had kept our word and after this we officially became Teatro de las Chicanas.

Teatro de las Chicanas

Soon we were asked to perform in the Los Angeles area. Most of us were in our early twenties, with shining flowing hair, and clad in jeans, anywhere on the spectrum between militant and flower child. We must have felt confident since we had recently performed and practiced our skit. The bright sun was warm, and details such as GPA's (grade-point average) and career goals were not on our minds. We were as excited as the first day of our acceptance into college. Our vehicle was not a van to me, but a chariot driven by Peggy.

We were practicing our lines, catching up on the latest gossip, waving at the cute males, and flirting with traffic on the 5-North freeway. One of us from the back of the van pulled out a clear plastic bag filled with a bunch of dry green grass and several rolled brown paper sticks that transubstantiated into the sacred weed of the celestial beings. Most of us were already excited and nervous about our trip and doubted little that we needed to trip out even more. But the logic kicked in; it was all right to smoke a couple of sticks and smooth out the jagged neurons. The funny-looking cigarettes were fired up, and the magic smoke was inhaled.

We were giggling, then laughing, and moments later our chariot of joy was floating among the traffic. I became soft and limp like jelly bouncing to the jerks of stop, go, and rolling to the curving swings as Peggy sped past the slower cars. I felt like a goddess witnessing the flow of life on a graveled road. I felt we were "all-glowing" and we were "all-knowing." We were flying, we were liberated, and we were invincible.

Out of nowhere in the midst of my artificially induced detachment, we heard blaring sirens and saw the blinding red lights of a black-and-white police car. Suddenly we were stiff with fright, trapped in an undeniable high and going to jail. The panicked voices of Gloria and Teresa, who were in the van's back seats, shrieked for us to start eating the rest of the dry grass. This would lessen whatever penalty it was for possession of dope. My ration doubled when I had to choke down the driver's share. Our cries intensified when the police car passed us and got in front of our vehicle while another patrol car appeared from behind. Our chariot of joy became a gutter littered with the *mota* that had flown out of our gagging throats. The long arm of the law was corralling us, and yes, we were crying for our mothers and praying for forgiveness.

By the time a third patrol car and a fire truck appeared on the scene we were frantic, and halfway passed out on dope and terror. Then we noted all the cars were slowing down around a huge cloud of smoke that was rising from the mass of traffic up ahead. This was followed by a strong stench coming from the burning flesh of corpses. There was a general silence, an intense message of human suffering. The police were not pursuing us, however we were mentally shot. We stayed in the slow traffic line until we were on our way again.

We had barely reached our destination but already we had been through extreme states of mind. In our collective stupor we piled out of the van and started carrying the props for our play toward the gym where we were scheduled to perform. I had to look down at my feet several times because I could not feel them inside my shoes or touching the ground. Unconsciously, I feared for the loss of my red handmade shoes, but I kept silent.

Because of the delay we entered a gym already full of college students, mostly female, ready to be entertained by an all-women *teatro,* and the crowd's curiosity was at a peak. I was very loaded but focused on our commitment that the show must go on. Unfortunately, everybody in the group was stiff and I asked, "What is the matter?" They looked like a bunch of cowering sheep with big bloodshot eyes. They nodded sideways, muttered and stuttered, and finally bleated that they could not do it. Our seated audience was glaring with at least three hundred pairs of eyes glued to the stage, and I felt like punching the remaining lights out of the actors, who were supposed to act. My head and heart were pounding; alone and abandoned, I took a deep breath and from the gym floor looked up at the rows of students seated on bleachers. I announced a song called *"Cubanita"* that we as a group favored. I began singing solo trying to show courage and howling in my uncertainty.

Cubanita	*Endearing Cuban Woman*
Cubanita soy, señores,	Cuban woman I am, sirs,
Cubanita muy forma	Cuban woman, very formal
Cubanita siempe he sido	Cuban I've always been,
Aunque usted lo tome a mal.	Even if you take it wrong.
Mr. Nixon está triste	Mr. Nixon is very sad—
Lo digo con disimulo	I say this as a matter of fact—
En Cambodia y en Vietnam	In Cambodia and Vietnam
Le están dando por el Cu . . .	He is getting it through the *Cu* . . .
. . . banita soy, señores!	. . . *banita* I am, sirs!

The *Cu* . . . was extended and completed with . . . *banita* because in Spanish it is insinuated that something is being delivered to the buttocks, as in *culo* (kick in the ass). By the end of the chorus I had ceased to be solo. I was joined by a howling pack of she wolves. Together we as a group completed this song and were ready to keep our commitment and perform.

Our performance was greeted by enthusiastic clapping, followed by a question-and-answer time in which audience and actors exchanged ideas. A female student seriously and strongly suggested we present ourselves to Hollywood. None of us mentioned what had happened on our way to this near "butt out" presentation. Night fell; we were quiet, all exhausted, and we listened to Carole King's songs on the way back to the SDSU campus. I, in the peaceful dark, slumbered into untold riches.

The image of the *vato loco,* or veteran of prison life, came to be idolized within the Chicano Movement on the SDSU campus. This was destructive, because it glamorized the overuse of drugs and encouraged spontaneous, valiant, short-lived action. Abusive relationships increased; there was a lack of continuity on community projects and we saw a decrease in the feeling of moral obligation to the labor struggle and human rights. Drug abuse by the student of life in general caused an outright neglect of the search for knowledge, understanding, and truth. I focused in on the group of women around and in *teatro,* and allowed no more dope when we were performing.

Experiences with *Teatro* and Women

The next *acto* we came up with was *Bronca,* which was a chant ventilating female rage against the inequality between the sexes. We don't know that it ever invited cooperation from the opposite sex, but it certainly attracted attention. We attended the beginnings of the first TENAZ (Teatros Nacionales de Aztlán) festivals. We performed *Chicana Goes to College* and *Bronca*. The main criticism was that our performance was at least ten to twenty years behind the times and that there was no longer any need to address the "woman question."

I clearly remember doing *Bronca* and lining up to sing toward its end, but we had to wait for Gloria Bartlett to join us. We were poised onstage waiting two or three minutes that seemed like an eternity. We were facing a silent audience, when I noticed my pin. This was the symbolic *huelga* eagle, about an inch diameter, black on the inside, and outlined in gold. I used to pin it on the outer middle calf of my bell-bottom jeans and liked seeing it whenever I happened to look down. Well, here I was up onstage and my pin was crooked, and I decided to do a slight adjustment since we were just sweating and waiting.

Slowly I lifted my foot off the floor and bent my knee high enough to adjust the pin. Well, this small maneuver was well noted by the very quiet audience. There was a subdued sound of laughter; I looked at the audience and smiled. And shit, where was Gloria? We had already done the *Bronca* strut and needed to wrap it up with a song. Finally, Gloria popped out from behind the curtain drop and we proceeded to sing, "*Yo quiero que a mí me entierren como revolucionario*" (I want to be buried like a revolutionary). Toward the end of the 1971 TENAZ festival, Luis Valdez called out the participating *teatros* and had the individual representatives come to the front of the assembly to be recognized. We were not included, but when we came back to our campus I saw us reinforcing our red handmade shoes.

Another *teatro* that had formed on campus was called Teatro Mestizo. I was asked to join by Marcos Contreras and Ernesto Hernandez. I agreed to check it out and when I got there, almost everyone present for the practice session was a familiar face from MEChA. I did the part of Ms. Puro Pedo, who was a teacher in the play *No Saco Nada de la Escuela*. I also requested that I be allowed to try out for the skit *The Militants,* which was about two males challenging each other as to who was the perfect image of a Chicano. This character assassination leads to a physical battle in which the males kill each other. I was given a fair chance to try out and got the part.

The males in Teatro Mestizo were reluctant at times, but overall cooperative. We shared a commonality of being in student activities and extracurricular activities. One evening after celebrating Cinco de Mayo we went to an afterparty held at an apartment that became stuffed with more than fifty students, thick pot smoke up to the ceiling, and loud music. As we sat crowded on the floor, this guy next to me tried to get my attention, but I chose to converse with Lupe Miranda. Soon after, my pants were soaked with beer. I made a big stink, calling out the suspect, but he stayed glued to the shag carpet. I walked out of the party with my supportive baby sister, Tere, and my cold wet ass.

Next evening we attended another festive event at the Centro Cultural de la Raza. I felt embarrassed by the spectacle that had taken place the night before and didn't even want to look at the eyes of these younger students, especially Laura Garcia and Lupe Perez; they quietly greeted me in a merciful manner. But it was at a later time that I learned that all the young men back at that party were left alone holding their joints because every single one of the women present had walked out as soon as I left. This had a profound affect on me because it made me realize how intricately I was weaving and woven into the net of the attuned female bond.

I didn't feel this same connection to the young males, but I was attracted to this one guy in Teatro Mestizo whom I thought I had scared away. I felt sorry for myself but focused on the many things I had to do, like acting or being involved with writing a skit or play. Writing a paper for my World Literature class was a terror for me to avoid. I opted to do a lecture chalking the whole board with the outline from the book *The Origin of the Family, Private Property, and the State*. It was a class of mostly Anglo students, some who came up afterward and thanked me for my class presentation. Right before this had happened I was in the library putting my final notes together and the guy I was attracted to sat beside me in the library. I said hello but was so intensely into preparing my material that, after a while, I was startled by his voice saying "Goodbye." Later I did get to see this desirable person joined by a beautiful

"Maiden." It was hard to tell if I grieved for my loss or if my heart ached for witnessing their union of such beauty and youthful love.

Miraculously, I experienced a lightweight feeling of completeness and calmness after my own personal success. What I truly knew and loved was doing my best before a group, whether it was in a class lecture or in a *teatro* performance.

I was either older than or felt more mature and experienced in comparison to the other *teatro* members. Sylvia Romero and I were pioneers in establishing the first Barrio Station in the summer of 1969. This was the first community extension of Chicano Studies from SDSU located in San Ysidro. In the coming fall and spring semesters, as an officer of MEChA I headed the volunteer students that built the foundation for the Supportive Services Program on campus to retain Chicano students. As the summer EOP director of 1970, I came in contact with every new student. My third year on campus I became the first MEChA chairwoman at SDSU and a member of MEChA Central. Under the guidance of Professor Carlos Vasquez, as a senior at SDSU, I was one of the teacher-students of a political science class in Chicano Studies. It was important for me to have some *saber* or at least point to the source of information for knowledge and as a female student of action set an example in the public eye.

Occasionally I would party with Peggy Garcia and Delia Ravelo in private. It was so relaxing, listening and saluting our favorite female singer, Janis Joplin, whose red handmade shoes were destroyed by fire. We would look to the infinite heavens and philosophize, act silly, cut loose, and become theatrical. One time this guy from out of town came to see me when Peggy and Lupe Miranda were visiting. We tried calling Delia Ravelo, but she was unreachable at the Indian reservation where she lived, so just the four of us smoked a joint and listened to Santana's music. I was using a pen to strike the coffee table, drumming away when my fingers felt sticky; I gawked at my hand in the dim light. Then Peggy started screaming, "Oh, my God. She is bleeding!" She and Lupe grabbed my arm, pulling it toward the sink while I dragged behind.

Peggy was yelling, "Are you in pain? Felicitas, look at me! Look at me!" I was laughing so hard my eyes were shut tight, my wisdom molars were fully exposed in my mouth, and my free hand was holding down my bursting stomach. Lupe wanted to get into medical school and Peggy into nursing school. I was in good hands but was literally running out of breath and turning beet red from nonstop laughing. "Elevate, elevate the hand and apply pressure," ordered Lupe. "Well, there is no cut on the hand and this blood is . . . Oh no! She is holding onto her stomach! Oh, my God! It is her stomach! Look at her, look at her! She is delirious from the pain!" assessed the nurse, Peggy. "Lift up her shirt!" ordered the doctor, Lupe. "Feliz, let go of your blouse. We are trying to save your life," said Peggy, and she slapped my silly purple face before Lupe forced my hand away. They pulled up my blouse, exposing my small flopping tits. Still they could not find a wound, just red stain on my stomach. By this time they started noticing that the red was not coming off onto their hands because it was ink. And the guy who came from out of town to see me was beside himself. Needless to say, he did not call again after this diagnostic and prognostic theatrical episode.

Laughing at ourselves and laughing it off provided a great release; for example, one night after a meeting we were upset at the men within the Chicano Movement. We as women had allowed ourselves to feel like a meat market in their presence and needed to shake this feeling off. It was difficult for any of us to enjoy or take pride in our sexual nature without being branded an idiot or a slut. We gathered in the MEChA office and started joking around with the concept "Aztec princesses of Aztlán"—"So what if you are royalty, you are still a stupid female." Teresa Oyos got on top of the office table and mimicked herself as a brainless "big ass and tits" participant of a beauty contest, wearing a paper band that read "Miss Ass of Asslan." This was an exaggerated view of the problem of separating the female body from the mind and spirit.

How far could this go? It was natural for me to see an attractive male and still see that his body was inseparable from his mind and his spirit. Once I got a phone call past midnight from the beautiful Rico Bueno, which wasn't uncommon because we worked together as officers in MEChA on events that needed attention. Surprisingly, he invited me to hang out at his apartment with the guys from the band Malo. Somewhere he said, "And you know, call the women." I was physically very attracted to Rico, but I also respected his mental capabilities and loved his spirited efforts to organize fundraisers for the UFW. I figured he was being polite, hung up the phone, and went back to sleep. Several days later, when we were in the MEChA office, he was unusually reserved, but we went ahead with business. Later I heard that I really had been expected to beckon the women like groupies for the band that Santana's younger brother played in. It was also pointed out to me that I had made Rico look bad in front of the men. I did not mean to hurt this special person. In joking terms, I was expected to round up the "Brown Asses of Asslan." I didn't care for being referred to as an "Aztec princess of Aztlán" and gravitated toward the term "*vieja bronca*" (wild woman) because it carried more dignity, essence, and wholeness.

Wholeness and such were not easily attained with unwanted pregnancies. One night we were partying at a house when I got the phone number of an abortion clinic from one of the women. I found it hard to believe that from a limp penis somehow a sperm must have found its way up my vagina. This was my punishment for having immoral sex. I was drinking Pear Ripple wine to drown my dilemma. One of the younger women in *teatro,* Kim, got everyone rallied to go to Tijuana and party in Mexico; we all willingly piled into a couple of cars and took off across the border. It seemed everyone except me was having a great time—until I went to the bathroom. I think it was the miracle of wine that made the ten-week absence of my period come to an end. The red stain on my underwear was as welcome as my red handmade shoes. I was pro-choice, but in my mind going through this psychological decision was traumatic. I was so grateful not to have to go through a physical abortion, but most of all I felt that regardless of what these women thought about abortion, they would always stand guard over my wounds of the body, mind, and spirit.

If we were called or referred to as whores, lesbians, bitches, witches, cunts, communists, or traitors like Malinche, we made an attempt to not to get all shook up. Yeah, right! Malinche as an object of possession was handed down from her own mother to bronze males, and they gave her to white males and both skins degraded women. Within our group we tried not to put each other down, but sometimes mocking each other was unavoidable. For example, at this one party somehow I had lost sight of Peggy and then spotted her coming out of one of the bedrooms. She had a big smile until she got sober and realized that she had taken on this small guy nicknamed *Pajarito.* Next day this little bird was fluttering around trying to keep up with my pace as he asked, "Where is she?" Who? I stopped to look at him. He said, "You know the one . . ." and then in desperation he fluffed out his little arms in front of his chest and winged the outline of these full, filled breasts. I pretended not to understand, but later with Delia and Peggy we dissolved into laughter.

Sex was personal, but when snide remarks or insinuations of degradation started in about one of us, we banded closer. How ironic that the very males who would take advantage of an over-intoxicated female had no problem putting her down. Here we were in a higher institution of learning that consisted of university professors, men in positions of administration, leadership, and power over students. We had politically conscious grown men "pulling trains" or taking advantage of over-intoxicated females when the opportunity arose. This was why we could not stress enough the importance of women educating themselves and becoming politically aware of the dangers of our society and how the male ego system feeds into this degrading train of thought. Feminine self-worth was impossible to implant overnight, though, and we made some pretty bad decisions.

The California Tour

Teatro Mestizo made plans for a tour up through California. Laura and I, who had major parts in Mestizo, requested that the Teatro de las Chicanas be included. The males did not readily accept our request. Before we started out Delia, Peggy, and I smoked a joint in private and floated over to where the two vans were parked for our tour. We got in the first van and kept on conversing, oblivious to the fact that we had chosen the most comfortable coach. The males piled into the second van, which had cracks that throughout the whole trip brought in cold drafts and rain on its male passengers. We started out in luxury, kicking back and enjoying each other's company; suddenly we realized that we didn't have a dollar between us. Lupe Perez, our treasurer, shrugged her shoulders. We were well acquainted with spontaneity and figured we'd call my sister Tere for help on our arrival in Pomona sometime before midnight.

There were two apartments, one with a telephone for the males and the other for females. Delia and I went for the phone, trying not to step over all the male bodies lying on the floor. Above all the whooping catcalls, I nervously dialed in the poor light. My sister Tere on the other end could barely hear me, thought I was crazy, and hung up. Tere had helped out in the *teatro* by keeping our props clean, pressed, and neatly stored, but not this time. The telephone was facing the wall of the living room so I had pulled the cord into the small kitchen area, pressed the phone to one ear and muffled the other ear by using a nearby kitchenette towel. I threw this towel at the wall above the stove before hanging up the phone and tramping out the door with Delia.

Next day, we got these suspicious looks from the males but thought nothing of it. One of the women came back with a story that she was told not to repeat. When we left the *hombres'* apartment everyone settled down to sleep and Ramon Sanchez, nicknamed Chunky, had a bad dream; he was being strangled by me! He slept on the kitchen floor next to the stove, where the towel I had thrown covered the burner, creating a deadly smoldering gas. In the dark, way after midnight, Chunky woke up to uncontrollable coughing and noticed that the whole top half of the living room was filled with white smoke. Males in their underwear vacated the apartment, to evade suffocation or strangulation. In the chilly dawn air they debated my intent to kill.

I was more than willing to apologize, but the woman held me back and begged me not to expose her, and no other words were said or heard. What happened next is that we would perform as Teatro Mestizo and then as the Teatro de las Chicanas. I sensed more sneering, suspicious looks from the *hombres* but heard no words. Lupe explained that the universities, which had made the contract only for Teatro Mestizo, decided that the pay should be divided in half for both *teatro* groups. So Lupe, treasurer for Las Chicanas, collected half of the contract money. Later we were in the cafeteria with these long tables; the men sat at one. Chunky was seated at the end of their table, looking at our table, which was pulled over to theirs. You would think Chunky had fashioned himself ruler of all males as well as las Chicanas when he held his cup high in the air and saluted.

Peggy walked in, noticed the set-up, and instinctively sat at our end of the women's table; in a domineering and authoritarian manner she returned Chunky's salute. "The Last Supper" was now balanced and celebrated with a torrent of laughter, whooping, and hollering from both tables. I clapped and stamped the floor with my red handmade shoes. This was the high point of our communication, with minimum words exchanged between *teatros* and sexes. In one play Enrique Ramirez and Chunky both played the roles of my male militant challengers. In one of our performances, when we killed each other off Chunky had the last laugh; his stomach was quivering as we both played dead on the floor. Afterward he said he didn't mean to punch me so hard, but this came too late, as he knew from the stark stare on my face. When Chunky apologized I felt that he knew I did not mean to harm him or anyone; after all, we were in the process of making the *Nuevo Hombre* and the revolutionary *Adelitas* in red handmade shoes.

In Teatro Mestizo I played the part of *Madre Patria*, who is a woman pointing to facts of history and addressing the plight of her children as they cross the border into the United States. Enrique Ramirez asked me to recite my lines to him in private quarters. I hesitated at first but went ahead with his request; he said I needed to be softer and more humble. I disagreed and explained that it was best to play the part in a stronger voice to get the lines across to the audience. He nodded and smiled in agreement. Since he and I played dominant roles it was rumored that we should be sweethearts. Not to my surprise, like most males, he was swept away by my hitchhiking buddy, Sylvia Romero (Chiva).

Sylvia was at the time working with a group of junior high *Adelitas* from the SDSU Barrio Station that had been relocated to Logan Heights. Sylvia and I had shared some 1969 road adventures. César Chávez and his guards picked us up on the outskirts of New Hall during one of our hitchhikes. I was embarrassed and said that we were going to see my sick aunt in San Jose. No! Lies!

We were going to explore the exciting Bay Area and party with my cousin, Manuel Delgado, one of the "Third-World Strike" students from UC Berkeley. But before Sylvia also swept my cousin's feet away, she had mapped my way to the Bay. And this is how I got to see the *The Mother* performed by the fabulous San Francisco Mime Troupe. I was struck by a desire for theater and could hardly contain myself, but Sylvia remained composed. Within our group she stood out as a slender, sharp-witted beauty; her hands and feet were so small that I felt like a clod next to her. She was born in Mexico and taught herself to speak perfect English. Sylvia to some extent became the official photographer of Las Chicanas.

The women in *teatro*, especially the younger ones like Laura, looked up to Sylvia. Laura Garcia was one of these younger women who started out looking quiet, but her Chinese eyes were always watching. One time after a performance at the Chicano Federation in Logan Heights, Sylvia expressed regret for not bringing her camera to take pictures of our version of *Rudolph the Red-Nosed Reindeer* at Christmastime.

Laura Garcia

The Teatro de las Chicanas did a Christmas play for the children, and Laura enthusiastically volunteered to be Santa and said she would be responsible for her costume. She was well known for taking her audience to the river of tears, and I was curious about the fact that she wanted a role outside her specialty. However, we were very busy making our reindeer horns out of cardboard and fastening them to our heads with bandanas, going over the idea of the lines, and putting on heavy mascara accentuated with white shadow to bring out the black eye outliner. Because of my bright red, lipstick-spotted nose I would take the lead of Rudolph during the crisis snowstorm.

During our presentation I was caught up in the moment of creating my lines to fit the concept of teamwork. I was the hero, a leader above all the other deer that had mocked and put me down before. I could feel the children's eyes on us as I pointed out each deer's special gift and contribution to the teamwork concept. But when Laura walked onto the stage, we the reindeer were snowed under the oohs and the ahs. She took the reindeer show by storm. Why?

First of all her body was perfectly elongated, rounded, and alluringly curved. Her skin hinted a glow of golden peach with yet peachier cheeks, complemented by springing, shimmering dark hair. Second, the outfit she wore was a red fitted suit topped with a Santa's hat. This crimson fabric delightfully caressed her upper torso, tightened at her waist, and snuggled her hips. Finally, this fabric dropped into a long skirt that had a split way above the knee that exposed her black knee-high boots and the fleshy long legs. Obviously we had had no dress rehearsal and about a week's notice to put this Christmas play together. My red deer nose was outshined, but can you guess why my red handmade shoes got a brighter red? I felt so proud.

Margie Carrillo

Somewhere in the middle of preparing for this Christmas play Margie Carrillo told me, "Felicitas, you look beautiful with eye makeup. You should seriously wear make up all the time." This would be complicated; it was more practical to stay simple in every daily activity, skit, or play. Working with what we did have was necessary for economizing costs. Effort and time set aside for learning was very precious. Margie would drive me crazy because she wanted to be sure of all her lines, yet we all needed to understand a concept or idea before presenting. Then we would have to convince her that she could make herself come out onstage; I got to the point of just shoving her or whoever out on the stage as a last resort.

Later on I would recall kicking Margie from behind our curtain drop so she would stop going on and on. We were performing for an event sponsored by the Women's Movement at SDSU. They probably thought kicking was not a gesture of sisterhood, but Margie just backed away from the curtain, got closer to the audience, and kept on blabbing. Usually it was the *teatro* that would listen to her ramble on about how she was a virgin on the night of her wedding and in general how virginity was important to her and so on. This voice was like a mosquito in my ear. Years later, during one of our performances, this little voice got to be more than annoying when we agreed that for Juneteenth we were going to perform at a park where black youths hang out. I was playing the role of Sojourner Truth, and the skit was basically acknowledging our constitutional stand against slavery. Well, Margie kept crying about how we were going to get beat up for going to a black neighborhood park and talking about people who are not like us.

But there we were, I with my head bandana, saying my line "and ain't I a woman?" There were about twenty black kids in their early teens, mostly male, and their eyes were intense. I could hear Margie whispering, "We're dead." Upon completion of our presentation we left in a hurry, "free at last," but not from our ingrained fears. I came away from that performance with sadness because those children we left behind seemed very alone and confused. They were not in a university setting, and I kept wondering to whom they would turn in a ghetto for personal growth and political knowledge. Margie's concerns reflected those of a society that focuses on the double standards between men and women, a society that divides, conquers, and creates ignorance by emphasizing differences between racial groups more than commonalities. Except when it comes to selling products, credit cards, and war; then everyone is common. Margie would say what the rest of us would not voice.

Lupe Perez

Then there was Lupe Perez, who with her nasal voice said very little but made an effort to be supportive, always adjusting her eyeglasses with her index finger in a very eloquent manner. I even got to visit her family in Fresno and met her little blond brother, who was the exact striking duplicate of the dark Lupe. She and Laura were tight sisters. Sometimes I would be with Lupe for several hours at a time but we never got past the visible aspects of our lives. I never told her I had an affair with a married artist or told her of my shame to see the eyes of his children and lovely wife. I felt comfortable being around Lupe and had asked her to be the treasurer for our *teatro,* and several times she called me to meet over *teatro* business at the International House of Pancakes. At first this was unheard of, but then there I was at night delighting my palette with pancakes. I still remember Lupe giving the order; her thick hair falling back, her eyes rolling up to the waiter, adjusting her eyeglasses, her voice rising an octave or two to say, "Blue cheese with my salad please, thank you." I lacked in elegance next to her blue cheese, but this did not get in the way of our agenda.

Before Lupe Perez left *teatro* she went with us to Brigham Young University, where we performed our *Bronca* strut in front of cameras and other groups. Among these groups was a young man I was attracted to who belonged to a *teatro* from the Los Angeles area. We wrestled a little on the shaggy carpet while Lupe and her tight buddy Laura Garcia looked on, so I was restrained. But I was not restrained when I decidedly assured this guy that we as the Teatro de las Chicanas would gladly perform on his turf. Once we got back to California, I berated Lupe and Laura for not showing up to practice; instead they showed me: I had made a decision without their approval. Respect to the group came first and personal animal attractions came second on our agenda. Our agendas usually called for new recruits especially for the plays *The Mother* and *Salt of the Earth;* both would require at least twelve characters. This is how I got to meet more young women, who were brought in by the other members, but Peggy was moving on.

Peggy Garcia

Peggy, Delia, and I had formed a trinity before *teatro*. On our ventures together, Peggy was more than ready to share her abundant loving energy. She did not hesitate to go onstage with other Chicanas from Northern California whom she had just met and perform as a united coalition for the Indo Chinese Women Conference. We had come together in 1971 for a Third World Women's conference in Vancouver, Canada, to form an international alliance protesting the inhumanity of the Vietnam War. You could hear the cry of the universe when we sang "La Llorona," exhorting our pain "to cleanse our bodies, to clean our rivers." Yes, our bodies are rivers. And Peggy kept "Rolling on the River" in the Tina Turner riveting fashion.

Peggy captured the singing soul of the spiritual revivals that I as a child loved to hear standing outside the Negro churches. At first sight, she was like a magical child with big rolling eyes and a joyous laugh, but when party time rolled around you got to see God move her body: bumping, shaking, grinding, and swinging to the beat of Creedence Clearwater, James Brown, and Carlos Santana. I would be transformed into a "Black Magic Woman." We parted in drunkenness and my blues gave a purple tone to my red handmade shoes.

However, Delia Ravelo and I had much to do. The newer members were in the process of exploring, discovering, and being connected. We needed to understand the importance of the rural and industrial working class to facilitate the message behind the acting. The death of Delia's father in a motor factory made her keener on the plight of the industrial worker. The first time we performed *The Mother* was in Logan Heights for a large group of Mexican females. Their community backdrop was a dying tuna factory and National Steel Shipping Company. I questioned whether these women would relate to our presentation. This play is about the hands that create colossal wonders, about the hands that "give us our Daily Bread."

This play is about awareness of the hands of creation that belong to a respectful working-class force. This labor force happens to be universal. May 1st is the Labor Day celebrated and recognized worldwide by all workers, except in the United States of North America, where the rights of the working class were first established. The book *The History of the American Working Class* by Anthony Bimba gave us some insight for this play. We were uneasy, but instead of jeers we got not only strong applause but a standing ovation from our audience of older women. And the younger *teatro* members must have seen and felt a sense of dignity and worth. "Above all be true to yourself." This was at the core of our quest, to learn with movement.

Our study groups and practice sessions involved learning elementary moves onstage, making most of the voices sound roughly male, and complementing the personal elements of each actor. But the voice had to be made strong through our understanding of theory. Sandra Gutierrez, who sauntered in with a graceful stride, made you think she had "been there, done that" as she stood strong as steel. And it's no wonder, because her family's ancestors were entrenched in the labor union battles of the New Mexico mineworkers where the movie *Salt of the Earth* originated. The big dark eyes of Clara Rodriguez (Cuevas) were like wells; her voice flowed like clear water once she plunged into her stage lines. Long, slim Kim made her moves and voice like wind song; she was like a breeze onstage that fed the "sparky" Kathy Requejo. Kathy was very petite, but when she learned what blocking was onstage: Beware! No one blocked her action or else her speech of accumulated knowledge came at you like a giant fireball. Virginia Rodriguez had a voice quiet like the earth; at first she reminded me of a nun, until she showed up in a halter-top and cut off jeans, glowing like earth covered in purple flowers. Virginia had to make an effort for her voice to be heard but her knowledge of human struggle sounded from the heart.

Teatro Laboral

It was Virginia who drove us to the 6th TENAZ conference in the summer of 1975. This is about the time we were toying with idea of changing our name to Teatro Laboral. Most of us were out of the university. I was apprehensive about not getting our notice of acceptance from the TENAZ organizers in San Antonio, Texas. Instead of worrying, I just imagined that we were the "the Magnificent Eight" driving into a southwest adventure.

What I recall most vividly about what happened that day is the slow-motion braking of our guardian angel's foot. Cubana was pregnant and dozing under the van's back window. I was kneeling in the opening between the driver and front passenger seats, blabbing to Laura and Virginia. Raquel, Margie, Irma, and Becky were minding their business in the back of the van. I was involved in my conversation, which suddenly ended when I switched my attention to Virginia's foot on the brake. I never saw the crash we avoided, but the force of the braking threw my head back, then forward. The front seats kept my shoulders braced between them. Then came this tremendous weight of five bodies piled against me. I heard Margie's voice, "*Chinga,* let go of my *chichi.*" Cubana said something like "*Chinga,* whas hoponing?" in her Cuban accent. I couldn't breathe. When we got free of our human pile-up, we laughed. Margie kept on griping about her squashed breast, while Cubana massaged her protruding pregnancy.

Maria Juarez

This event would be the first time I saw Cubana as a *mulata* dance native. Her features were very soft and delicate. Her voice was fast and lively in conversation, but if she needed an item, a favor, or to steal a smile from you, then her voice would turn to honey. Her hair and skin tone was a honey brown, and her eyes were hazel and very coquettish. She was extremely shy when it came to expressing herself onstage. She had this one liner, "But what am I suppose to do, prostitute myself?" At practice everyone would be sending encouraging energy, lip-serving her line, but she was still nervous. When she did say her other line, *"Ay, matarón al Arzobispo Romero,"* she sounded and carried on like she had been having a love affair with the archbishop who got killed. We did not want to discourage her but we just busted out laughing.

Back at the 6th TENAZ conference we were waiting, lying around, getting some sun, and fanning ourselves when we heard the sound of the conga. This was Cubana's call; she showed us a dance step where the knees are semibent, feet spread about twenty inches, and the hands clutching the waist. Then the body is thrust forward in small jumps accompanied by thrilling shoulder and hip moves. Her facial expressions and her dancing eyes dared and provoked me to question our inhibitions. Here was Cubana creating life, in scant clothing: displaying, teaching, and celebrating the beauty and the feminine magic of our natural temples in broad daylight without shame and without reservations.

I was shocked the following day by an accusation from some of the men at the conference, who said that our dancing in broad daylight was a seductive plot to snake our way into the conference. I was also reminded of my careless attitude, and rightly so; I was to blame for mailing in our fee and application late. But what made me feel worse was our dismayed newer members, Raquel, Irma, and Becky. Their confusion reflected that of the attending *teatro* groups, which seemed to be barely evolving under the guidance of TENAZ. I had rationalized that because we had already paid somehow we would be given some slack and accommodated. We were, but only after a big ugly scene took place. We could participate as observers, but would not be allowed to perform. Now we were officially labeled and restricted as Teatro Laboral. At this event I did not cry in public; only in solitude did my tears wash my bloody red handmade shoes. Virginia and Laura went on their individual paths and the *teatro* kept dancing into controversy.

It was during the controversy of the Allen Bakke case in September of 1976 that we came up with a play called *No School Tomorrow.* We even took in two smart handsome knights, Gene and Marco, who seemed to admire our red handmade shoes. Then there was the vibrant *Italiana* Maria with golden rose-wine hair with tight curls and sparkling blue eyes. Delia Rodriguez, we knew from her presence at our past *teatro* rehearsals. We took a position on the Bakke case because it was limiting accessibility to higher education for less affluent students by questioning the validity of holding university admission slots for the children of the labor force.

Our universities are where books of knowledge are studied and awareness is increased. Our universities are local environments where the individual connects to the wider world. UNI (one) and VERSE (song) make the world one song with knowledge and understanding. A true love for knowledge combined with a passion for understanding can lead us to compassion. Knowledge with (COM) and rapture for (PASSION) understanding of the self and the world can lead to LOVE for our universal selves. This truth is what I learned from a university.

When I entered the higher echelons of education I already knew that the hands of my mother as well as my own were of great value. This inherited value and the privilege of a higher education convinced me that all children born of women and the world they live in are valuable. We teach values, not with greed or weapons of destruction, but with intelligence and energy that evolves into love for our world. I believe our society will excel in compassion for our universal self when higher education and knowledge become the priority of every individual. The Bakke case questioned the right to an education on the basis of nationality, economic class status, and grading system, and to me it posed a further threat in questioning our religion, color, sexual preference, and gender.

The *teatro* collective focused on and considered the needs of the individual, whether personal or educational. Delia Ravelo was the social leader, and I saw myself as a not-so-popular leader. We did what we could to nourish the individuals within *teatro.* However, we willingly became followers when the individual or individuals presented their superior insight and education. Four individuals—Gene, Marco, Maria, and Delia Rodriguez—taught us about the Bakke case. They seemed to embrace and present the controversy of the Bakke case with thunder, and then like lightning they also exited at the same time from teatro. The Bakke performance would be rated atrociously bad by a theater professional. A liberal would say it was full of energy, and an apologetic would explain that the members were first-timers onstage and its content needed to be organized, but otherwise it was informative. In *No School Tomorrow* our underlying message was, "It is the right of every individual to be cultivated to their highest potential."

Delia Rodriguez

Delia Rodriguez was a newly cultivated teacher with hazel eyes that complemented her apple-white skin and ruddy lips. It was not easy for her to understand that the world did not revolve around her theatrics. Oh, Delia would freeze. We would lift her stiff body offstage and stand her in the sun to thaw. I could almost read the *teatro* critic headliner, "And She Froze with Her Red Handmade Shoes." One time she said, "You know, I feel like I've had children all my life, and I don't know what it is to think or how to make choices without my children in mind."

I was stunned by her sincerity and remembered my mother experiencing motherhood and spousal abuse at age fifteen. No divorce, no birth control; how did she do it without drowning herself or her children in desperation? I witnessed the strengthening of her inner spirit when she folded her strong hands in prayer every day of her life. Years passed and I got to see Delia when she was on one of her trips back from Mexico. She was chattering away with her sweet smile and told me that her husband had commented on her wide thighs in a bathing suit. She told him, "You see these tapioca pudding thighs? Well, feast your eyes honey, 'cause it doesn't get any better than this." This was the familiar person I knew offstage.

Hilda Rodriguez

Hilda Rodriguez trespassed into our stage in her arrogant manner, offering instant scolding and lecturing to the dangerously innocent, criminally stupid, and lunatics in heat. "Where's Hilda? There she is heading this way." "Hey Margie, Cubana, come over here. They are asking if we want to go for a ride." "Feliz, let's go checkout this other bar." "Yea, but these guys . . . Here comes Hilda, oh shit!" I was bent over, flirting, looking into the window of a car that was parked on the curve of one of Tijuana's busiest streets, Revolución. About five of us had gotten out of one bar and Hilda was behind us, but she caught up to me first.

"*¿Qué chingados estás haciendo?*" "Who me? I am just here talking with these guys." *"¡Con una chingada, vente!"* "Hilda, lower your voice, they want to drive us around." *"¡Pendeja, te llevan a las lomas y te chingan!"* "These guys don't look dangerous, they look cute." *"No la chinges. ¡Vámonos!"* This was Hilda in the raw and I was the lunatic in heat. There was one scene where Hilda was playing the role of "Mother" in a meeting to unite the workers; she was warned of approaching danger and had to hide but she was like an octopus suctioned to the stage floor and had to be yanked and dragged away. We did not know her stomach was upset and about to blow out the other end. Recalling this eventful improvisation onstage brought tears of laughter to Delia Ravelo.

Whether it was a dirt floor or gold dust, it was our stage; we had numerous ideas and skits to present. I once played the role of Barbara Wala (Walters) interviewing a steelworker from the shipyards. The skit pointed out the need to improve communication among workers in their union. We also did a presentation for the cabinet workers and reenacted an incident that had taken place in the parking lot, causing concern and illustrating the need for workers to unite. Our cars were painted cardboard boxes and the workers who saw this skit started laughing when they realized we were replaying that event.

We attended the 1977 TENAZ conference, held at the University of California, Los Angeles (UCLA). We did a skit, based on a true incident, in which the teacher forces a student to pick gum off the floor with his mouth. At this moment we would freeze and I would sing out, *"América, América, yo me acuerdo de ti"*(America, America, I remember you). Our biggest laugh at that conference came from Margie, who gave a vivid description of her male workshop leader on body maneuvers. He was wearing very short pants and every time he stretched, all the "little fellas" would sneak a peek at Margie. Delia Ravelo let out a high shrieking laugh when told of this sensational highlight.

Delia Ravelo preferred to create new material for the *teatro* and yearned for more elaborate props. I preferred fewer simple props and didn't want to let go of the play *Salt of the Earth*. I recall one time in between scenes of this play I ran around the stage picking up the props as fast as I could; when I heard the gasping sound from the audience I realized that I had dumped the rubber baby head first into a pail. I took the baby out, held it in my arms, and announced the next act. I thought how oversensitive the audience was, but this also meant they were paying close attention.

I had paid close attention to the film *Salt of the Earth* when I saw it during my first year of college. It gave me a great sense of assurance that I was involved in the student movement not only to better the males, but also to better myself. Now I belonged to a generation that wanted to better the whole world. I dropped out of college after five years and short of a degree to work in a sewing sweatshop. Delia went to work at the tuna factory. We kept our *teatro* and settled for joining the working class and bringing positive change to the workforce. The tuna factory closed down, and I went through multiple jobs. Eventually, I returned to school and Delia went to work for San Diego Gas and Electric, but *teatro* was timeless in our hearts.

Teatro Raíces

We became Teatro Raíces in the summer of 1979. We hadn't done *teatro* for two years but had kept in close contact; we were close to thirty years of age. Among other jobs, I had gained the experience of being a student teacher of *teatro* for a semester at Hartnell Junior College in Salinas, California, and recently graduated as a registered nurse. Most of us were earning a living, well into motherhood, and experienced in marital matters. We felt so prepared and ready to put every ounce of energy we could afford into our joyful reunion as mature women. We as a group agreed to honor guidelines that would remind us of our purpose in *teatro,* and Delia Ravelo generously contributed by putting the "Principles of Unity" (see the addendum to this book) for the *teatro* in black and white. This was useful for the new as well as the old members, especially when I was distracted by the makeshift nursery full of children at our practice sessions.

If it were not for Delia Ravelo we would have written fewer skits and plays. As I mentioned, she always felt we needed new *actos,* but I felt we needed fewer in order to focus and strengthen our presentations. But as long as the majority was willing to put in the work, there we were. The material we had to read and understand was educational, and this encouraged everyone to express and contribute to the skits and plays. Delia Ravelo spearheaded commercials such as *Anti Nuke, United Negro College Fund, Cheese Manfatten Bank,* and *Círculo Vicioso.* She did a comedy stand-up routine of President Jimmy Carter on conserving energy. I was Billie Holiday singing "Strange Fruit"; Guadalupe Beltran sang and danced to the lyrics "Hit the road, Jack, and don't you come back no more." We loved using commercials and music for introducing and resolving issues.

Kerry

Kerry, an Anglo Amazon who joined us, would play on the piano, "Did I ever tell you, you're my hero? And I am the wind beneath your wing." She was involved in our play *This Is Your Life*, and her minor roles were magnified by her stance, solid as an oak tree, and shaded by her thick rust-gold hair.

A special gift to us from Kerry was her mother, who would always warmly welcome us into their home. Kerry had first-hand knowledge of politics through her mother, who was a parent of action in her community. I felt like we had the "Mother's Seal of Approval" when we practiced at Kerry's home. She also learned to play "The Rose" for us while Lupe and I sang our hearts out. Kerry contributed to our effort to incorporate popular music in our repertoire in order to address issues in our immediate world. We were sad to see her move on, but still I remember fondly when we howled under the moon.

Guadalupe Beltran

Guadalupe Beltran met with the *Coyote* under moonlight and danced herself into the role of E.T., Enriqueta Tejeda. The first time I saw her it was like seeing a baby girl at nighttime who had gotten separated from her mother and was lost at SDSU campus. I was sitting on a couch talking with other students. The big room was dimly lit. Her eyes were so open that she looked scared and about to burst into tears. She had wild hair with a tight wave and a round creamy face. I watched from a distance and when she finally smiled at her companion, the dim room was illuminated. I never imagined that she would want to join *teatro*.

When we first talked, direct eye contact was avoided. She was always very polite and gracious. Foul language was never part of her vocabulary, but this child had dignity and stood her ground. She had a ringing laugh that reminded me of children, puppies, and kittens running and playing. Later she took on the responsibility of being treasurer and secretary correspondent. I was impressed by her dedication, especially because she more than the rest of us struggled with writing. One time I noticed a pack of cigarettes rolled up in the sleeve of her T-shirt, and I sarcastically asked her about it. She explained it went with her role in *So Ruff, So Tuff.*

We were working on the play *Archie Bunker Goes to El Salvador*, and I was surprised that she was so intent on playing the Archie character. Sure, Guadalupe Beltran, go ahead. Practice time came around and everyone was in place, ready to go, and here came Archie. I could not believe the detail Lupe had put into this character. She had done it to the utmost perfection; no one in the group wanted to or would try out for this role after Lupe. I cannot to this day get over the impact this "Maiden" had on us. I knew she had special red handmade shoes. To me this play with the Archie character, put together by the group, was the most successful of all.

The 11th TENAZ festival, in September 1981, was the last I had the privilege of attending with the group. I got to see Sylvia and Enrique, and this was where Long Slim Kim also spotted me. I took my nephew Amado and Gloria Escalera took her son Alex. Very close attention was given to caring for the children; thank goodness, because I would forget about the kid until I spotted him in line getting his own food. Childcare was a high priority and I give a lot of credit to the organizers, because by this time people like Carolina Flores in WIT (Women in Teatro) had started implementing measures to ensure that women and young mothers were retained in *teatro*.

However, I did not have children and it seemed that not being a mother got in the way of my coming across sincerely to the members of *teatro;* Delia Ravelo was the biggest squawking mother hen. I still recall the plopping of her two-gallon breast where we sat so that her kid, who was running around our meeting table, could sip from the nip. I would sneer at Delia and she in so many motherly words would come down on me like the wrath of nature. I really couldn't understand how the women wanted children when they had to struggle even harder working full-time jobs, keeping house, going to night classes, struggling with their mate, and practically raising their children solo. Yet deep down inside I could not help but love and respect them.

Evelyn Cruz

Evelyn Cruz of Puerto Rican background was the youngest and last member of Teatro Raíces. She was tall, with bottle eyeglasses, but you could see that she was very attractive, yet very pensive. I remember her being so excited about attending the 11th TENAZ conference. It became obvious to her that we were seen as lesbians. I pointed out that this was just a maneuver to get us to have sex with men. It was up to us as individuals if we wanted to prove or disprove being lesbian, but if sex with the males did take place it was usually followed by disrespect.

In July 1982 Evelyn and I tried out for a theatrical project connected to the Shakespeare Globe Theater that was headed by Jorge Huerta and Bill Virchis. We were accepted into Teatro Meta; of all the members in Teatro Raíces only we were able to commit long hours of practice. We figured on learning from this project's techniques and using this experience for our group. I understood that we as Meta were to make a presentation that was reflective of working together. At a practice we were given a scene and I was told to act the role of a submissive wife. I looked at Jorge and immediately expressed that I did not believe in being a submissive woman. He immediately reminded me that it did not matter what I thought and that I was there to act. So act I did, but I could not help noticing that Evelyn kept daintily covering her mouth and coughing.

It wasn't until she had to take my place that I understood what she was going through. It was so awkward for me to see her in such a weak position under the dominating male actor. I could barely control my cackling, but it was worse because no one else thought this was funny. Trying to hide my hysteria, I was coughing, hacking, and burying my face on my knees. We got out of that practice torture session without exploding but once inside the car we rocked it, booming with howling laughter into the night. To this day I still remember waking up in the morning with this intense jaw pain. Sadly, after this Evelyn had to drop out because of her children. I stayed to the end through the fall season, playing the role of a tuna fish, a lizard, a wealthy snob, and other bits. Gloria Escalera said I looked professional on opening night and a female member from the Teatro de la Esperanza said that I was not strong like she had seen me before in the women's teatro. Without thinking, I blurted, "I am not in control."

I remember a practice session in Meta when we were asked to spontaneously get up and express whatever came into our head. I got up and pretended I was an Indian goddess, Coatlicue. I looked up and held my arms out, expressing that I was a powerful deity who overlooked the earth, in both life and death; when the Spanish came with their religion, my head was lowered, my eyes downcast, and my hands were folded. I was dressed in a concealing cloak and left looking like this; I had mimicked each change and posed submissively, like la Virgen de Guadalupe. I don't recall being challenged or getting feedback on this exercise, yet I did put all my time and effort into this project, faring well as a student actor of Meta. Years later I was happy to hear from Delia that Evelyn Cruz had moved on to obtain a Masters in Theater Arts; there again was the timeless apparition of my red handmade shoes glowing in the dark.

Unfortunately, my involvement with Teatro Meta backfired with the members in Teatro Raíces after we did a joint presentation at the Centro Cultural de la Raza. First I played the part of a woman in a scene with a photographer under Meta, then as Teatro Raíces we did our play *So Ruff, So Tuff.* I had stayed up the night before reconstructing with wood sticks and cloth the low-rider car we used in our play, because our old cardboard car was torn up. Not having practiced with the new heavier model made us look very awkward. It was embarrassing fumbling onstage. This new car model in black velvet would become the most concrete reason to put our Teatro Raíces to rest, but we kept on pressing. I transformed into "La Llorona," wailing and then howling like a she-wolf under a waning moon.

Gloria Escalera in My Past

Gloria's first impression of me must have involved awkwardness and embarrassment for her, as an eighth grader in a predominantly Anglo-Catholic school. Basically, all I had going for me at that time was knowing how to fight. The books under my desk inexplicably spilled out to the floor that first time, and by the second time I noted that the students next to me—including Gloria—were laughing in muffled tones. When the books spilled onto the floor the third time I already had my reserve books in my hands, and with all my might I landed a hard blow to the head of the menacing culprit, named Dennis.

I had transferred into seventh grade as an honor-roll student from Miguel Hidalgo School but was no match for the high quality of education in this private haughty school, including Gloria herself. She was a beauty with rich cream skin with a touch of raspberry glow, and thick straight eyelashes lavishly fanned her dark curious eyes. We both crossed the train tracks to get to a parish school that strangely had no Virgin de Guadalupe or brown mother of God in the school's church.

At that school my first name was Phyllis and my last name pronounced like Nones. But my school name did not impress anyone, including Gloria. During a school recess both of us faced the mirror, and from behind she called me, "Negraaaa." At home, I had four older brothers: Seferino, the conservative, called me Pelona; Genaro, who wished I were a boy, called me Pelon; but to Fidel and Rafael, I was Negra. I was used to hearing "Negra," and so the name usually resonated inside me with a wave of acceptance. However, from Gloria's contorted lips, the name vibrated with hate. I reacted with a slap to the side of her beautiful face.

From this moment, instantly and instinctively we bonded in mischief against this school and its church that had no Virgin de Guadalupe or brown mother of God. We reacted by stealing students lunches, cheating on our homework, and dressing atrociously. Three times in front of the nun, my widowed mother's hands were folded in desperation, making a plea to not expel me but to give me another chance. Gloria graduated from eighth grade, while I stayed behind to finish my time. To the shock of this school and its church community, I got to crown the Virgin Mary, or the white mother of God. This was the result of a draw from a hat filled with pieces of paper that had all the names of the female eighth graders. My mother, upon hearing this, lifted her devoted hands up in the air and said this was a sign from God that I was destined to be a nun.

Gloria started high school and my mother was a nurse aide in the hospital where Gloria ended up in isolation with yellowing skin. My mother raised her hand and commanded that my contact with Gloria end. Neither my mother nor Gloria ever said that the real cause of hepatitis was drugs. I stayed home with a heavy heart on the day of Gloria's shotgun marriage. A year went by, and she returned and joined me in high school. We still side-lined in moderate mischief, but otherwise we were using our hands opening books and learning. That is, until one day after school as we crossed the train tracks Gloria's cheeks were tracked with tears. She was pregnant again. We returned to our homes in silence and saw less of each other after that.

The next time I saw Gloria, she was a cherry-blond certified beautician with eyes made up like Cleopatra. At my desperate request, she came to examine my scalp. I felt all my hair was falling out. She reassured me that it was not and cracked the apple of my tight skull with the trained maneuver of her hands.

And off to college I would go to open more books with my hands. My mother was in the midst of prayers with the rosary wrapped around her hands pressed against her heart. For the third time her third and youngest son was off to war, this time in a place called Vietnam. But my mother's wishings for her children were powerful. Her eyes welled and she made the sign of the cross as I distanced myself from maternal tears and the beautiful Gloria.

When I saw Gloria in 1970, she was dressed as a flower child with two beautiful little girls. I was enamored with her renewed image, but it pained me to see her so young with children. She left them with her mother, and we partied in our hometown, covering both sides of the train tracks. Then her estranged husband approached us outside the liquor store, where he tried to drag Gloria away. I got in between them to fend him off and posed in my new learned karate stance; this worked, but only after he had a big laugh at me. I kept in contact with Gloria throughout the years either by chance or allegiance. She even got to join me on a double date when I brought two of the Young Lords from urban city Chicago to our rural town in Brawley.

In 1978, as a student nurse in pediatrics at Children's Hospital, I saw the back of a woman sighing softly over the bed of this sick child. It was such a forlorn scene that I hesitated to enter the room, but I knew it was Gloria before she even turned her tear-streaked face. Gloria quietly kept constant care over the permanent debilitation of her daughter Elizabeth. And Liz would laugh and smile when I addressed her by her old nickname, Lizard.

In the fall of 1979, even knowing how busy Gloria was, I still asked her to join *teatro.* She did come around to practice, but she was partial to the cute female roles. One time she had to fill in for the role of a clown taxi driver. Delia Ravelo told me under her breath that Gloria did not seem capable of playing this role but we had no choice. Gloria, to my triumph, made the audience crack up with laughter. I did note that her taxi cap was covering her eyes, but she was exceptional in "clowning" the public.

Delia Ravelo

Delia Ravelo was my beloved monster, who first appeared to me on a college campus with a black *rebozo* and downcast eyes. But when her eyes finally came up and mirrored my vision, unknowingly, I was in for the stage-dancing of a decade and more. And did we dance in our red handmade shoes! We even came to the point of throwing our shoes at each other in times of frustration and disagreement. But whether we were doing *teatro* or living life, we were to remain connected from that first day our paths crossed in a wondrous university environment.

Delia, while working full time, got her Master's degree in literature. Tears rolled when she finally decided that she could not afford to pursue a doctorate and become a professor within a university setting while still raising her children. She loved reading and expounding on all great literary works. We could talk for hours and would listen to John Lennon sing, "Imagine there's no countries . . . and no religion too . . ." We agreed that when her last child left for college we would become writers. Meanwhile, we talked about her adventures in education. She once told me she was going to play the part of the oppressed Mexican and have the Anglo student play the part of the oppressor for a class presentation. I suggested the actors be reversed; this would be a way of challenging a stereotype and introducing compassion at the same time. She did play the oppressor, causing great discomfort in the class, but instead of compassion this incited anger. Delia said this idea was taken to a stage where only the aesthetic could view this as entertainment.

I had been living in northern California and partially due to Delia's encouragement I decided to finish my Bachelors at SDSU in Chicano Studies when I moved back to San Diego. I took a class in Women's Studies in which our professor pointed out the exploding market for reshaping female breasts in order for women to be loved. Jokingly, she questioned how men would feel if they were being encouraged to enlarge or reshape their testicles in order to be loved. Delia and Evelyn Cruz put a skit together about this idea. The three of us also worked on a skit titled *Moco Loco,* which was about newscasting in the fashion of the *Saturday Night Live* TV show. Delia and I further developed the skit on testicle augmentation by including different kinds of "Victor's Secret" underwear. We as a team presented this skit *Bola Job* at several events, including the twentieth anniversary celebration for Womancare, June 19, 1992.

We started as if we were already living in the future, and she wrote her part for our *teatro* project before all her children left home and before she retired. She worked full time for San Diego Gas and Electric, sat on its committee that made decisions on how to allocate charity funds, and was an avid member of her labor union. She also volunteered for a childcare program in Tijuana, was a parent community organizer, and was an educational consultant. Her body came to its end under heavy medical treatment and now she lives in my heart.

Ashes of a Chicana in *Teatro*

Ashes of a Chicana are all that remain of my beloved Delia Ravelo. In addition to the roles we acted out in life, we created more roles for ourselves through *teatro*. As Chicanas in *teatro* we battled and searched to find out why and who we were. Chicanas in *teatro* to us meant knowledge put into an action of love onstage that continued into life. Through *teatro* we discovered a world that became our stage.

Teatro facilitated for us the process of changing, interchanging, and transforming our roles onstage and in life. Costumes, titles, labels, diagnosis or prognosis, and disguises that come with attachments and addictions cannot define who we are or dictate how we feel. Truth, knowledge, and compassion led us to use *teatro* as a connection to life. *Teatro* as a dark magic cradle rocked us on the rivers of the world. We all share our rich darkness emanating light in many forms. I cried myself back into this cradle to find a bed of ashes. And in my dark void discovered an eternal radiance, revealing the spirit of Delia Ravelo.

I was in *teatro* with a Chicana named Delia Ravelo. We danced in step with other "Maidens" who created and proudly wore their red handmade shoes. I have laid my beautiful mother to rest in the rich glow of the moon. My heart overflows with treasures. I center myself in the universe and turn as my hands bless the four-corners and its winds that carry maternal tears and fertile ashes.

Conclusion

THIS BOOK REPRESENTS the labor of seventeen women who formed a collective in order to put together their recollections of the work of a beloved theater company, which was first called Teatro de las Chicanas and was later known variously as Teatro Laboral and Teatro Raíces, but was always *teatro chicana*. These women, now heading into middle age, were university students in San Diego from the late 1960s into the 1970s. The process of producing this book was like stitching together a patchwork quilt, one piece at a time, not quite knowing what the final product was going to look like. As the women progressed with the book they knew that each precious patch had to be used, because without it the quilt as a whole would be incomplete.

Their goal has been to respectfully pass on to a new generation of young women and men a record of experiences and lessons learned during that crucial period of reflection and protest—not because the writers felt that their experiences were unique, but because they believe that each generation adds its own sweat, labor, and intellect to the advancement of humanity. We are links in a chain of history. In the tradition of Native American storytelling, the women aim to pass on their story to this current generation of warriors. It is their hope that generations to come will learn from their failures as well as their successes.

The generation that came of age during the Chicano Movement strove to create awareness of civil rights, to continue the struggle for women's equality, and to mobilize opposition to the Vietnam War. Many of the same political issues, in different guises and disguises, confront us today. And the work of the *teatro* women resonates with relevance. For example, the issues raised in an *acto* written in the early 1980s, *Archie Bunker Goes to El Salvador,* would easily be recognizable today in an *acto* revised as "Archie Bunker Goes to Iraq." The *acto* titled *E.T.—The Alien,* which was about the immigration issue, is still valid today as we witness the virulent attacks on the undocumented immigrant population and those who dare to defend them or sympathize with them.

Controversial issues were the core of the *actos* the *teatro* women wrote—issues such as discrimination on the job, drug abuse, and abortion. These women researched, wrote, and performed the plays on campus and in the community, all while struggling to pursue their own higher educational goals. In the *teatro* play titled *So Ruff, So Tuff,* the protagonist, Rudy, is pressured by his friends to sell drugs on the street while his sister Rosie becomes pregnant and decides that an abortion is her only option for dealing with this unplanned pregnancy. Both Rudy and Rosie find it difficult to pursue their dream of going to college, just like so many of today's working-class young people who are faced with similar challenges and obstacles.

As demonstrated in the *actos,* the foremost goal of the women was to stimulate community action through political awareness. They used the medium of theater to raise social consciousness. They strongly believed—and believe today—in the freedom to express political views without persecution. Freedom of speech—whether in the written word, public performance, or music—must be protected, because it is through dialogue and debate that we exercise and ultimately preserve our democratic rights.

The writers of this book are a microcosm of society in the first chapter of the twenty-first century in this country. Some of the women obtained their degrees thirty years ago, while others returned to college while working full-time in order to earn their degrees. Some of the women married. Some divorced. Some were single mothers and others raised children with their partners. Three of the women are cancer survivors and one was lost to cancer during the early stages of the writing of this book. In the years that it took to write this book, some of the women suffered the loss of parents, sisters, and friends.

The *teatro* women are elementary school teachers, university professors, nurses, linguistic translators, administrators and administrative assistants, counselors, community and school liaisons, and labor union officials. In their varied capacities they touch the lives of many people in their communities, including children, students, the sick, the elderly, workers, and prisoners.

In their daily lives the writers of this book apply what they learned in their years with the *teatro:* to treat everyone with respect regardless of nationality, language, color, or gender; to value every human being and to passionately advocate for the rights of workers, the poor, and the most disenfranchised among us in society. And, more important, to encourage others to add their *granito de arena*—their own contribution—for a better society and the advancement of humanity. The *teatro* women are devoted to peace, reason, and compassion.

II

Actos / Scripts

Chicana Goes to College

Characters

Lucy	Ricardo
Mom	Dad
Mailman voice	Bullhorn police voice
Chona	Class Teacher
Class Student 1	Class Student 2
Class Student 3	Anglo Student
Amado	Nando
MEChA Student	MEChA Student
MEChA Student	Dora

Scene I: Home

(Lucy Garcia in this scene explains first to her boyfriend, then to her parents, that she wants to go to college. Conversation is outside the door with her handsome boyfriend. On right back side stage is door with a sign on easel that reads "Home of Mr. and Mrs. Jose Garcia." On rest of stage are the still figures of the

parents with backs to the audience. Boyfriend is trying to get Lucy sexually aroused just outside the door.)

LUCY: Stop, please, Ricardo, my parents are inside.
RICARDO: Then let's get back in the car and go to back to Lover's Point.
LUCY: I'd rather not because you can't listen to me.
RICARDO: Listen, you love me don't you? Or are you just playing hard to get? You are teasing me. Besides, what is the point of holding back, baby?
LUCY: I am not ready for this.
RICARDO: I love you more than I love my mother. Do you understand what that means? I am putting you above my mother and you are playing hard to get. What else do you want?

(*Lucy with one hand holds onto a small cloth pouch that hangs from her neck and looks nervously and humbly at her lusting boyfriend.*)

LUCY: I'm sorry if . . . uh . . . I have this hope, this wish to go to college.
RICARDO: Oh no, you ain't going to no college. You are going to marry me and have my children. Where do you get this silly idea of going to college? You are mine and I love you. Soon you'll be Mrs. Ricardo Chavez.
LUCY: Do you mean that I'll lose my whole name?
RICARDO: You see the sign here on your door? This is the right and proper way. The woman gives it all up for love and in return takes the name of her husband.

(*Ricardo hugs Lucy tighter, she shows her worried face to the audience.*)

LUCY: Okay, one more kiss from you so I can dream, dream, and dream.
RICARDO: Okay, but dream only of me, me, and me.
LUCY: You know dreams also have a background.
RICARDO: I know. You're thinking of the whole enchilada. Your crowning veil, the puffy dress, and your new name.
LUCY: Ay, Ricardo, good night.

(*Ricardo grabs her butt before he exits and as she opens the door. Parents come to life in their living room.*)

DAD: It sure took some time for you to get in. I almost went out to bring you inside.
MOM: *Ay, viejo,* how soon you forget when we were dating.
DAD: And you were playing the part of hard to get.
LUCY: Dad . . . . Mom, I need to talk to you.

DAD: What! You are PG, *panzona?*

MOM: Papa, let her talk.

LUCY: No, I am not pregnant, and I have been giving this a lot of serious thought. I have decided that I want to go to college.

(*Parents stare in disbelief at their daughter.*)

LUCY: I found out through the recruiters who came to our school that there are grants and student loans. And . . . and I put in for an application and maybe . . .

(*She clutches the hanging pouch.*)

DAD: Except for girls who become nuns, all females who leave their home to go to school or anywhere become whores!

LUCY: What about Frances next door? She got a degree.

DAD: That Frances got involved with a married man. What was the point of her degree? What is the use of being highly educated when you turn out to be a laughing joke?

LUCY: She made a mistake.

DAD: And you are not making a mistake. You are staying here in this home until you either become a nun or are properly married.

MOM: Lucy, *m'ija,* maybe I was too harsh and set against you dating Ricardo, but actually he is a nice boy. He could give you a name and a place in society. And you could give him children and be a good happy wife.

DAD: Do you think you can be better than us? We love you. Why do you want to separate from us? *M'ija, los hombres* and only men leave home because they are men. Women stay home and do not stray out into the world alone. Men do not get pregnant! Let her go, Lupe. Just remember anything (*points finger at Lucy*) bad, ugly, awful, and dirty that happens to you will be because you brought it upon yourself.

LUCY: I will call Ricardo and tell him I am not ready for marriage.

(*Her eyes fill with tears and she exits stage left, crying. Her parents are left facing each other and slowly exit stage left. Sign saying "Next day" is carried across stage from left to right. Knocking on the door is heard. Lucy responds, enters stage on left, and goes to right back stage and opens door to find a letter on entry. Lucy picks it up, opens it, and gets very excited.*)

LUCY: I have been accepted to go to college!

(*While Lucy dances with joy, Ricardo appears unexpectedly at the door.*)

RICARDO: What do you mean by saying on the telephone that you don't want marriage? And that we have different roads!

(*He grabs Lucy by the arm. She struggles to get out of his grip and shouts.*)

LUCY: Please, let go of my arm, Ricardo! Mamá!

(*Because the door is still open the sound of police bullhorn comes on the loudspeaker addressing the couple. The mother enters stage left and runs in to stand between Lucy and Ricardo, notes that the door is left open.*)

BULLHORN: Is everything alright?
MOM: Yes, officer, thank you. He is just leaving. Aren't you, Ricardo?
RICARDO: Yes! Shit, yes!

(*Ricardo exits and Mom locks the door.*)

MOM: Why are you crying, Lucy? Do you still love him? If you do, then don't leave. Like him you won't find another. He is very hurt.
LUCY: I feel bad that he is hurt, because in a way I do love him.
MOM: Lucy, you are not making any sense.
LUCY: Mom, I love you and I still want to go. I need to go away.

(*Lucy puts the hanging pouch softly to her cheek and hugs her mother.*)

MOM: *M'ija*, if you stay I would help get you an old car and with the both of us working, a new car!
LUCY: Mom, are you trying to bribe me?
MOM: Well, maybe. Yes, I am.

(*They both exit. The sign on the easel stage right is changed to "College," and about five chairs are set up facing at an angle on right side of stage. Stage left, a chair, a podium or table for the teacher, facing students.*)

Scene II: College

(*Lucy is in college and she is very flustered as she speaks to her friend Chona. Both are in front stage right and they enter class through back right stage door. They wait for the English teacher. The three other students enter randomly through right side stage door and take a seat.*)

LUCY: I am having a rough time getting around this huge campus.
CHONA: Hell, I thought psychology and psychiatry were the same so I ended up in the wrong class. Everything sounds confusing. I don't know if I can make it in this *gigante* school.

LUCY: Well, let's try to take many classes together so we can help each other out.

CHONA: Yeah, maybe two *cabezas* are better than one mind.

(*Teacher enters as Chona is reapplying her makeup and Lucy is writing notes.*)

CLASS TEACHER: Okay, class, I am handing out the syllabus for the semester at the end of class. Next, pull out paper and pen and write in twenty minutes a two-hundred-word essay of who you are and what you are doing in your life.

CHONA: Shit! (*Raises hand, teacher motions.*) You mean right now?

CLASS TEACHER: Yes, write. Right now. You *sabe* or you *no sabe*?

(*Chona is embarrassed and Lucy reaches out to touch Chona's shoulder for support. The other students either sneer or give a muffled laugh. All the students concentrate on their class assignment and teacher reads a magazine. Chona shows the most frustrated movements of all—pulling her hair, putting her head down then overextending it, scratching and rubbing her head, tapping her feet, swaying knees. Lucy writes with one hand and holds her hanging pouch softly to her cheek. The other students seem pretty relaxed, and then Class Teacher looks at his wristwatch and calls for end to writing session.*)

CLASS TEACHER: By now you need to be wrapping up your story.

CHONA: (*Loud whisper.*) Lucy, I can't write, there is nothing to say about me that sounds right. It is too messy, boring . . .

(*Lucy looks at her own paper and shakes her head.*)

CLASS TEACHER: Hand in your papers, make sure you get the class syllabus, go over it, get or buy the required books. Do your assignment for the next class meeting. Ask any questions.

(*Students hand in their work. Lucy and Chona, being the last, face the teacher.*)

CLASS TEACHER: What is this scribbling with smears of lipstick, mascara, and eyeshadow? You got to be joking, or you are in great need of a remedial course. This is an English 1A class.

CHONA: What is a remedial class?

CLASS TEACHER: It is an elementary approach to learning the fundamentals of the English language. By the look on your face, you'd be better off learning a trade in facial makeup. I believe it is called cosmetology.

(*Chona goes into a slump and Lucy gives her an elbow nudge.*)

CLASS TEACHER: And you, Ms. Garcia. From what I see you did make an effort to write but it is very poorly done. Both of you certainly could use help. Both of you would feel more comfortable learning to be beauticians but not here in this environment. Get some counseling. You need to start from the beginning, or go back where you came from.

(*He exits right back stage door, leaving Lucy and Chona alone.*)

CHONA: (*Crying.*) I told you I can't make it in college; this is not where I belong.

LUCY: Look, he might have sounded like a jerk but he did say there are classes where we can learn to write.

(*They exit the class right back stage door and walk a semicircle to the front center stage, going through motions of conversing with each other. Three chairs are removed. Two chairs are placed center stage, four feet apart, facing the audience. Chona and Lucy sit down.*)

CHONA: Yeah, but how embarrassing we have to go back to baby class and learn English. And you, Lucy, are smarter than I am. Still, even you messed up. Makeup artists sounds better to me. Oh! Look at this campus (*toward audience*), full of beautiful green grass and trees.

LUCY:. Look, Chona, we can easily learn how to apply mud on our face, but wouldn't it be great if we can also learn to write? So what if we have to start from the beginning. What have we got to lose?

CHONA: You sound like we are on an adventure or some sort of fairytale.

LUCY: I don't think so. Cinderella, Sleeping Beauty, and *la* Snow White never went to college. Didn't you notice? They waited for Prince Charming to rescue them.

CHONA: I wouldn't mind being rescued myself. It is not a bad idea.

LUCY: Yes, well then, all we have to do is sit, wait, and look out the window.

CHONA: Do you hear that Mexican music in the background? Let's go check it out.

LUCY: You go. I'll wait for you and check out the schedule for a remedial English course.

(*Chona exits and Lucy goes over the schedule while clutching her hanging pouch. An Anglo boy enters stage right. He pretends to be minding his own business and makes his moves to nestle close to Lucy.*)

ANGLO STUDENT: Hey, *chula*, you are some fine hot stuff. How about some chile and free holes?

LUCY: Put the *frijoles* up yours and have some respect. If you don't know what respect is, get a remedial class in human manners.

ANGLO STUDENT: Excuse me, I just thought we could have a little fun.

(*He shakes his head and exits stage left. Chona enters stage right, all excited.*)

CHONA: Lucy, guess what—the organization for students like us is having a meeting tomorrow evening!

LUCY: What are you saying?

CHONA: You know, the Chicanos on campus who belong to MEChA.

LUCY: I really am not interested at this time. It's just that we have a lot of homework.

CHONA: Yeah, but remember it was partly through the efforts of MEChA that we got to college and are sitting here on this beautiful campus.

LUCY: Yeah, but we still need to learn writing better English plus all these other confusing classes.

CHONA: I feel that we need to make time for a good cause.

LUCY: What *causa?*

CHONA: Well, look at this pamphlet. MEChA is planning a fundraising concert for the United Farm Workers. We could help out in this planning to support the struggle of the *campesinos.*

LUCY: I came to college to get away from *campesinos.* I don't want to go back and work in the fields.

CHONA: And I don't want to end up working in a factory sweatshop either but there is a need to improve wages and working conditions.

LUCY: I'm saying I don't want to go backwards.

CHONA: Backwards?

LUCY: I mean, I don't want to return to those horrible working conditions. And that old couple . . .

CHONA: What old couple?

LUCY: The big trucks came to pick us up at 4:30 this one freezing morning to harvest the crops. This old couple was shivering, we all were, but being crowded inside the truck we huddled together. I tried not to stare at their bent bodies and tired wrinkled faces.

(*Chona hands a tissue to Lucy, who is trying to stop the tears from running.*)

CHONA: Well, what happened?

LUCY: The old man must have noticed me as they shared a bottle between them. He offered me a drink. So, not to hurt their feelings, I drank. It was cold coffee.

CHONA: *Ay*, and you don't like cold coffee?

LUCY: No, it is just that I don't want to have to do hard labor as an elderly person.

CHONA: Just kidding, this little story is just one more reason for us to show support by demanding better work conditions and benefits for the elderly folks. As students we can volunteer some time.

LUCY: Well, yes, but remember, we also have a lot of studying.

(*Lucy clutches at the pouch hanging from her neck.*)

CHONA: How can I forget with you reminding me?

LUCY: Yeah, and then as college graduates someday we can help in this struggle as nurses or teachers.

CHONA: There you go diving into the future. And what is it with that bag you keep hanging on to?

LUCY: Oh, it is a broken broach I found on the edge of this water fountain. It is like my good luck charm.

CHONA: Well, hang onto your charm because I'm saving the best for last.

LUCY: What, tell me? What?

CHONA: Girl, there are some fine-looking dudes parading and announcing the meeting for tomorrow. One of them is called Amado and the other is Nando. *Ay, Papasotes.*

(*Lucy and Chona exit right back stage door as Chona describes the good-looking dudes. The sign on door is changed to "Movemiento" with same arrangement of chairs as in classroom scene. A table or space should made for UFW literature facing right front stage. The MEChA students can start entering to fill up the seats. The speaker's podium should have a Huelga flag or some insignia referring to this MEChA meeting.*)

Scene III: The MEChA Meeting

(*Enter Amado and Nando looking like militants, wearing shades and strutting their importance as they enter stage left, come around to front center stage, and enter through right back stage door and end up in mid-center.*)

AMADO: Nando, my man, there better be some new chicks that volunteer to clean, cook, and type because we got so much work ahead of us.

NANDO: You are the president, Amado. It's your show.

AMADO: How do I look? (*Strikes a pose.*)

NANDO: Huh, don't take it personal but you look *firme.*

AMADO: You don't look so bad yourself, man.

(*Entering right back stage door is Dora, a woman modestly dressed. She approaches Amado and Nando.*)

DORA: My name is Dora and I am the representative for the United Farm Workers. I understand you want me to speak.

AMADO: There must be some kind of mistake. We were expecting . . . well, we thought that . . .

DORA: If you have any questions here is the number to the UFW office. I have done this before.

(*Nando and Amado look at each other and shrug their shoulders, put their palms up, and look confused. By this time they also notice Chona and Lucy making their way in and taking a seat. They elbow each other while Dora gets her notes and information in order.*)

NANDO: Okay, Dora, we'll let you know when to speak. (*He makes his way towards the novices.*) Good evening, my name is Nando and I want to get to know you better after the meeting.

CHONA: Oh, we would like to stay a while, wouldn't we, Lucy?

LUCY: Maybe, but we can't stay too late.

(*Nando goes back to where Amado is getting ready to chair the meeting.*)

CHONA: Are you trying to ruin my chances? He is so cute. Oh, I know, Lucy, you are making us hard to get. (*She waves at Nando.*)

LUCY: What?

AMADO: Could I have your attention, please! There is a party after this gathering and we want to make this meeting as short as possible. As most of you know, we are planning a fundraiser for the United Farm Workers next month. Dora, who is a UFW representative, is also on our agenda. Dora, do you think that you can handle this, now?

DORA: Yes, thank you, Amado. On behalf of my organization, we are very gracious that you as students are doing what you can to acknowledge and participate in our efforts to better the working conditions of the *campesinos y campesinas*. Any funds that come our way will be used in our drive to organize the farm workers.

(*Chona raises her hand and Dora acknowledges her.*)

CHONA: Can we choose the day and time it is best to volunteer?

DORA: Yes, I brought some literature that gives you more details on what we are all about and also how you can participate in other activities such as walking in our picket lines. Please come forward after the meeting and I'll be here to answer any questions. Thank you for contributing in any way possible. *¡Y que viva la Huelga!*

(*Everyone joins in a loud clapping. Lucy and Chona look at each other. The shout is repeated three times in chorus.*)

NANDO: Chicano Power!

CHORUS: Chicano Power! Chicano Power!

NANDO:. And now we present the man of the hour, Amado, the chairman of MEChA.

AMADO: *Orale, carnal,* you're alright. I want to talk about our beautiful culture and as you can see for yourselves, the beautiful *Chicanitas* in this room. These women are our Aztec princesses who bear our children and continue the ways of our people. Our people who have been repressed, compressed, depressed, and oppressed. We men must rise up as proud Aztec warriors to defend our helpless children and women.

(*Amado reaches for a glass of water and rearranges his hair and shades while Nando fans him with a paper. Lucy and Chona give each other a puzzled look.*)

AMADO: And our women will keep and tend our beautiful culture that gives us pride, that feeds us the *maiz,* the *frijoles,* and the *nopales* that make us unique to all the others. We are special. We are a proud people. And now we are calling forth our beautiful women to help us by volunteering in the typing, clean up, and food committees. Please step forward and sign up. This meeting has been adjourned.

(*Nando hand-carries the sign-up sheet to where Lucy and Chona are seated.*)

DORA: May I remind those that are interested in more information about the UFW, to please come forward and see the informative material. There are pamphlets for free.

LUCY: Chona, while you talk to Nando, I'll check out what Dora has on her table.

CHONA: Okay.

(*She flutters her eyelashes at Nando. Amado notices Lucy coming toward the front and can't believe that instead of talking with him, she goes to see what information Dora has to offer. This reaction is frozen with other students attending the meeting and focus goes to Nando and Chona.*)

NANDO: You can sign up for all the committees but I do want you to pay attention to only me.
CHONA: Well, I don't see a problem with that.

(Chona smiles and signs her name on the sheet Nando gives to her. Nando then gives the sheet to Amado and introduces her to Amado.)

NANDO: Chona, this is Amado.
AMADO: Thanks for volunteering, maybe your friend can also sign up.

(Chona rearranges her clothes and her hair and sneaks on some lipstick. Other students examine the sign up sheet that Amado places on a nearby chair, and another student wanders over to where Dora has her table of UFW information to the left side of the podium.)

NANDO, *loud whisper to Amado*: What do think about Chona? *¡Está bien chichona!*

(Nando puts both hands out in front of his chest.)

AMADO: Hey, man, you have scored!
NANDO: Chona, you want to look at the stars while your friend looks at the UFW information?
CHONA: I don't know.
NANDO: Well, I do know! Let's go.
CHONA: Okay.

(As Nando and Chona exit, Amado nods approvingly and puts his thumb up, grabs the sign up sheet from the students who have signed it. Amado goes over to where another student stands next to Dora and Lucy by the information table. Dora has her attention on the other student and Amado directs his attention toward Lucy.)

AMADO: Excuse me, I'm Amado, and you are?
LUCY: Lucy.

(She lightly holds on to her cloth necklace.)

AMADO: Are you going to sign up for any of the committees that will be helping out at the UFW concert?
LUCY: Do you have a place for a mistress of ceremony?
AMADO: You mean a master of ceremony? You are looking at the master.

LUCY: I see.

AMADO: But these committees are just as important and we need all the help we can get.

LUCY: I will help out but first I would like to check it out before I make a decision.

AMADO: And what about me, don't you want to know me now?

LUCY: I already know that you support the UFW. I'm sure that we will get to know each other.

AMADO: Why waste time?

LUCY: I don't think that I'm wasting time.

(*The student who was frozen in communication with Dora exits. And Dora comes into the conversation between Lucy and Amado.*)

DORA: Is there something that I could help you with?

AMADO: No, we are getting ready to leave, thank you.

LUCY: I do have some questions.

AMADO: I am going to the party, ask Nando, and he can take you and your friend later. (*He exits.*)

DORA: Sorry if I interfered.

LUCY: It's all right. I was looking at this UFW pamphlet. The pictures show all kinds and colors of people who are involved. I thought it was only for people of Mexican background.

DORA: We are open to anyone who is able to give the UFW support. The struggle of the farm workers reaches every table where drink and food is served.

LUCY: So you include all people whether they are white, black, red.

DORA: Yes, indeed, even female students like you.

(*Lucy chuckles and holds on to her necklace pouch.*)

LUCY: You seem so sure of yourself. I mean it in a positive way.

DORA: That is a compliment because when I first started out I was very scared to speak out. What is that pouch you hold?

LUCY: It is a broken broach. It is has an image of a female who is very young and very aware.

DORA: May I see it?

LUCY: Yes, of course. (*She pulls it out.*) I find it so interesting because she is carrying a bow and arrows strapped to her shoulder, like a hunter yet very respectful.

DORA: It is a woman of very ancient times, and there is also some kind of hound or wolf at her side.

LUCY: Yes, she looks so relaxed, yet so strong and independent. In a strange way she makes me feel that I need to look out for myself.

DORA: I'm sure that you will find out what this figure stands for. Especially because you are in an environment full of books and knowledge. I think it is great that you are in a university.

LUCY: It has been hard for me and my friend, Chona. But I am excited to be here.

DORA: Oh my, time goes fast. Read over the rest of the information and here is the number to contact the UFW office for ways to get involved in activities as a volunteer when you make time.

LUCY: Yes, I'll read it.

DORA: Remember, don't let go of your goal. I have three kids but still someday I want to get a degree in teaching. Take care, goodbye. *Y que viva la Huelga.*

(*Dora exits and Lucy waves goodbye. Then enters Chona. Her hair, makeup, and clothes are messed up. She is trying hard not to bust out crying.*)

LUCY: Chona, what happened?

CHONA: Nothing, I'm okay. (*She wipes her tears.*)

LUCY: Chona, why are you crying?

CHONA: Nothing, just hold me.

(*Chona is tenderly hugged by Lucy.*)

LUCY: Come on, Chona, let's go, we'll get some sleep and in the morning we will figure out what to do.

(*Both exit. The stage is emptied except for one chair facing the audience. Lucy enters with her backpack, sits down, opens her bag, and pulls out a paper and reads.*)

Scene IV: Chicana Resolution

(*Lucy starts out sitting and for emphasis stands up, does some pacing, acting out with emotion certain parts of the paper she is about to read as she addresses the audience.*)

LUCY: I would like to share a letter that is meant for my mother. I have given it much thought, but I am still very nervous and also excited. It starts:

Dear Mom,

I've already been here at this university for two years and there is so much to learn from books and teachers. I have also learned from examples, experiences, and even mistakes. But my being aware, getting involved, and caring for others has made my life very rich. Chona and I have been volunteering to help out with the United Farm Workers. Our involvement with the UFW also has taught us to respect our roots. *Campesinos* who work the land are to be respected like all other workers for their contribution to society. I am proud of my working-family background. Chona and I have gotten to know other women like us. We have been talking about holding a small gathering of daughters and mothers at our campus. It is called Seminario de Chicanas. I really want you to come to our university event and spend the day with me.

(*Enter Chona onstage to see what Lucy is reading.*)

CHONA: I thought I heard you mention my name. Can I read the rest of this? Oh, it's a letter.

LUCY: Promise not to make fun of me.

CHONA: I can't promise but here we go.

Mom, I want you to know how I see the world: My views may be different from yours but this does not mean that you are less important. You are the one who gave me life. And in spite of problems and hard times, it is a very exciting world that I am experiencing. I am glad to be alive and to be able to communicate with you. I realize that you did your best in raising me to be strong and responsible for my actions. I really am fortunate to have a mother like you. Please understand that even though I'm not under your care, all that you have taught me has not been forgotten. I have also learned that change is difficult but it can also mean a better life for me. Even if you do not agree with my changes, I still want you to know what I feel and what I sense. I love you with all my heart. Get ready for our mother and daughter seminar. Your daughter, Lucy

LUCY: Well, do you think my letter makes enough sense so that my mother will come to our seminar?

CHONA: I say that your English grammar skills make sense and I think your mom will come to be with us. Later, you will go over my history paper before I turn it into my teacher?

LUCY: Of course, I will. So, let me read you the last part of my letter. P.S. Mom, remember when we dropped a coin and made a wish by the water fountain? This was the place where I found that old broken broach. I still have it in my treasure box. Well, it has a story like your necklace of La Virgen de Guadalupe. The name of the female image in the broach is Artemis. She is a link to an ancient "Sweet Virgin," the goddess of animals, childbirth, and instinct, and a protector of young women.

End

Bronca

CHORUS: *Bronca, Bronca, Bronca,*
Bronca-Bronca—BroncaBronCabrónCabrónCABRONCABRONCA
MUJER 1: Bronca, *¿por qué solo me quieren de cocinera? ¿Porque soy mujer?*
Why is it that when it comes to the preparing of food, automatically men see me stuck to pots, pans, and dishes?
Cooking food is the task as well as the many joys of life.
Carnales, don't put yourself above this task.
Pitch in and let's divide the work equally.

(*Mujer 1 steps back into the Chorus.*)

CHORUS: Bronca, Bronca, Bronca!
MUJER 2: Bronca, *¿por qué solo me quieren de secretaria? ¿Porque soy mujer?*
Why is it when it comes to taking the minutes and notes of and for men, automatically men look blankly at me?
The typing and writing of words is the task as well as the joy of anybody.
Carnales, don't put yourself above this task.
Take notes and let's divide the work equally.

(*Mujer 2 steps back into the Chorus.*)

CHORUS: Bronca, Bronca, Bronca!

MUJER 3: Bronca, *¿por qué no me quiere escuchar? ¿Porque soy mujer?* Why is it when it comes to speaking and making speeches, automatically men ask each other and not one of us Chicanas?
Verbal expression and direction is the task as well as the joy for anyone.
Carnales, don't horde yourselves with this task.
Listen to women's words of wisdom.

(*Mujer 3 steps back into the Chorus.*)

CHORUS: Bronca, Bronca, Bronca!

MUJER 4: Bronca, *¿por qué solo me quieren para cuidar a niños? ¿Porque soy mujer?* Why is it when it comes to childcare and child-rearing, automatically, men point at women and mothers?
The caring of lives is the task as well as the joy for both men and women.
Carnales, as responsible parents don't run away from this task!
Embrace the knowledge of being or becoming a loving father.

(*Mujer 4 steps back into the Chorus.*)

CHORUS: Bronca, Bronca, Bronca!

MUJER 5: The *machismo* hurts men and women alike.
The *machismo* is a tool of the oppressor.
Man is not the enemy that breeds inequality and disease. The oppressor is!
Brothers, unite with your sisters to fight the oppressor. Down with *machismo*!
Brothers, unite with your sisters to fight the oppressor. Down with the enemy!
We are both members of the same class: the working class!

(*Mujer 5 steps back into the Chorus.*)

CHORUS. Only by men and women uniting as equals can we attain the liberation of our class!

(*Chorus sings song, "Yo quiero que a mí me entierren como revolucionario."*)

End

So Ruff, So Tuff

Characters

Mrs. Martinez
Rudy Martinez
Rosie Martinez
Rod Sterling
Mrs. Fuller
Girlfriend
Leo
Gas Attendant
G&E Receptionist
Sassco Personnel
Sassco Striker
Policeman
Old Man

Songs

"Low Rider"
Theme from *The Twilight Zone*
"So Rough, So Tough"

Scene I: The Graduation

(*Backstage music recording from* The Twilight Zone. *Rod Serling enters.*)

ROD: You're traveling into the unknown arena, not only of sight and sound, but of mind. A traveling into a wondrous land whose boundaries are that of the imagination. At the next sign, posted up ahead, the next stop, the Unknown Arena.

(*Enter Rosie and Rudy.*)

ROSIE: I'm glad the graduation ceremony is over . . . hey, there's Linda (*waves at audience*). Oh no, look, my buddies Art, Fernie.

(*Enter Mother.*)

ROTHER: Oh, my children! I am so proud of you. I am so happy. (*Hugs Rosie and Rudy.*) Oh, oh, my children, so intelligent.

RUDY: Ma, my friends are watching.

ROSIE: Oh, Mom, my makeup is rubbing off.

MOTHER: Oh, my children, I can't help it. I'm so proud you are the first in the family to graduate from high school. And Rosita you made it without getting pregnant.

(*Enter Mrs. Fuller.*)

RUDY: Say there goes Mrs. Fuller, the counselor. Remember, *Jefa,* she said I was never going to make it through tenth grade. Mrs. Fuller, this is my mother.

MOTHER: Rudy, don't be so rude. My pleasure to meet you.

MRS. FULLER: Rudy, I must say I am surprised you have graduated after having been such a troublemaker. Now my advice is to go put your application into Sassco so you can start working and roll with the punches!

RUDY: I graduated the top ten from my class.

ROSIE: So did I.

MRS. FULLER: So?

ROSIE: So we're thinking of going to college. We spoke to the recruiter from MEChA and we have a good chance of getting a grant and loans.

MRS. FULLER: Well, I wouldn't say that since so many educational benefits are being cut off. (*Turns to mother.*) Mrs. Martinez, I think you should set your children straight on what's real and put an end to their dreams. Good day to you.

(*Mrs. Fuller exits.*)

MOTHER: (*Baffled look.*) You mean my children are not for college?

RUDY: Oh, *Jefita*, it's just an opinion.

ROSIE: I want to go to college.

Teatro Raíces. Kerry performing *This Is Your Life* on a homemade stage for a backyard party. Courtesy of Felicitas Nuñez.

A Teatro Raíces backyard performance of *Círculo vicioso*, a spoof on pharmaceutical advertisements. Courtesy of Felicitas Nuñez.

Teatro Raíces members kick it up. *Left–right:* Kerry, Delia Ravelo, Felicitas Nuñez, Maria Juarez, Gloria Escalera, Margarita Carrillo, Maria Pedroza, and Guadalupe Beltran. Courtesy of Felicitas Nuñez.

Teatro Mestizo performing *Soldado razo* (1973). *Left–right:* Ramon "Chunky" Sanchez playing the trumpet; (*back*) Laura Cortez Garcia, Dolly, and Mercedes Cueva. In the background is Ernesto Hernandez in the role of "La Muerte." Courtesy of Laura Cortez Garcia.

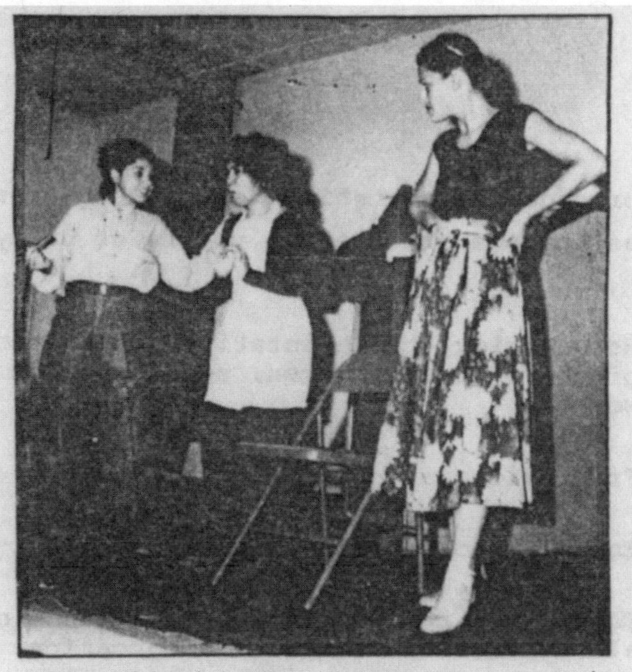

Members of the Chula Vista group, Teatro Raices, stare in disbelief as Archie explains his solutions for Latin America in their original play "Archie Goes To El Salvador" performed at this year's celebration of International Women's Day.

Teatro Raices is a street teatro,
it performs in garages, at parks, at
peoples back yards or in their homes
and auditoriums, wherever they are
asked to perform.

For more information write to:

Gloria Escalera
2033 Prospect St.
National City, CA 92050

Or phone (714) 426-4233 ask for
Guadalupe Beltran

Teatro Raíces brochure.

Evelyn Cruz as "Rod Serling" in *So Ruff, So Tuff* (May 1982). Courtesy of Felicitas Nuñez.

TEATRO LABORAL PRESENTS

NO SCHOOL TOMORROW

No School Tomorrow is a play that is intended to alert everyone to the dangers present in the Bakke Case. While some may feel it is only a problem for minorities, it is not. We feel that every student, including Allen Bakke, should have an opportunity to a higher education. The problem is the educational system and the fact that it is not serving the needs of society. So we see it is not just the minorities who are excluded but that also a majority of the anglo students are too. A solution to this problem would be the Nationalization of Education. Let us force a cut in the military budget and put that money into schools, jobs and peace. Then education will become a right in reality and not the priviledge for a few that it now is. Equal, Integrated and Quality Education will not be given to us, but it is what we have to fight for!

Teatro Laboral flyer for the performance of *No School Tomorrow* (1977). A synopsis was given on the back of the flyer.

4 — THURSDAY, MAY 3, 1973 — Daily Aztec

Chicano amateur theatre group conveys political message through satire, humor

By Henry Acevedo

A group of Chicanas have organized a theatre group here, which espouses before campus and community audiences, the ideals of dignity, equality and respect for women.

"Teatro de las Chicanas," an informal association of women, is scheduled to perform at 11 a.m. today at Montezuma Hall as part of a Cinco de Mayo program sponsored by MECHA.

Members of the group, none of whom is a student of drama in the conventional sense, use actual experience as the basis for skits performed in guerrilla theatre style. Most presentations are ad libbed, with the group specifying among themselves beforehand only the general social or political "message" intended.

When scripts are used, they are of material written by the members for a part which may eventually be played by all other participants. The actresses rotate character roles among themselves to create an opportunity for all to express themselves in various roles.

The group, which was formed in April, 1972, has performed at colleges throughout California, parts of Mexico and at various Chicano community events in San Diego.

The membership, which varies from six to 10 women, pay their own way in transportation and other expenses and design the costumes and props used in their performances.

The group is unique in that its members are exclusively Chicanas; that is, women of LA Raza.

While at first glance this makeup might seem female chauvinistic and reversally racist, it is not, members say. Its makeup, explained in social and political terms, is actually a realistic first step toward eradicating sexism, racism and more, according to group members.

The group recognizes a three-tiered structure of oppression and its members say their position now is one at the bottom from which they will eventually work upward.

The first tier of oppression is that suffered by women throughout the world, they explain. As Chicanas, they are struggling against that oppression first, the one closest to home.

To advance at this level, they say, they must promote womanhood in such a way as to show its ability to achieve on a par with men.

Thus, men are excluded from "Chicanas" participation to emphasize a positive rather than a negative point, the basic equality of women to men.

The next tier of injustice is that of racism whose victims are mostly people of color, it was explained. As brown-skinned women, they bear this burden as do all people of the Third World.

As they or their successors begin to realize success at the first level of tyranny (sexism) the struggle will move to racism. Other nationalities are excluded from "Chicanas" participation, but the move is explained as a constructive effort at rebuilding confidence among the various nationalities in themselves.

That is, all Third World people are urged to free themselves of overwhelmingly white dominance and to strengthen confidence in their

Though struggle at this level is far away the women are urging caution now not to develop a reversed form of racism against Anglos.

"Exclusion" of Anglos at the "Chicanas" present level of development is purely theoretical, they explained, as Anglos have expressed no interest in the group's activities.

When the effort passes this second tier of involvement, as explained by members of the group, the result will be the eradication of sexism and the strengthening of peoples of the Third World.

The third tier of the struggle

"TEATRO DE LAS CHICANAS," is a unique organization of women who present, through entertainment, a serious socio-political message. From left: Peggy Garcia, Delia Ravelo, Maria Perdoza, Lupe Perez and Felicita Nunez. Not shown are Laura Cortez and Lupita Gonzales.

teaching people and implementing ideas; for politicizing and teaching my people."

The notion of a struggle, or a movement pervades the performances of the "Chicanas" as well as their conversation.

These women, conscious of a class-, race- and sex-based purpose in their work, seek to educate as well as entertain. In methods calculated to this end, they employ satire, exaggeration and humor in getting their message across.

"We present a ridiculous look at the different attitudes which people have of the Chicana Movement," said Peggy Garcia, a "Chicanas" member.

"If you exaggerate, people are better able to see the point," another member added.

Getting the point across is recognized as often being quite difficult considering the complexity and subtleness of the problem.

The problem of sexism, they explain, is real and happens everyday. If it were presented as it really occurs, a polished and sophisticated art after so many centuries of practice, much of the audience might miss the point.

"We don't do it in a sophisticated way; we do it in an exaggerated way, so people can take it from the stage and relate it to reality," a member said.

If men are not actually on the stage, they are represented there. Teatro members don men's clothes for parts and play men's roles since, in reality it is chiefly men who oppress women.

"Generally speaking, most men can't understand our position," said Lupe Perez. "So we women work to inform other women of our movement."

"When we play in the community, it's the women and the older men who just love us," said Ravelo. "The people in the barrios are aware of the problem, they just don't know how to solve it."

Azteca article 2 psd

Article by Henry Acevedo, *Daily Aztec*, May 3, 1973. Used by permission of the *Daily Aztec*.

Campus , Government Reform is Chicana Goal

by CINDI HUNTER

Tuesday, January 16, 1973
California State University, Sacramento
Volume 26
Number 45

Felicitas Nunez and Angie Avila, both active in the Chicano and Women's movements in San Diego spoke before a sparse crowd last Thursday morning.

The thrust of Ms. Avila's efforts have been aimed at reforming local government in San Diego to make it more representative of the Chicano population. San Diego county has more than 250,000 Chicanos and 17 Indian reservations, in addition to a sizeable Black and Asian population.

Widespread reforms in San Diego county have been realized as a result of Ms. Avila's and several other Chicanas' efforts. The women were instrumental in the creation of a Mexican-American Community Affairs office which set a national precedent. The creation of a M[illegible]rity Recruitment Officer f[illegible] county as well as

Their work is by no means complete for Ms. Avila stressed that much more needs to be accomplished. For instance, only two Chicano psychiatric social workers are employed by the County Welfare Department. Only one Chicano psychiatrist is employed in a half time position.

Ms. Nunez and members of "Teatros de las Chicanas" arrived late and began their planned panel discussion by sharing their experiences as members of a Chicana group at CSU, San

and anger. Chicano men, they claimed, contributed to their lack of confidence in speaking before groups in the Chicano movement. As women they were put down by men for attempting to raise their own consciousness and awareness.

In the afternoon the members of "Teastros de las Chicanas" presented a short skit in Spanish dealing with the problem of rasing consciousness and awareness among Chicanas.

The women were presented by Cultural Progra[illegible]nd Consualo

T[illegible]sday, January 16, 1973, The State Hornet

Article by Cindi Hunter, *State Hornet*, January 16, 1973. Used by permission of the *State Hornet*.

INTER-
NATIONAL
WOMEN'S
WEEK

MARCH 2-5 1981

UNIVERSITY OF CALIFORNIA AT SAN DIEGO
PROGRAMS FREE— CHILDCARE

MONDAY
Mountain View Lounge
(Third College)
6:00pm Opening Reception
Music by: Carlota
7:30pm "Raices"
(Guerrilla Theater)

TUESDAY
International Center
(Gilman & Hutchison)
6:00pm Women's Poetry
Selected Readings of
Community Poets

WEDNESDAY
NORTH CONFERENCE RM.
—(STUDENT CENTER)
1:00pm Asian/Pacific
Slide Show
International Center
(Gilman & Hutchison)
6:00pm Pot Luck Dinner
7:00pm Panel on:
"Opportunities
& Barriers"

THURSDAY
TLH-107
(Third College Lecture Hall)
6:00pm Women's Film Series
Chicana, Double Day,
Bush Mama, Children
of Resistance,
Mother of Many
Children.

Sponsored by: The Women's Resource Center, Mujer, B.W.A. and S.A.A.C. —MECh.A.
B.S.U. U.A.I.S. and A.A.S.A.

Art & Design by Magda Reyna

Poster for International Women's Week celebrations (March 1981). Teatro Raíces performed at the event.

MOTHER: College! You certainly can't; you will find a decent man and get married.

ROSIE: Oh, Mom, really!

MOTHER: Don't talk back to me, my precious; you know I'm only thinking of your welfare.

(*Enter Girlfriend.*)

GIRLFRIEND: Hey, Rudy, you're the first boyfriend I ever had who has graduated from junior high and high school.

(*She seductively ambles toward him and puts her arms around him.*)

RUDY: Cool it my *jefita* is watching!

GIRLFRIEND: *Ay, ¿y a mí qué? ¡Hola, Doña!*

ROSIE: Oh, she is a wacko.

MOTHER: You mean she can't cook?

GIRLFRIEND: Oh Rudy, now we can get married.

RUDY: What! (*All choked up.*) This is not the place to discuss these things.

GIRLFRIEND: Oh, sorry, big boy, we can discuss this tonight under the romantic moon, the glimmering stars, and the dreamy clouds at the alley on the corner of J and 12th Street. (*She sings*) Going to the chapel (*and she swings her hips, singing*), ohhh, we're gonna get married.

(*Girlfriend exits. Rudy looks blank and puts hands into pockets.*)

MOTHER: *Ay,* to me that girl is not good for you.

ROSIE: What now, big stuff?

RUDY: Shut up, Rosie!

(*Enter Leo, carrying six-pack of beer.*)

LEO: *Ese* Rudy . . . *Te aventastes,* congratulations (*hands him and his mom a beer*) ¿Gusta una, señora?

MOTHER: *Ay, sí, es bueno para la bilis, tú, no, Rosita,* and Rudy, you are too young (*takes beer away from Rudy*).

RUDY: *Simon ese pués,* I finally did it.

LEO: Well, that's what I want to talk to you about. First I got some bad news.

RUDY: What?

LEO: *¡Mataron al Mantecas!*

RUDY: You mean our homeboy, Lard, got killed? How come?

LEO: Well you see . . . the *bato* burned Big Daddy Loco Joe. They found him stone stiff in a garbage can. Now we need someone . . . (*Mother and Rosie have wide-open eyes and ears*) . . . to take his position. And you, Rudy, have a lot of status with your new diploma. The community looks up to you.

RUDY: *Ese,* I don't know. I've been thinking about going to college.

LEO: Look, if you work for Big Daddy Loco Joe, you will make the big times.

RUDY: What can it get me? (*Tries to keep low tone away from Mom and Rosie.*)

LEO: Man, you can get a better car, more chicks, and some sharp threads.

RUDY: Like yours?

LEO: Most important is that you can always stay loaded and be high like me.

RUDY: I don't know; it means getting in too deep.

LEO: Well . . . think it over and if you want to talk business, I'll meet you under the violent moon, the searing stars, and the cruel cold skies at the corner of 12th and J in the alley. Think it over.

RUDY: I will, *ese.*

LEO: I encourage you very much, we need you. Hey, give me my beer back.

(*Grabs extra beer away from Mrs. Martinez and exits.*)

ROSIE: Rudy, you know what that guy does?

RUDY: Shut up, Rose.

MOTHER: I don't want you hanging around with that kind. You know better than that.

ROSIE: He's nothing but a dope pusher.

RUDY: He's offering me a job, isn't he?

MOTHER: *M'ijito,* but I don't want you to end up in a garbage can like Mantecas.

ROSIE: You're so dumb you would go for something like that.

MOTHER: *M'ija, no le hables así a tu hermano.* Not one more word.

(*Rudy frowns, slumps; Mother worried; Rosie flustered—all three freeze onstage.*)

Scene II: The Cruise

(*Enters Rod; background music is from* The Twilight Zone.)

ROD: Meet Rodolfo and Rosie Martinez. They are about to embark on a journey that may very well change their lives. They have brown and pensive faces and a quest for the impossible, a normal and decent life; despite a background of poverty and near-illiteracy, Rodolfo and Rosie may fulfill their dreams in the Unknown Arena.

(*Exit. Characters on stage unfreeze.*)

MOTHER: The both of you are always arguing. Now stop, Rudy, we have to make several stops before you take me and your sister to work. So come on we have things to do, places to go, people to meet.

(*They all get into a cardboard car.*)

ROSIE: Hurry up, Rudy. You're always too slow.
MOTHER: This car is a little bit too small with the little bit of weight I put on.
ROSIE: Come on, Rudy . . . move.
RUDY: Shut up, Rosie.
MOTHER: *Ay, ay, ay,* my dress, careful.

(*Music "Low Rider" turns on and start cruising through the barrio waving at people. The car starts slowing down and chuckles to a dead stop.*)

MOTHER: *Ay, madre mía de las carreteras amparanos . . . ay, ay.*
RUDY: We are out of *gasofa*. Ma, you steer, Rosie and I will push.
ROSIE: I'm not gonna push.
RUDY: Hey, you want a ride?
ROSIE: I got my good clothes; I don't want to get dirty.
RUDY: If you want to get to work, you better push.
MOTHER: *Ay, yo no sé que hacer, ay, ay.*
RUDY: Come on, Ma, the brakes.

(*Car is swinging sideways, mother almost runs over gas attendant, mother screams. Gas attendant enters.*)

RUDY: Cool it with my car, *Jefa*. (*Turns to attendant.*) Give me two gallons worth of regular.
GAS ATTENDANT: (*Makes sound with voice as gas is going in.*) That will be $3.58.
RUDY: Hey, I said two gallons, why is it so expensive?
GAS ATTENDANT: I only work here. (*Extends hands.*)
RUDY: (*Searches in empty pockets, looks embarrassed.*) Ma, do you have three dollars?
ROSIE: Mom, don't give him any money. He always asks.
RUDY: Do you want to walk?
MOTHER: *Ay, m'ijo,* well, let me see . . . I have it in a special place.

(*Tries to get small purse hidden in bra so no one would notice and gives it to Rudy, who then gives to the gas attendant.*)

GAS ATTENDANT: Thank you.

(*Gas Attendant exits. Rudy starts up car and music continues.*)

MOTHER: I said careful . . . *mis nahuas* . . . Now we have to go see about the gas and electric bill.
ROSIE: Here's parking . . . there's another over there.

(*Park stage left. Enter stage right G&E receptionist, who sits down and files her nails. Stagehand walks across stage with a "So Damn Greedy and Expensive" sign—big capitals "OIL" and in small letters, "Opportunists International Looters" Company. Rudy and Mother get out of the car and walk up to G&E receptionist.*

ROSIE: I'll wait out here, you two go ahead.
MOTHER: *Halo, ah,* yes . . . I need (*broken Spanish. Rudy behind mother, smoking a cigarette*).
G&E RECEPTIONIST: (*Shakes head.*) Oh my, do you need help . . . the bilingual clerk will be in later. You can wait an hour or come back another day.
RUDY: (*Moves Mother gently to the side and puffs smoke into worker's face.*) My mother speaks English.
G&E RECEPTIONIST: Step right up, Ma'am.
MOTHER: We need an extension on our bill.
G&E RECEPTIONIST: No wonder you learned to speak English. Well, there are several forms you have to fill out. First here and here . . .

(*Both freeze. Rudy storms out to where Rosie is waiting in car.*)

ROSIE: What's wrong, Rudy?
RUDY: (*Angrily gets into car and Rosie is in his way.*) Get out of my face. These people get me so mad, they act like they own the company. She is just a worker for that rip-off oil company.
ROSIE: Hey, Rudy, don't take it out on me.
RUDY: You don't understand; what do you know about discrimination.
ROSIE: Hey, Rudy, first of all I am poor, I am brown, and I am also a woman.
RUDY: You're only a broad.
ROSIE: And I don't need you discriminating against me!
RUDY: Who, me?
MOTHER: *Ya basta con este* crimination . . . *y quién sabe que más* . . . you two argue. Come, Rudy, let's go take in your application to Sassco.

(*All get situated in car, music continues with same tune, turn in and park at Sassco on stage left. Bald man with a cigar enters stage right.*)

ROSIE: Park here . . . park there, this is where the Sassco office is located (*points at bald man with cigar*).
RUDY: *Jefita, pase la aplicación.*
MOTHER: *M'ijo*, here it is, I put it next to the *chorizo y se le hizo una manchita de manteca.*
RUDY: And you want me to get a job with a stain on my application?
MOTHER: *Ay, m'ijito* . . . just go, and you, Rosita, put on your makeup so you can be beautiful like me.
ROSIE: And Rudy, don't take too long.

(*Rudy combs his hair, tucks in his shirt, and wipes his shoes and walks to stage right.*)

RUDY: Ah, I came to put in my application for a laborer position.
SASSCO PERSONNEL: So, you want a job.
RUDY: I just graduated from high school.
SASSCO PERSONNEL: You might have graduated from high school but you didn't learn a damn thing. Half the answer is wrong, and the other half of the answer is spelled wrong and there's even a grease mark! (*Rudy is embarrassed.*) And you want me to give you a job!
RUDY: Well, ah, . . . you know what, I've been too busy graduating but I can do anything you ask me to. I can start right now if you need me. My sister can take my car and . . .
SASSCO PERSONNEL: Don't give me all the details, I'm not interested. Tell you what . . . We'll keep the application and don't call us, we'll call you. One thing about your type—you come begging for a job, then you can't even hold down the freaking job.
RUDY: I would do my best.
SASSCO PERSONNEL: Well, if the strike continues longer, then you can expect we'll keep you in mind.

(*Sassco Personnel exits, Rudy shakes his head, goes toward car. Worker with strike sign approaches.*)

STRIKER: Hey, Rudy, Rudy Martinez. Do you remember me, José Lopez?
RUDY: Oh yeah, José—you're in this strike?
ROSIE: (*Approaches and breaks in on conversation.*) Why is there a strike?
SASSCO STRIKER: We are fighting for higher wages and more benefits. What's the occasion? You guys are all dressed up nice.
ROSIE: We graduated.

RUDY: *Simon*, so I'm now looking for a job.

ROSIE: We've also thought about going to college. I want to be a lawyer.

SASSCO STRIKER: (*Ignores Rosie.*) Rudy, if this is what you want, it's hard work, but I hope you get in after the strike.

ROSIE: That's right, Rudy; you wouldn't want to scab.

SASSCO STRIKER: On the other hand, if there is an opportunity to go to school, think about it seriously. We need lawyers and doctors. Wish you both all the luck. *¡Huelga! ¡Huelga! ¡Huelga!*

(*Sassco Striker exits.*)

ROSIE: He is very nice.

RUDY: Rosie, you're always embarrassing me.

ROSIE: I didn't do anything.

MOTHER: Will you two stop. Rudy, you should help your sister look for a decent husband. It's only natural that she is interested.

ROSIE: Yes, Mom, but that doesn't mean I'm desperate for a husband; maybe you are?

MOTHER: (*Swings her purse at Rosie.*) *Malcriada.* I just want you to be properly married someday.

(*Rosie shakes head. Car starts up again with music; engine shakes and rattles.*)

MOTHER: Watch my skirt. Now you can take us to work, *m'ijo.*

RUDY: Yes, Ma.

MOTHER: *Aaah, ¿qué está pasando*?

RUDY: Calm down, there is something wrong with the car.

ROSIE: Rudy, just get down there and fix it.

RUDY: Shut up, Rosie.

MOTHER: *Dios mío de las carreteras, por favor sácanos de este apuro.*

(*Rudy gets off car, uses crank-motions to put front end of car up. As he cranks Mother elevates car and Rudy gets under.*)

RUDY: It's no big thing, Ma.

ROSIE: I hope we're not late for work.

MOTHER: *Ay,* yes, *m'ijo.*

RUDY: Ma, when I tell you to turn the key, do it.

MOTHER: This makes me so nerrrvous . . . (*car gives a clucking noise*). Start, oh God, oh God.

(*Policeman enters.*)

POLICEMAN: You called, what's the problem, did you run over someone?
MOTHER: Oh, no, Ociffer . . .

(*Policeman starts to look closer.*)

MOTHER: My son is fixing up the car, it only broke down for a little while.
RUDY: (*Gets out from under.*) Oh, officer, ah . . .
POLICE: Listen, you better get this piece of junk off the road.
RUDY: What junk!
POLICEMAN: This junk. (*Kicks front of car. It falls with a bang. Rudy is very angry.*)
MOTHER: *Ay, dios mío, ¿qué está pasando?*
ROSIE: Well, who does he think he is?
MOTHER: Ay, my God, my God.
POLICEMAN: Listen, boy, don't give me that look; you just better move on out of here.
RUDY: (*Restrains anger.*) Officer, I was just taking my sister and my *jefita* to work . . .
POLICEMAN: Don't want to hear it, just get this trash and these weird people out of here.
RUDY: Wait a minute (*raises his fist*).
POLICEMAN: (*Puts club up.*) Just try it.
ROSIE: Hit him, slam him, Rudy!
MOTHER: (*Grabs Rudy.*) No, *m'ijo,* don't . . . let's just go. *Por el amor de dios que no vaya a pasar nada.*

(*Policeman exits, laughing.*)

RUDY: I have had it! I am tired of being pushed around! I can't get a job, I find it hard to educate myself! I've been pushed around and discriminated against.
ROSIE: Hello, Rudy, join the club.
RUDY: I might as well give up and go work for Big Daddy Loco Joe and die in style like Mantecas.
MOTHER: Oh, no, wahha!
ROSIE: Who do you think you are, Rudy, somebody special? You don't think we all have problems? Damn.
RUDY: You think you got it all together. I happen to know you got an abortion when you were only fifteen.
MOTHER: Rosa, *¿pero cómo?* Oh no, wahhaaa!

ROSIE: Mother . . . I didn't want you to know; I'm not proud of myself . . . at that time I just wanted to die of shame. I'm sorry.
MOTHER: Wahha . . . Dear God, save my children.

(*Rosie stares at Rudy.*)

RUDY: Well, don't look at me, I don't have your problems . . . it's nothing to do with me!
MOTHER: *Cállate, muchaco malcriado* (*aims to hit Rudy with her scarf*). Oh, my heart is broken. Rosita is not a virgin and Rudy, you are thinking of dying like Mantecas. Stop it, the both of you. Rosa, you ask for forgiveness for taking a life.
ROSIE: Ma, I had to decide. Abortion was my choice because I am not ready to give up my life to raise a child. I've learned from my mistake, I hope you can forgive me someday.
MOTHER: *Ay, tú también cállate. Los dos me han hecho pasar por tanto.*

(*Keeps hitting both with scarf. Rosie and Rudy dodge her blows. Mother gets down on knees, wailing. Around this time an old man sweeping the street can't help but notice. Old Man enters, sweeping the street.*)

OLD MAN: *¿Pero qué está pasando aquí?*
RUDY: Please just go, we got enough problems and you don't understand.
OLD MAN: (*Swings at Rudy with broom.*) Don't you talk to me like that after making your mother cry.
RUDY: But I didn't mean to.
OLD MAN: Now if you believe an old man like me does not understand problems, you are wrong.
ROSIE: Great, now everybody knows our problems!
OLD MAN: Problems have always been. But you young people have to get out there and struggle with all the contradictions like your ancestors did.
RUDY: When was the last time you were young?
MOTHER: *Cállate, malcriado.* (*Hits Rudy with her purse.*)
OLD MAN: Nothing in this life will be given into your hand, even the gains you benefit from have to be fought for. Especially, now that they are being taken away.
ROSIE: So is this why you are pushing a broom?
MOTHER: *Respeto,* he may not be pushing a pencil but he can be especially wise.
OLD MAN: Every chance you have to educate yourselves, do it. I don't care if

all you do is push a broom. Learn from history and you will cherish the future.

RUDY: Times have changed and it is harder than you think.

MOTHER: Wait a minute, my children; have you not listened to my stories of my own past? To this moment I have struggled to give you a better life in the best way I could.

ROSIE: Mother, you are right. You may not be in fashion but you have been an example of courage and given us hope.

RUDY: Yes, Mom, and love like yours will be forever. I guess problems in society will always be around, but so will love, hope, and courage to solve our problems in society.

ROSIE: It would seem that you are a hero, Mother. And you, sir (*faces the old man*), also have much to teach from your experiences. It is true, we as the youth must also continue struggling in this society to make it better.

OLD MAN: And what better way to live, struggling together to build a society worth living in.

RUDY: It's like the song says, "So Rough, So Tough." *Gracias, señor.* Ma, the car is ready to go.

ROSIE: (*Gets Mom by arm.*) Come on, Mom.

MOTHER: Oh yes, well, *muchas gracias, viejito.*

ROSIE: Thank you.

MOTHER: Oh, I'll be late for work.

(*Rudy starts car, Rosie and Mom get in. Music starts playing the song "So Rough, So Tough." Everyone on stage swings to beat . . . also old man with broom. Music lowered. Enter Rod Serling with* Twilight Zone *music.*)

ROD: Rodolfo and Rosa Martinez: Two young people who have discovered something about life—that life can be rich, rewarding, and full of beauty—if one would only pause to look. In retrospect it may be said that they achieve that final dream. You can find Rodolfo and Rosie on every street corner; you can find them in every mirror. You can find them in the Twilight Zone.

(*Music goes up louder, everyone onstage dances off.*)

End

Salt of the Earth

Characters

Esperanza
Ramón
Jenicks, Anglo union organizer
Worker 1
Worker 2
Worker 3 (Anglo)
Worker 4
Ruth, Anglo
Connie
Administrator (Anglo)
Foreman (Anglo)
Sheriff (Anglo)
Deputy (Anglo)
Soledad
Alberto
Mary
Female at union meeting

Scene I

(Esperanza—Espe—is pregnant, nearing nine months, wearing a plain dress. She is busy sweeping. Stage left there are a table, two chairs, a high bench with two bowls sitting on top; next to these are a cooking pan and coffeepot sitting on stove burners and sink. On stage right is door entry and close by is a box with

radio on top. On an easel sits a portrait of Benito Juarez and a guitar at its side. Esperanza stops in center stage and looks at the audience.)

ESPE: How can I begin my story? On this day, I am thirty-five years old and it is my Saint's Day. I am the wife of a miner, a mother of two children and another on the way. My husband, Ramón, has been working in the mines for eighteen years with dynamite and darkness. Before the Anglos came, Ramón's grandfather owned the land that my husband works on. The house is not ours but the flowers, the flowers are. And the radio is still not ours but the music gives me company in my solitude after a hard day's work. At times I feel that no matter how hard we work our living conditions do not improve. I worry about the future of my little boy and girl. We barely make ends meet and have to be constantly scraping for a living. But my heart feels heavier today because all I can wish on my Saint's Day is for this next child not to be born. "Not into this world." And I pray to the Virgin Mother to forgive me for having such a thought.

(*Ramón, her husband, enters from right back stage door.*)

RAMÓN: Today I almost got blasted to pieces. Working alone when setting the fuses is very dangerous. I don't think that I can go on working this way.

ESPE: I feel that way at times about my work, just having to boil the water because we have no sanitation. If we had plumbing and sanitation it would make a big difference.

RAMÓN: There are other more important issues then sanitation. The safety of the workers comes first. I see no other way out but to go on strike.

ESPE: Strike! We will get behind on the payments and all the bills we have to pay. My radio will be taken away.

RAMÓN: Is that all you care about, the plumbing and your radio? Because we got this instrument on the installment plan, now we are tied to this object! This thing called credit, this installment plan is the curse of the working man!

ESPE: You don't understand. This radio is very important to me.

RAMÓN: Is that all you can think about, yourself?

ESPE: You don't think about me when you go out to the bar and spend all night out. I listen to the music from my radio and that makes me feel good. (*Crying.*)

RAMÓN: I can't put up with you and your selfishness and crying.
ESPE: Where are you going?
RAMÓN: Where else, away from you!

(*Ramón exits stage right door, Espe exits left. Song "Paloma Negra" is played in the background.*)

"Paloma Negra" [1]

Ya me canso de llorar y no amanece
Ya no sé si maldecirte o por ti rezar
Tengo miedo de buscarte y de encontrarte
Donde me aseguran mis amigos que te vas
Hay momentos en que quisiera mejor rajarme
Y arrancame ya los clavos de mi penar.
Pero mis ojos se mueren si mirar tus ojos
Y mi cariño con la aurora te vuelve a buscar
Ya agarraste por tu cuenta la parranda
Paloma negra, paloma negra, ¿dónde, dónde andarás?
Ya no jueges con mi honra parrandera
Si tus caricias han de ser mías, de nadie más
Y aunque te amo con locura ya no vuelvas
Paloma negra, eres la reja de un penar
Quiero ser libre vivir mi vida con quien me quiera
Dios dame fuerza que estoy muriendo por irla a buscar
Ya agarraste por tu cuenta la parranda.

Scene II

(*Stage is set up to be a bar while song is being sung behind the curtain or on side of stage. The bowls, pans, and pot are put under the bench and covered with a cloth. Bottles are set on top with glasses and bartender is serving drinks. Bartender puts over Benito Juárez's portrait a poster reading "End of Road's Bar." Workers 1, 2, and 3 enter stage right and stand at the bar to get their drinks. Ramón and Jenicks sit at the table front center stage.*)

RAMÓN: I see that Anglos have better working conditions, they work in pairs, while we Mexicans work alone setting fuses. I am supposed to do the work of two men and be grateful for a job, even if it kills me.
JENICKS: You are right. It is an unfair treatment of workers. You also have to

realize that because Mexicans have worse working conditions, that this is used against the Anglo workers.

(*Workers gather to hear what Ramón and Jenicks are talking about.*)

WORKER 1: Explain what you mean.

JENICKS: The bosses are always pacifying and controlling the Anglo workers by pointing out that Anglos have it good in comparison to Mexican workers. Therefore Anglo workers should shut up and put up. This weakens the value of not only the labor of the individual but also the value of the whole working force.

WORKER 2: Still, Anglo workers have more rights than Mexican workers.

JENICKS: Yes, but the bosses make the Anglo workers think that because of color their work has more value. It is not skin color that gives value to work.

WORKER 3: I agree, the real value of work comes from the labor of the worker's blood, sweat, and tears. It is the labor of the worker that gives value to labor. It is labor that builds civilizations and makes miracles possible.

JENICKS: So, you see, all workers are valuable. Disunity and division turns workers against each other. We end up selling ourselves cheap. We end up betraying our society, our world, and ourselves.

(*Worker 4 enters and whispers to the bartender. Bartender goes to the table.*)

BARTENDER: Message from your son who is outside. He says it is your wife's Saint's Day.

RAMÓN: Oh no, I forgot. Let's go, men, so we can sing *Las Mañanitas* to my wife. I hope she forgives me.

(*Ramón, Jenicks exit first and start singing "Las Mañanitas" behind the curtain or side of the stage. The rest stay behind and help set the stage, which is to be left empty. A basket of laundry is placed at the center of the stage.*)

"Las Mañanitas"[2]

Estas son las mañitas
Que cantaba el rey David
A las muchachas bonitas
Se las cantamos así.

Despierta, mi bien, despierta—
Mira que ya amaneció
Ya los pajaritos cantan,
La luna ya se metió.

El día en que tu naciste,
Nacieron todas las flores
Y en la pila de bautismo
Cantaron los ruiseñores.

Ya viene amaneciendo
Ya la luz del día nos dió.
Levántate de mañana
Mira que ya amaneció.

Scene III

("Las Mañanitas" is being heard sung in chorus behind the curtain. This chorus sound is lowered as Espe enters with a big smile. She starts to fold clothes and talks to the audience.)

ESPE: I can't keep from thinking what a wonderful night it was when Ramón brought me the gift of music. *"Las Mañanitas"* is still singing in my ears. There was dancing and laughter. I couldn't dance, but Ramón did. I was happy to see him smile. And all our neighbors joined us to celebrate.

(Ruth, Connie, and Mary enter and approach Espe where she is folding clothes. They carry a poster on a stick that reads, "We Want Sanitation, Not Discrimination.")

RUTH: That was a great evening yesterday for your Saint's Day. We are here because we would like to talk to you about an idea.

CONNIE: We want to talk to the men about our need for hot running water in the home, as part of their union demands.

ESPE: The men have more important issues to deal with than sanitation and hot running water.

MARY: We women also have needs and sanitation is necessary, just as safety for the men is on the job.

CONNIE: Esperanza, other company houses have sanitation. Why not us? Look at our sign, sanitation is especially good for us who work in the home.

RUTH: Before everyone in the house takes a bath, chop wood, before everyone is fed breakfast, chop wood, lunch, chop wood, dinner, chop wood. The clothes need to get washed, chop wood. My husband comes home from work and what does he say? You've been sleeping all day?

(The sound of siren is heard, and there is a look of alarm on all the women's faces.)

MARY: Trouble in the mine!
RUTH: Who is it this time?
CONNIE: Esperanza, I'll help you.

(Connie grabs the basket of clothes Espe was folding and takes it to the back of the curtain. The women exit stage right. Enter Ramón from stage left all dirtied from the near-fatal accident. He is met by the foreman and the mine company administrator, who enter from stage right. Other men start gathering around this encounter. Leave one person in back of stage, a woman who will raise the poster that reads "We Want Sanitation, Not Discrimination.")

RAMÓN: I told you this was going to happen. If the work is not done in pairs there is no protection.
ADMINISTRATOR: It is being done in pairs, the foreman is your cover. (*Points to foreman.*) Are you not covering him?
FOREMAN: Yes, I checked the fuses but Pancho here was sleeping.
RAMÓN: You're a lying . . .

(He goes to punch the foreman and the workers hold Ramón back.)

ADMINISTRATOR: Now come on. Get a hold of yourselves. A man has been hurt. This is no cause for a holiday. Get back to work, all of you.
RAMÓN: We need to be assigned in pairs and work together from beginning to finish. I'm not going back to work by myself.
ADMINISTRATOR: Fine. You will be replaced.
RAMÓN: Who is going to replace me, a scab?
ADMINISTRATOR: An American worker will replace you. What is everyone standing around for? Foreman, get them back to work!
FOREMAN: You heard him. Move!

(No one listens to foreman or moves.)

ADMINISTRATOR: Jenicks, you are the union representative. Get them back to work.
JENICKS: They don't work for me. I work for them.
WORKER 1: He is right; we need to be assigned in pairs for protection.
WORKER 2: We are asking for safe working conditions.
WORKER 3: We are not going back to work until you meet our needs!

(Then the poster sign appears behind the curtain or to the side of the stage, "We

Want Sanitation, Not Discrimination." Everyone is momentarily distracted, the stage is emptied, and Espe enters to front of stage holding the poster in one hand. She addresses the audience.)

Scene IV

ESPE: On this day the men did not go back to work. It was the beginning of the strike. A union meeting was held that evening to make the strike official. Towards the end, we the women came to the union meeting to be heard. We asked that sanitation be one of the demands and a part of the union strike. We were for the most part politely set aside, scorned, and scolded for making fools of ourselves. At a later time the women would become involved in the strike, but for now only the men were at the forefront.

(*Espe exits and men who are on the strike come onstage. The mood is positive comradeship.*)

WORKER 1: So, the foreman who is an Anglo tells me, "If you don't accept the company's conditions, go back to Mexico."
WORKER 2: Did you explain that you were here before the Anglos came?
WORKER 3: I was also told that, and I am from Oklahoma.
WORKER 1: Salinski, oh no. Oklahoma? We don't want to see you go.

(*Everyone hugs or pats him.*)

WORKER 2: Yeah. New Mexico is now your home with us.
WORKER 3: If you say so.
RAMÓN: I agree, we *hombres* must stay united.
WORKER 1: Yes, we want safe working conditions just like our Anglo fellow workers.
WORKER 2: We want equality for all.
WORKER 3: We must picket for our rights.
RAMÓN: We have begun a strike that may be a long one. Let's not waste any time and may we endure what lays ahead.

(*The men start to picket and an older woman appears knitting on the side stage, watching the men as they say their slogans of solidarity.*)

RAMÓN: Come on, men, let's see the real *hombres* who have more courage and *huevos!*
WORKER 1: We workers must be respected for our labor that creates wonders!
WORKER 3: Yes, join us in our struggle for safe working conditions!

WORKER 1: There is Soledad.

WORKER 2: I had not seen her since we buried her husband who died in one of the mine accidents.

RAMÓN: *Buenos días, señora.*

SOLEDAD: *Buenos días a todos ustedes.* (*She keeps on knitting.*)

WORKER 3: I think that the women must be seen as our partners.

WORKER 1: There is more partnership between men.

WORKER 2: I consider my wife my partner.

RAMÓN: I consider my wife my bed partner. Ha, ha.

(*Worker 2 laughs with Ramón. Worker 1 gives Ramón a nudge to watch his language in the presence of Soledad, who keeps knitting.*)

WORKER 3: Now that woman's bed partner is gone. Yet her partner shared more than a bed in her life. The partnership between them is still alive in her memory and in support of our struggle.

WORKER 1: Well, she is a special case, I guess.

WORKER 2: I sure am glad to see my wife when she brings me my *tacos.*

RAMÓN: Now there is a great partner. (*He hugs Worker 2.*)

WORKER 3: I wonder which of our wives is going to make our coffee and bring us our lunch this morning?

(*All people onstage go into slow motion and Esperanza appears on the side front of the stage and addresses the audience.*)

ESPE: Yes, we started coming around to feed our men. Señora Soledad was the first woman to be at the picket line every day showing her support. Then one day she joined the picket line and started marching with the men. It was all very natural. Meanwhile, the women's auxiliary became crucial to the survival of the strike. We handled all the correspondence. Letters of support and donations started to come in from other mineworkers as far away as Chicago and New York. The men at first did not think it was necessary to build a women's auxiliary shelter. Later they built us a headquarters.

(*Espe hands two cups to Worker 3 and he gives one to Ramón, who has not noticed his wife's presence. He sips from the cup and gives a big smile.*)

RAMÓN: Esperanza, I knew by this great cup of coffee that it was you!

ESPE: I got tired of you complaining about bad coffee. (*She indicates a sudden pain by frowning and holding on to her side.*)

RAMÓN: Are you all right?

ESPE: Oh, it's just the baby kicking.
WORKER 1: Ramón! There is trouble. Someone is hiding in the distant bushes as if wanting to harm us!
RAMÓN: I'll go see what is going on. Don't break the picket line and keep guard over my wife.

(*Ramón exits to back of stage curtain.*)

WORKER 2: I'll stay with her. Maybe you should sit down, Esperanza.

(*This scene freezes. Worker 2 assisting Espe and the others is facing the back of the stage. The voices coming from the back of the curtain are pronounced.*)

RAMÓN: What are you doing, spying on us, Alberto?
ALBERTO: Let me go, Ramón, don't hurt me. Sheriff, help me.
SHERIFF: Ramón, my deputy and I are going to give you a lesson. Alberto, you have done well, now run off.
RAMÓN: But, Sheriff, I didn't hurt him.
SHERIFF: It's all the same to us, Ramón. Deputy, handcuff him.

(*The noise of a beating is taking place behind the curtain and the screams of Ramón unfreeze the actors onstage. Esperanza goes into labor with screams that coincide with her husband's agony.*)

ESPE: *Ay, madre santa, cuida a mi esposo y que estes a su lado cuando dé luz.*
WORKER 2: Mrs. Quintero, don't worry about Ramón now. We need to get you to the doctor.
RAMÓN: *Ay, madre santa, cuida a mi esposa.*
SHERIFF: Pancho, you don't need no mothering. What you need to do is show us how you can take a beating.
RAMÓN: *Ay, madre santa, ayúdame. Ten piedad.* Esperanza!
ESPE: *Ay, madre santa, ayúdanos a todos.* Ramón!

(*The men decide to carry Espe offstage, each holding a corner of a blanket. The stage is set for the union meeting. High bench faces chairs at an angle. Song "God Bless the Child" is sung while stage is getting set.*)

"God Bless the Child"

Them that's got shall get
Them that's not shall lose,
So the Bible says and it still is news.
Papa may have, Mama may have,

But God bless the child who's got his own,
Who's got his own.

Money, you've got lots of friends
crowding round your door.
When it ends and the splendor is gone,
They don't come round no more.
Rich relations bring crusts of bread and such,
You can help yourself
but don't take too much.
Mama may have, Papa may have,
But God bless the child who's got his own,
Who's got his own.

Scene V

(*Scene should be set up for a union meeting before song above is completed. Esperanza enters with a bundled up baby and as she reaches the front center stage there is silence.*)

ESPE: As my child Juan came to light, Ramón was imprisoned and charged for assaulting an officer and resisting arrest. He spent two weeks in the hospital and thirty days in jail. Upon his release our baby was baptized. Our baptismal celebration was interrupted by the police. They came to take my radio, my music away. So we picked up the guitar and sang our hearts out. The strike was taking so long. Some of the miners' families moved away; we never saw them again. The union decided that some of the miners should get jobs on the outside. Those who were able to get work split their pay with the rest of the striking miners' families. This is how we got our basic needs met, helping one another. What we don't know is how we are going to face the court injunction that was filed against the miners' picket line. A union meeting is being called to address this matter.

(*Espe takes her place stage right behind the chairs facing the high bench. Jenicks, who is the Chairperson, stands behind the high bench. Stage left next to high bench on easel is poster "International Workers' Union." The men enter stage right door and sit on the chairs. Espe and the women slowly come in and stand alongside.*)

CHAIR: This meeting will now come to order. We have here a sanction filed by the court against the miners. It is illegal for the miners to continue the picket line. If we vote to strike, we will be arrested. If we do not strike, the strike will come to an end. Floor is open for discussion.

RAMÓN: Brothers, what is the use of us returning to work, if there is no protection in the workplace? I motion that we strike!

WORKER 1: Yes, but if we picket we will go to jail and there will be no picket line anyway. Our hands are tied.

WORKER 2: He is right, brothers. We have no choice.

RAMÓN: We can't just let all our efforts go to waste. So what if we get arrested. Let's all go to jail!

CHAIR: Brothers, I just want to clarify that either way you vote—to end or to continue the strike—the International Workers' Union will back you up on your decision.

MARY: Brothers, the court injunction is against the miners, not against the wives and sisters of the miners. The women can legally continue the picket line.

WORKER 3: What kind of men allow the women to take over the picket line? We'll be the laughingstock.

RUTH: But you have not been able to find a solution. We have. The women can carry out the picket line.

RAMÓN: I am against this solution. We men can't be hiding behind a woman's skirt.

FEMALE: I agree. Women should not be allowed on the picket line. This can even be a mortal sin.

WORKER 2: I am for the sister's proposal to continue the picket line.

CONNIE: I say, let's put this to a vote.

WORKER 1: Women are not allowed to vote. It would be unconstitutional.

CHAIR: Brothers, he is right. The women are not union members. Their vote will not count.

MARY: Point of order. (*She nudges Espe to speak up.*)

ESPE: Brothers, how can we as women not vote on a motion that involves our participation? We must be allowed to vote.

CHAIR: The only way our sisters' vote can be counted would be as a community meeting.

WORKER 2: I move that we adjourn the union meeting.

CHAIR: All those in favor?

(*Votes are in favor of motion to adjourn.*)

RUTH: I motion for the community meeting to commence.

CHAIR: Motion on floor for community meeting to resume. All those in favor?

(*Majority votes for motion to start community meeting.*)

WORKER 2: I move that we put to vote the motion for the women to take over the picket line.

WORKER 1: I second the motion.

CHAIR: All those in favor of the motion for the women to take over the picket line? (*count*) All those against? (*count*) The motion for the women to take over the picket line has been approved and carried by the members of this community meeting.

(*The meeting breaks up and a conversation between three couples is to follow. Meanwhile in the background there will be quiet motion of figures putting away the furniture to empty the stage and set it up for the picket line.*)

CHAIR: Ruth, I am worried about you and the women taking over the picket line. In a way your solution is best but I'm not sure you will be able to handle it.

RUTH: I have followed you around every campsite in the country. I have put up with your constant preoccupation in organizing the workers around union issues. Don't you think I have learned anything?

(*Jenicks and Ruth exit.*)

WORKER 2: Mary, my beautiful wife, I am very uneasy about this motion. Yet I can't express how grateful and proud I feel for the support that you and the sisters have voiced. God bless and protect you all.

MARY: *Ay, mi corazón,* I love you for expressing yourself to me. And the blessed mother will see us all through this troubled time.

(*Worker 2 and Mary exit.*)

ESPE: Ramón, the women want to be supportive. We are not about making men seem less important. I want to walk the picket line. Beside it will be good for the baby. It will help him burp.

RAMÓN: I forbid you to walk the picket line. You have your place in the home, taking care of the children and me.

(*Ramón exits and Esperanza faces and addresses the audience right front stage. The women who will picket come in slowly while Espe talks.*)

ESPE: Even though I didn't walk the picket line, I showed up every day and stood watching the women coming in from near and far. The word of the women's strike had reached across county and state lines. The word also reached the sheriff and company men. They tried tear-gassing and waving their guns to scare the women's picket line. But they could not break our strike. The husbands stood nervous on the sidelines, watching from a distance.

(The sheriff and deputy are shown in motion to be teasing women and motioning to aim with their guns but the women keep their ground. They sing "We Shall Not Be Moved" and they dance.)

MARY: The union is our leader, we shall not be moved. The union is our leader, we shall not be moved.
CHORUS: Oh, deep in my heart, I do believe. We shall overcome someday.
RUTH: We are, we are not afraid. We are, we are not afraid. We are not afraid today.
CHORUS: We are, we are not afraid. We are, we are not afraid. We are not afraid today.
CONNIE: We are, we are not alone. We are, we are not alone. We are not alone today.
CHORUS: We are, we are not alone. We are, we are not alone. We are not alone today.

(The sheriff and deputy turn the high bench over and the top side is used as the front fender to hit Connie, one of the women on the picket line. The deputy is scared so he runs away to back of curtain. The sheriff gets out of the car with his gun waving in the air. Mary and Ruth are struggling with him but he will not let go the gun. Espe hands Ramón the baby, takes off her shoe, and goes to hit the sheriff's hand. The gun falls to the ground. This scenario freezes. Ramón with baby in his arms goes over to talk to Jenicks.)

RAMÓN: Jenicks, we need to help the women out!
JENICKS: They seem to be handling themselves well. Besides, you have your hands full.
RAMÓN: There is no way that I will take care of the baby, and whatever else Esperanza does! She knows how I feel.
JENICKS: I don't approve of how you feel but that's between you and her.
RAMÓN: You're damn right. No union is going to run my house. And I'm not taking care of no baby!

(Both men exit to the back of the curtain and the frozen actors also exit. The picket line in the back disperses to set up the next scene quietly. The song "Mixteca" is sung. The table is brought to right of stage at an angle facing the

audience and the high bench is placed on top of the table and one of the chairs is placed on its side on the top of the table and under the high bench. This is the jail behind bars.)

"Canción Mixteca"[3]

¡Que lejos estoy del suelo donde he nacido!
Inmensa nostalgia invade mi pensamiento,
Y al verme tan solo y triste cual hoja al viento.
Quisiera llorar, quisiera morir de sentimiento.
O tierra del sol, suspiro por verte,
Y ahora que lejos estoy sin luz, sin amor.
Y al verme tan solo y triste cual hoja al viento.
Quisiera llorar, quisiera morir de sentimiento.

Scene VI

(As the song comes to a close Esperanza appears with baby in arms to address the audience.)

ESPE: The insults and actions against the picketers did not end but continued with more violence and anger against the women strikers. But they did not know we would also grow stronger to keep the picket line from getting broken. The sheriff came later to make arrests of the women, including me with my baby Juanito.

(The sheriff and deputy in the background start putting the women strikers behind the jail bars. The women are feisty and try to show no fear. Espe goes to the far back of the jail space.)

SHERIFF: Get in there, cuties. This is where you belong for misbehaving. What you all need is a good spanking.
RUTH: We are not children. We are practicing our right for better working conditions.
SHERIFF: You must be joking. Just shut up.
SOLEDAD: Yes, we are practicing our freedom of speech and equality.
SHERIFF: Who asked you?
MARY: And now we want beds, baths, and food. Right, women?
CHORUS: Right! *Queremos camas, queremos baños, queremos comida. Queremos camas, queremos baños, queremos comida.*

(Espe is trying to hush the baby up because it is crying [make crying baby

sound]. Mary hears sound and goes to talk to Espe in the back and returns to front of jail space to address the sheriff.)

MARY: Sheriff, listen . . .
SHERIFF: Shut up, all of you!
MARY: We have a baby and the baby needs its special formula!
SHERIFF: I gave you milk already!
MARY: It has to be the special formula.
SHERIFF: Do you think I'm running a pharmacy drug store?
MARY: We need the formula!
CHORUS: *¡Queremos la fórmula! ¡Queremos la fórmula! ¡Queremos la fórmula! ¡Queremos la fórmula! ¡Queremos la fórmula!*
SHERIFF: Pleeeeaassseee, shut up!

(*Around this time Ramón appears.*)

SHERIFF: Haven't you already seen enough of me? What do you want?
RAMÓN: I came for my baby.
SHERIFF: Step aside and let him take the baby!

(*Esperanza makes her way to the front of the jail space. She and Ramón look at each other for a moment and she hands him the bundled baby. Ramón exits with baby and Espe looks at the Sheriff in defiance as he shoves her back into the jail space. Espe regains her balance behind the bars and speaks with determination.*)

ESPE: *Queremos camas. Queremos baños. Queremos comida.*
(*Chorus repeat, repeat low volume, repeat lower volume, repeat whisper.*)

Scene VII

(*As the volume of the chant/chorus goes down the stage is set up for the home of Esperanza and Ramón. Table and chairs on one side and high bench with two bowls for sink; next to this the stove with coffeepot and pans, easel with portrait of Benito Juárez. Ramón enters with bundled baby and sets it down in the box that serves as a crib. Ramón starts to wash the pot and pan in the two sinks and looks frustrated and talks to self.*)

RAMÓN: The dishwater is cold and I still haven't finished hanging up the clothes to dry.

(*There is a knock on the door and Ramón goes to side stage to answer. The neighbor next door enters.*)

WORKER 3: Ramón, the kids outside are playing with the damp clothes in your laundry basket and I came to borrow some soap.

RAMÓN: (*Looks out the door behind stage right.*) Hey, kids, get away from those baskets, go play elsewhere!

(*Closes door.*)

WORKER 3: This is crazy not having any hot running water, so much time is spent chopping wood and boiling water.

RAMÓN: It takes three hours just to get the water hot for washing clothes. Salinski, we have to make hot running water one of the main demands in our union contract.

WORKER 3: I agree, especially if our wives are going to jail. This is the fourth day of their incarceration.

RAMÓN: You needed soap?

(*Sound of baby crying. Ramón gets bottle and gives it to the baby.*)

RAMÓN: This time the temperature is right, you should not be crying. When I get my cold bottle of beer, I feel better. There, drink up your milk. Now, Salinski, where were we?

WORKER 3: Have you ever heard of the "Woman Question?"

RAMÓN: No, what's that about?

WORKER 3: Well, the way I understand, it is about having equality in the home, as well as equality outside the home.

RAMÓN: Oh yeah!

WORKER 3: Yes, and it also talks about sex equality.

RAMÓN: What do you mean?

WORKER 3: You know. What is good for the man is good for the woman.

RAMÓN: (*Gets a cup of soap from the sink.*) Here, soap. Is that all?

WORKER 3: Guess I better go; you is not in a good mood.

RAMÓN: I have a lot of work and . . .

WORKER 3: And "Ain't no sunshine when she's gone."

(*He exits singing, leaves Ramón thinking.*)

Ain't no sunshine when she's gone.
Ain't no sunshine when she's gone.
And she gone four days and nights
Ain't no sunshine when she's gone
Only darkness every day
Ain't no sunshine when she's gone

And she's gone four days and nights.
Ain't no sunshine when she's gone.

(Ramón sits at the table and puts his hands over his face. Esperanza enters stage right door with a big smile. She picks up the baby and hugs it, puts it back, and gives Ramón a kiss on the cheek.)

RAMÓN: Am I glad to see you. I've been here doing all this housework. I have had these kids all this time.

ESPE: I've had them since they were born.

RAMÓN: Did you sign the pledge not to go back to the picket line?

ESPE: No, they couldn't make us.

RAMÓN: Then how did they let you go?

ESPE: They did not like hearing our voice.

RAMÓN: Esperanza, I wanted to talk with you.

ESPE: Later, Ramón, I have a meeting with the women. It won't take long. We need to go over our next steps.

(Knock on door, Espe answers. Enter Mary and Ruth, cheerful and ready to plan for action. Then there is the sound of a slamming door as Ramón exits.)

MARY: What are you going to do about him?

ESPE: That's something I have to work out between us.

RUTH: I went to see Connie. She is better from being bumped with the sheriff's car and will be back on the picket line tomorrow.

MARY: We still need to watch her, maybe she can do work behind the counter handling the mail.

ESPE: Yes, I'll get the first aid kit ready for tomorrow.

RUTH: I'm taking the coloring books and crayons for the children.

MARY: The mail correspondence continues to grow. We are getting donations from Anglo and Mexican working families. We have gotten supplies and support of the women walking the picket line from both the mill and the mine-working families.

ESPE: Including contributions from the industrial workers across the country. This is an example of unity and a big step towards solidarity.

RUTH: Yes, we must continue sending out the letters of appreciation to each and every person, family, and organization.

ESPE: I feel good about our progress and how far we have come in our struggle.

MARY: Yes, I do too. We better go home and get some rest, women.

(The women give each other hugs say their goodnights and exit. Esperanza yells out to the children to come inside and turns her attention to the baby.)

ESPE: Come inside, children. We'll fix a snack and get ready for bed. Let's see if you need your diaper changed. Look at you, what big eyes. We can see each other's hearts. It's bedtime for you. (*Cradle tune, as in "Rock a Bye Baby," in Spanish to be sung by Espe.*)

"Duerme" [4]

Duermete, niño, duermete.
Ya yo estaré cercas, cercas de tí.
Sueña, mi niño, sueña de amor
Cuando amanezca yo estaré aquí
Junto a tu lado, llena de amor. .

(*Espe holds the baby in her arms and puts it back in the box-crib and carefully takes it to the bedroom behind the curtain. Stage is empty for two seconds. She reenters, humming the lullaby, sits at the table, puts her arm on top of the table, and rests her head. She falls asleep and wakes up suddenly and goes to peek behind the curtain. Talks out loud to self and audience.*)

ESPE: My children went to bed without me giving them their snack. I fell asleep. Guess I was very tired. Ramón is still not home.

(*Noise coming from the direction of the door. Ramón enters stage right staggering and exits left, makes noise as if searching in back, and comes out with a box where he keeps his rifle and will proceed to polish it.*)

ESPE: Ramón, please don't wake the children, it's past midnight. You wanted to talk?
RAMÓN: No, not anymore.

(*He looks for a rag in the kitchen.*)

ESPE: Can you not bear the sight of me?
RAMÓN: You don't have time for me. You don't care about me.
ESPE: I do, Ramón. I waited and I'm here to listen.
RAMÓN: Then what? So the Women's Auxiliary can tell me where to go?
ESPE: (*Notes him taking rifle out of box.*) What are you doing?
RAMÓN: Me and the men are going hunting in the morning.
ESPE: What, at this crucial time in our struggle? But you can't, we need you.
RAMÓN: What is the use? The company men and the bosses are stronger and they will starve us workers. That is the whole picture.
ESPE: What do you mean, the whole picture?

RAMÓN: The company bosses will outlast us. We might as well go down fighting.

ESPE: Ramón, I don't want to go down fighting. I want to stand and walk with dignity. I want to win! And we are not weaker; we are stronger!

RAMÓN: You are getting all these ideas from your friends.

ESPE: I like having friends and I respect them.

RAMÓN: I don't like what is going on. I rather go back to the old way.

ESPE: We can't go back to the old way. You just want me to stay in my place. And you look down at Anglos when they try to keep you in your place.

RAMÓN: Say no more.

ESPE: You need me, Ramón, like I need you. And you cannot win this strike without me.

RAMÓN: *Te dije que callaras. (He gets aggressively close to Espe.)*

ESPE: Can you only have dignity if I have none?

(Ramón motions to hit Espe on the face.)

ESPE: Never try that again. It would be the ultimate act for you to hit me. Sleep wherever you like but not with me.

RAMÓN: When day breaks I will be gone hunting. I am going hunting with the rest of the men. Just like a real man.

(As soon as Espe exits left and Ramón exits right there is a resounding knock on the door. Espe comes from behind left stage to answer door on stage right.)

Scene VIII

MARY: ¡*Buenos días!* It is a beautiful day. Are we ready?

ESPE: Yes, I'll get the baby.

(Espe goes to left and behind backdrop speaks while Mary looks around.)

ESPE: Children, I will be taking the baby for a walk. I need for you both to get ready.

CHILDREN *(offstage)*: We can eat at the place where you write letters, Mama. And we can play in the bushes!

ESPE: Just stay close by, don't go far.

(Espe enters from left stage where Mary sits checking on her notes.)

MARY: Where's Ramón?

ESPE: He went hunting with the men.

MARY: How can he do that? We may need him close to us.
ESPE: That's what I tried to tell him.
MARY: He got a taste of what it is to be a woman and ran off.
ESPE: It has been very hard on him. (*Turns to right.*) Kids, wait for us.
MARY: Esperanza, anything that brings change is going to be difficult. Anything that makes us learn is going to be painful. Some will react strongly against change but if change benefits the majority then the pain we bear is worth the happiness we can gain.

(*Imaginary kids exit. Espe, baby, and Mary go to the right door stage and curve towards the audience in slow motion, facing the audience. Enter the sheriff and his deputy into the home setting through stage right door and curious neighbor enter from left stage and come out to watch from left outer stage.*)

SHERIFF: Now we got to get all this trash out of this dump.
WORKER 3: Hey, what are you doing? I'm the neighbor and I know that you were not invited.
SHERIFF: We have an eviction notice. This house belongs to the company. They sent us here legally to have this house evacuated. Deputy, start throwing out the trash!
DEPUTY: All right. I will enjoy destroying the trash in this dump.

(*Worker 3 runs towards Espe and Mary, almost or in the audience space.*)

WORKER 3: Esperanza, you are being evicted. Where is Ramón?
ESPE: He went hunting with the men.
WORKER 3: What? Where?
ESPE: I don't know.

(*The Sheriff and his deputy go out the door right side and curve to the outer front center stage next to dump the household items. They even go behind the curtain where the bedroom is to get blankets, basket, clothes, and whatever is available for trash. Meanwhile more people come around and stand alongside Mary and Espe.*)

SHERIFF: Where the hell do all these people come from?
DEPUTY: I'm ready to arrest those kids. They are throwing rocks at us!

(*Enter Ramón; he pauses to looks apologetically at Espe, who acknowledges his silence until Salinski interrupts.*)

WORKER 3: Ramón, it was about time!
RAMÓN: Salinski, we can start picking up the furniture and putting it back.

MARY: I'll get the children to stop throwing rocks.
RAMÓN: Yes, please.

(Ramón motions for those witnessing the eviction to pick up what has been dumped near the audience and take it back into the house. The sheriff and the deputy try to stop them, but all the household items keep getting returned. People in the audience can also return some of the household items, or they can stand in the path of the deputy and sheriff, who are bringing out the furniture. The deputy and the sheriff after a while give up.)

SHERIFF: I don't understand all this, to hell with everyone! Let's go!
DEPUTY: Yes, let's get the hell out. And I'll be back for those ignorant rascals!

(Sheriff and deputy exit stage right. Enter Jenicks left stage to addresses everyone.)

JENICKS: I bring good news. The company has called the International Workers' Union to the table to negotiate the demands that have been put forth by our union rank and file. And as law-abiding citizens we will continue to stand for our right to peacefully assemble and petition for just compensation.
RAMÓN: I want to thank all you brothers and especially the sisters of the Women's Auxiliary for supporting us in every way possible. Everything that our union brotherhood members have gained could not have been without the wisdom of the women on our side.

(Those who participated break out into joy. Music background or a song is optional. The actors playing the parts of sheriff and deputy come out and join as common folk. When Esperanza gets ready to speak to the audience she motions for silence with one hand while holding the baby with the other arm. She hands the baby over to Ramón and he accepts. Everyone participating becomes still and silent. Espe comes to the front center of stage and addresses the audience for the last time.)

ESPE: This is my story to you and my children. So, you see, my brothers and sisters, equality between us does bring strength and harmony to our struggles. Ramón came to understand that equality between men and women does and will continue to better our society and our world. What was more valuable for me from my story is that we got something that can never be taken away. This is hope. This hope that makes us women, the inheritors of the earth and our children, the Salt of the Earth.

End

Notes

1. Translation of "Paloma Negra"

Black dove, I am tired of crying and no break of day.
I don't know if to condemn or pray for you.
I fear looking and finding you
Where my friends assure me that you go.
There are moments that I would rather give up
And tear out the nails of my suffering,
But my eyes die without seeing your eyes
And my love with the dawn again looks for you.
You are indulging yourself in drinking binges.
Black dove, black dove, where, where are you?
Do not play with my honor, drinking binges,
If your caresses should be mine and no one else's.
Even if I love you with madness, do not return.
Black dove, black dove, imprisonment of sorrow.
I want freedom, to live life with one who loves me.
God give me strength because I'm dying to find you.
You are indulging yourself in drinking binges.

2. Translation of "Las Mañanitas"

These are the break of days that King David sang.
To beautiful girls, this is how we sing.
Wake up, my beauty, and see the break of day
Now the birds sing and the moon takes cover.
The day that you were born, the flowers were born.
And on the baptismal font sang the nightingales.
Here comes the break of day, its light shine on us.
Get up and see that the break of day is born.

3. Translation of "Canción Mixteca"

How far I am from the earth where I was born.
Immense nostalgia invades my thoughts.
And to see myself alone and sad, a leaf in the wind
I wish to weep, I wish to die of tormenting sentiment.
Oh land of the sun, I sigh to see you.
And now how far I am without love, without light.
And to see myself alone and sad, a leaf in the wind
I wish to weep, I wish to die of tormenting sentiment.

4. Translation of "Duerme"

Sleep now, my child, sleep sweet dreams.
I will be near you, close at your side.
Dream, my child, dream of love.
When the day breaks I will be here.
Close to your side and filled with love.

E. T.—The Alien

Characters

Enriqueta Tejeda (E. T.)	Guard
Coyote	Güera
Migra 1	Mr. Union
Migra 2	Boss
Tiffy	Juan
Mom	Farm worker 1
Husband's Voice	Farm worker 2
Bus Depot Announcer	Migra 3
Bag Lady	Migra 4

Scene I: Introduction of E. T.

(*Enriqueta enters stage right, selling gum.*)

ENRIQUETA: *Chicle, chicle,* please buy some gum, anyone, please.

(*She is ready to burst into tears and notes her audience front center stage and slowly moves to the left, telling her story.*)

ENRIQUETA: My name is Enriqueta Tejeda—call me E. T. I am from the continent of South America, across the Mexican border. In Latin America the poor are not as hidden as in the United States. Once you cross the border poverty is vast and naked. There are the super-rich who have taken all the land and are protected by the government, and then there are the foreign companies, many of whom are runaway shops from the United States of North America. They pay their workers a meager $6. 75 an hour, while they only pay South American workers a $1.00 a day. But now even these factories are closing down. There are many organized protests in South America against injustice and hunger. Those in power have smothered these sparks of revolution. In spite of this oppression, people like me will continue to struggle for a better life at whatever cost.

(*E. T. says all this as if saying a story. She is unaware of the presence of el Coyote. She stands stage left, facing away from center stage. The Coyote sneaks up to center stage with a dry bush, enters stage left, drops bush in mid-center stage, and gets in front of it to address audience.*)

COYOTE: *Yo soy el coyote.* For a price I will pick up wetbacks from the border, for a higher price I will personally escort them across the border. I make a living off these pitiful creatures and all because of a border. So, you see, I am not their enemy. These creatures need my services. Most are escaping their miserable squalor, which I did not create, but which I take advantage of. Come, my sweet. Let's dance.

Scene II: The Bait

(*Dance between E. T. and Coyote to "Samba Pa Tí" by Carlos Santana.*)

E. T.: *Me dicen* that there is work in the U.S. My friend works for a very rich family. She sent me an address of one such family who needs a maid.

COYOTE: Heh, heh Enriqueta, there is much *chamba en los Estados Unidos* (*taps her on the shoulder*), *tus servicios* are much in demand.

E. T.: *No se,* I don't want to leave my country and its beauty, with its vast open valleys, the songs of the birds, and the richness of its culture.

COYOTE: You have to make up your mind, *linda;* it may be your country, but you do not own the land; it belongs to a very select few. Yes, your country may be beautiful, but you still live in crowded shantytowns.

E. T.: *Es cierto,* it is this love for my land that makes it much harder to migrate: How can I leave my brothers and sisters and my madre *que tanto quiero?*

COYOTE: Queta, you and your family have been stripped of your land and everything it gave. How far can you go on love now that the factory has closed down, now that your mother is ill, and your father? . . . Your father has disappeared. You are just another mouth to feed.
E. T.: I have saved some money.
COYOTE: With that money I can take you to a richer future; come, Queta, we waste time. I will meet you when you cross the border.

(Coyote exits stage left. E. T. hurries behind him as if looking for a safe place to cross the border. She tries to secure her bag of belongings to her shoulders.)

Scene III: The Catch

E. T.: The river current is strong but I must be stronger.

(E. T. is swimming in motion from left to right, front stage, in front of dry bush, across the water to get to land, and almost on the verge of drowning. Finally she gets to shore, to be greeted by the Migra, who enters stage right.)

MIGRA 1: Where do you think you are going?
E. T.: *Suéltame (struggling), me lastimas, por favor, suéltame.*
MIGRA 1: No way! I am not letting you go, my little *frijolito.*
E. T.: Please do not hurt me. *Tenga compasión.*
MIGRA 1: You know you like it, my little *tamalito.*

(Migra laughs for some time. Takes E. T. to the floor behind the dry bush on center stage. Migra bends, choking her. E. T. stops screaming when Migra stands up, fixing pants, pulling zipper, and laughing. Migra 2 enters stage right.)

MIGRA 2: Martinez, quit wasting time; we have an emergency! Come on!
MIGRA 1: Holy moly, Smith, you came on time. I'm through with this wench.

(Migra 1 and 2 exit stage right. E. T. regains consciousness; in shock over her violation, gets out a paper wrapped in plastic. She walks across stage as if in a daze and stands at center stage. Coyote enters stage right to meet E. T.)

COYOTE: What happened to you? Come on, the car motor is running.
E. T.: *Llévame a Los Angeles. Aquí está el dinero y el domicilio. (She hands him the paper wrapped in plastic.)*
COYOTE: *O sí,* the address of Mr. and Mrs. Megabucks.

(Both exit stage right and the Coyote uses dry bush as a cover to sneak away.)

Scene IV: *La Criada Malcriada*

(*Tiffy enters stage left carrying a pillow, a recorder, and a magazine, and a chair with cover is handed to her; puts it mid-stage left. Sets stage while grooving to Valley Girl music.*)

TIFFY: Oh Mickey, you're so fine, oh Mickey . . .

(*Mom enters stage right, wearing flowing nightgown, holding her head and a cup.*)

MOM: Tiffy, lower that racket! That noise is upsetting, and to top it off that maid was so filthy I sent her out to the greenhouse to clean up. She was disgusting, to say the least.

TIFFY: It is about time we got a maid. I am tired of this awful housework; it's totally gross!

(*Tiffy settles herself right mid-stage on the floor, props herself on the pillow, looking at magazine.*)

MOM: Oh my, I do have a headache. (*Pops several pills and sits with head back on chair.*) Tiffy, did you know that your father never came home last night?

(*E. T. enters stage right, tripping over Tiffy's purposely placed foot.*)

MOM: You will have to lift your feet up En . . . Eri . . . We will just call you E. T., okay? You'll have to stop shuffling when you walk.

E. T.: *Como usted diga, señora.*

MOM: You should know you have responsibilities besides housework. You have to wash windows and clothes, do the ironing, walk the dog, shop for food, and perform other related duties as they arise, etc., etc.

E. T.: *Sí, señora.*

MOM: I hope you have this place dazzling before tonight.

E. T.: *Como usted diga, señora.*

MOM: Here is some money for you to go grocery shopping. Tiffy will drive you there and back.

TIFFY: Do I have to be seen with her? How gross, so totally, utterly gross.

MOM: (*Looks out the window and fixes herself.*) Your dad is here. *Tiffy. Come on.*

(*Tiffy hits E. T. with the pillow on the way out. Both exit stage right. Mom goes to left front stage and waves with a scarf.*)

MOM: Oh, darling! Up here on the terrace. Did you have another important meeting last night?

HUSBAND'S VOICE: Yes, dear.

MOM: Oh, you must be terribly exhausted. I will ring the butler to fix us a martini. Would you join me?

HUSBAND'S VOICE: No, dear.

MOM: Well, perhaps after you have rested (*turns to the audience*). I will have the butler fix me a double. (*Exits stage right.*)

Scene V: Close Encounters

(*E. T. enters stage left and is looking around for her ride at center stage.*)

E. T.: *¿Dónde estabas?* I been waiting for you. I finish half hour ago.

(*Tiffy in a loud whisper comes up to E. T. from stage left.*)

TIFFY: The car is close by. Walk behind me. Oh, my God! Gag me with a spoon, hurry up. And get in the back and keep your head down.

E. T.: Gag me with a spoon? *¿Qué es eso?* You told me to wait at the street corner and now we go to the alley!

TIFFY: I can't stand it when the hired help get uppity. Come quickly, and remember—peons in the back.

E. T.: Why do you treat me like a fool? I know how you feel about me, but I never gave you reason to dislike me.

TIFFY: Do I actually have to engage in a conversation with this peon? The nerve! You are attracting attention!

E. T.: No, you are! And I will not hide in the back of the car.

TIFFY: I am going to make you sorry.

(*Both exit stage right and Mom enters from stage left as if in deep thought. E. T. enters right behind with scrub brush and pail and starts to wash floor.*)

MOM: (*Clothes in her hands*): Decisions, decisions; what shall I wear . . . my Gucci . . . my Fiarrinchi . . . my Tucchi . . . I'll wear my Tucchi. E. T., is my bathtub ready?

E. T., *looks up.* Yes, ma'am.

(*E. T. goes back to work and Tiffy enters stage left.*)

MOM: I will be soaking a while, Tiffy, so if Daddy wakes up, have the butler fix him a drink (*exits*).

TIFFY: Okay, Mom.

(*E. T. takes off her white hat and apron, moves to center stage, and continues *to scrub floor. Tiffy sneaks behind E. T. with a smirk and takes hat and apron, and then exits stage right behind Mom.)*

E. T.: Tonight I will write a letter to my family and tell them the great news. Then later, after my second week's pay, I will send them some money. My *mamacita* will be so happy and proud of me. It would break her heart to find out what happened to me at the border. (*Almost starts to cry.*) But I must be strong and work very, very hard.

(*Tiffy enters with recorder, dancing to song of "Mickey," attired like a cheerleader. E. T. watches for a while and joins in. The two seem to enjoy each other's company, but Tiffy draws away and E. T. backs off also. Mom enters in bathrobe with a towel around her head.*)

TIFFY: Mom, guess what! This servant of yours was in Daddy's room.
MOM: What!
TIFFY: If I had not come in, well. . . . Anyway all she was able to take off was her hat and apron.
E. T.: (*Aware of missing items, looks worried.*) No, señora, I've been cleaning.
TIFFY: You were not cleaning all the time.
E. T.: I stopped to rest a little.
MOM: So, you admit you are guilty. My daughter does not lie. Get out now! Tiff, I am going to call the immigration office. Don't let her get away. (*She dials the phone.*) Immigration office, I have just sighted an extraterrestrial alien.

(*E. T. runs out stage left.*)

TIFFY: Mom, you just ran her out! You have to find her because I am not!

(*Tiffy and Mom exit stage left. And E. T. enters as if running from stage right to center mid stage and faces audience.*)

Scene VI: On the Run

E. T.: I was not able to get all of my belongings but at least I've made it this far to the bus depot. I barely have one week's pay to get my fare, but to where?
ANNOUNCER: Next bus leaving for Fresno on door B. Be ready for departure in 20 minutes!

(*Bag Lady enters stage right, stands behind E. T., and checks her out.*)

BAG LADY: You are not from here, are you?

E. T.: No . . .

(*Güera enters stage left and listens in on the conversation.*)

BAG LADY: I can spot your kind a mile away. You are one of those that come and take all the jobs away from us, live off our welfare, take away our men.

E. T.: *Estás equivocada.*

BAG LADY: *Equivocada, avocado* yourself, and *patuti* to you too.

GÜERA, *approaches* E. T.: Do not pay attention to her. *No sabe lo que dice, y está perdida también.*

E. T.: Yes, I know, poor woman . (*E. T. turns to lady.*) We are in the same boat. We both seem to be homeless and lost.

(*Bag Lady continues to make awkward movements as if demented.*)

E. T., *talking to Güera*: Where are you from?

GÜERA: *Pues yo soy del sur* and I have a temporary *mica.*

E. T.: So you work temporary, and are you going back to Mexico?

GÜERA: Well, I just came back and am returning to work in the fields.

E. T.: *¿Vas a trabajar al campo?* I am without papers and need help.

GÜERA: I can help you get a social security number.

E. T.: Social security number?

GÜERA: Social security, you know, a card that the government uses to take money from people's wages for old age retirement, but of course, you cannot claim it.

E. T.: If there is work in the *campo,* will you take me with you?

GÜERA: Yes, come on with me, it is cheaper to hitch a ride.

(*E. T. and Güera exit stage left and Bag Lady points her finger at them.*)

BAG LADY: Yes, I know them all, nothing but troublemakers. But they shall repent; the Lord will see to that.

(*Bag Lady sits on the floor and with a spoon starts eating out of her purse. Guard enters stage right and sees Bag Lady.*)

GUARD: All right, can I see your ID? Did you understand?

BAG LADY: Mmmmm, yummy.

(*Guard takes away purse, gets out a can of dog food.*)

GUARD: Are you by any chance an illegal alien? I have to take you in.

BAG LADY: *No sabe, no sabe.* Ha, ha, ha.

GUARD: Do not get funny with me, lady. You know that since Simpson

Mazzoli came into effect, you have to have a special ID. You are coming with me.

BAG LADY: (*Looks at audience and covers mouth partially so guard will not hear.*) All right—3 meals and a cot!

(*Guard and Bag Lady exit stage right. Enter E. T. and Güera stage left.*)

Scene VII: *Para el Campo*

E. T.: *¡Que frío!* It was so cold in the back of that truck.

GÜERA: It is good I had the extra jacket for you. Well, it is 4:00 a.m. and that ride got us here just in time to sign up for work.

E. T.: You mean we start right now?

GÜERA: *¡Ay! Como estás tapada.* Don't you know that here in the fields the Boss needs to know that you are eager to start picking grapes.

E. T.: Where we are going to stay?

GÜERA: Later we will fix a place to sleep with cardboard boxes and sticks. I will show you. Here comes the Boss—show him your card!

(*Boss enters stage right and spots E. T.*)

BOSS: Are you new?

GÜERA: She is with me, boss.

BOSS: Okay, start at dawn and finish at dusk.

(*Boss stays on right side of stage, posing authoritatively while E. T., Güera, and two other workers start to pick grapes. All spread out back stage. Union organizer enters stage left and goes to front stage, faces the audience.*)

MR. UNION: My name is Max, or Mr. Union. My role is to organize the farm workers. Farm labor is hard work, but worst of all it pays low wages and hardly any benefits.

(*Mr. Union freezes. Boss comes to life in background.*)

BOSS: E. T., you take too many bathroom breaks. You are not being paid to frolic in the vineyards (*turns his back to audience*).

MR. UNION: Whether you are a garbage collector, construction worker, or a farm worker the whole labor force deserves decent wages.

(*Mr. Union freezes. Boss turns sideways to audience and his workers.*)

BOSS: E. T., you've been here for weeks and you speed has not improved. Now work faster. I'll be back. (*Exits stage right.*)

MR. UNION: I've been watching that E. T. for several months and she does not seem to have a clue about what is going on (*freezes*).

E. T.: I've been here 3 months already, time goes by so fast.

GÜERA: Better not let the boss know that you are sick.

E. T.: But I cannot help it. Who is that man?

GÜERA: That's Max, he is with the union.

MR. UNION: Hey, why don't you aliens go back to Mexico. You are taking our jobs.

E. T.: But we are here to work.

MR. UNION: We are organizing the farm workers for better wages and you are in the way.

E. T.: I am not against your organizing, but why don't you get us into the union and together we can be more organized and stronger?

(*Güera and Mr. Union look astonished.*)

MR. UNION: That is unheard of.

E. T.: Yes, that is why we keep losing from both sides.

MR. UNION: Well, I do have to go now (*exits stage left*).

GÜERA: E. T., it makes sense what you say. Is it possible that in our lifetime we will see workers joining and uniting from different countries?

E. T.: Maybe in this little one's lifetime, workers on an international stage will unite for fair, decent wages worldwide.

(*E. T. touches her stomach and the boss reenters stage right.*)

BOSS: That is enough for today. (*Two other workers exit stage left and Güera follows.*) You, wait! (*Points to E. T.*) Now, pack your belongings and go!

E. T.: But why?

BOSS: I heard about your union ideas. I do declare, when the foreign workers unite with the workers of the great U.S. of A., our democracy will surely crumble. Get lost.

(*Boss exits stage right. E. T. looks at Güera, who has been waiting at end of stage left. She goes to center stage with E. T.*)

GÜERA: Look, E. T., I have a cousin in another city and he said that there is plenty of work in the clothing factory. Let's go.

E. T.: Güera, you don't have to do this for me.

GÜERA: Oh, it is time for a change anyway. Come on.

(*Both exit stage left.*)

Scene VIII: Urban Love

(*Factory sweatshop, sewing pants. Two workers enter with chairs and small tables or boxes to lay the cloth. They set up to work, making zooming noises of machines and hissing steam irons. E. T. and Güera enter.*)

E. T.: I am glad you came. I am very grateful and this time I am really glad we got a ride in a van.

GÜERA: Well, you have to take the rides as they come. *Andale,* no time to talk. We will take turns carrying the bundles.

(*E. T. takes bundle of cloth to Juan. First time E. T. and Juan's eyes meet. Two workers in the background start swooning and singing "The First Time Ever I Saw Your Face," by Roberta Flack. E. T. and Juan each go to opposite ends of stage as if working assembly style and rejoin to smile at each other.*)

JUAN: E. T., I've known you only for a month, but I am in love with you. I want to marry you someday.

E. T.: Juan, I am attracted to you, but to marry you *es complicado.*

JUAN: Complicated! Don't be foolish. I have enough love for both of us.

E. T.: Juan, it is not that simple.

JUAN: *Díme, no me importa.* Nothing can separate us.

E. T.: Juan, when I was crossing the border (*pause*), I was raped. Now I am pregnant.

JUAN: What are you saying? Why did this have to happen to me? Now I cannot make you my wife; you are not a virgin. I have too much pride to accept this.

E. T.: I also have pride, and you are mistaken if you think that I am less of a woman because of what happened to me. All I wanted was to work and to better my life. I have chosen to keep this child and make a living for the both of us. I will do what I can to help my family back home. I, (*pause*) we, will go on with or without you.

(*Music starts again, "Samba Pa Tí." Shows E. T. and Juan avoiding each other as they cross the stage five times, during which E. T.'s stomach grows to the fullest nine months. She stays on stage left. Meanwhile Juan goes over to the two workers and they start a silent discussion which leads to finger-pointing, and the two workers exit stage left. Juan waves his hands as if in frustration. Güera continues to work until she takes note of E. T.*)

GÜERA: E. T., are you alright?

E. T.: Just my feet ache. I am so tired.

GÜERA: It seems almost time for your baby to come.

E. T.: Yes, nine months ago I crossed. Well, you know the rest of the story (*eyes tearing*).

GÜERA: Rest a little; I will bring you something to eat (*exits stage left*).

JUAN: (*Stops his frustrated movement and walks toward* E. T.): It seems that I am the only one interested in working today.

E. T.: It looks that way (*shy manner, labor pains keep increasing*).

JUAN: Well, back to work (*tries to be indifferent*).

E. T.: Yes.

JUAN: E. T., I . . .

(*Migra 3 and 4 enter stage right at moment of Juan's hesitation, and Juan helps E. T. to hide behind a chair draped with cloth. The Migra searches in all directions, until they catch Juan and handcuff him. Güera peeks from stage left and waits for the Migra and Juan to exit stage right. Güera follows them out and E. T. drags behind her. They stop at center front stage.*)

GÜERA: E. T., what are you doing?

E. T.: *Se llevaron a Juan.* He is gone (*crying, face showing, feeling more pains again*).

GÜERA: We must get you to the hospital!

E. T.: I do not think I can make it (*face shows lots of pains*).

GÜERA: Hurry, E. T., the child is coming.

(*Both go behind place where E. T. hid from the migra.*)

E. T.: Güera, promise me you will take care of my baby and return her to my family if I die.

GÜERA: E. T., you cannot die.

E. T.: Forgive me.

(*Sounds of labor cries and a baby crying.*)

GÜERA: I will do my best to care for this beautiful baby girl.

(*Migra 3 and 4 enter stage right, coming back for E. T. after she has delivered. Güera hides behind stage left backdrop. The Migra drag E. T. to stage right and push her behind backdrop.*)

MIGRA 3: Well, she may be dying or dead but at least she was returned to where she came from.

MIGRA 4: Yep, this is all in a day's work.

(*Migra 3 and 4 wipe their hands clean and exit stage right. Güera emerges from left backdrop, carrying baby to front center stage, and faces the audience.*)

GÜERA: Why does it have to be this way? What is the future of this child?

End

Anti-Nuke Commercial

Characters

Gas & Electric Representative
Teenage Son
Show Host
Mother (homemaker type)
Teenage Daughter
Two Cleaners (in radiation suits)

(*Show Host enters stage right toward left, kazoos in background blare tune of "Rocky Raccoon."*)

SHOW HOST: Good evening, ladies and gentlemen. Let me welcome you to your favorite T.V. show—THIS IS YOUR LIFE!! (*Kazoos blare.*) But now a word from a representative of our sponsor, your favorite and *only* utility company, the Gas and Electric Company!

(*Blare of kazoos. Host exits stage left. Enter stage right G&E Rep.*)

G&E REP: Yes, we've heard lately about the oil shortage and we've heard about Three Mile Island and the accidents connected with nuclear energy, but this is a one-sided view. The reality is that we need nuclear power to provide and meet our current and future energy needs. Today I want you to meet a family whose total energy needs are provided by nuclear power.

(*Entering left stage, Mother and two teenagers, Mother wearing an apron and mixing food in bowl. She faces the audience. G&E Rep. stands proudly, still right stage.*)

MOTHER: Yes, our family was continually suffering the loss of electricity and spontaneous blackouts, but that was before they built the nuclear plant. Now every day we have all the atomic electricity we want, don't we, children?

SON: Yes, Mom! I can hear and even feel in my body all the different sounds coming from my stereo all the time. I get so automatically charged just by playing my electric guitar. But you know something, Ma, I've been feeling tired. I don't feel like doing anything (*yawn*). Besides, my hair is falling out. (*He pulls out a chunk of hair and laughs.*) Look, Ma, hair!

DAUGHTER: That's funny, I'm not tired, but I do have a skin problem even though I use the Epidermis Zapping Machine to relax and tone my skin.

(*She exposes her arms. One arm is full of boils and dark scars, the other arm looks normal until she scratches, and takes off a layer [ace tape] of skin. Mother gasps.*)

DAUGHTER: You see what I mean, Mom?

MOTHER: When did this start happening, kids?

SON: Oh, I don't know . . . not sure, even though I feel all these vibes. It's like that earthquake.

DAUGHTER: Wait a minute! The earthquake six months ago! The nuclear plant was already in operation, but they did say the deadly nuclear waste is safely buried in barrels under the earth.

SON: So, if the earthquake sprung a nuclear waste leak, the Earth dies, but not us? Right, Ma?

MOTHER: Oh no! Is this why I am . . .?

(*She clutches her right mid-torso as if in sudden awareness of increasing pain, screaming and pointing at the G&E Rep. and children get very scared.*)

MOTHER: You are contaminating the earth! You are polluting all of us! You liars! You killers! You never told us we had to pay for this automatic nuclear power with our LIVERS!

(*The family drops to floor with arms and legs shaking in air, dying like roaches.*)

G&E REP: (*Flustered at first, regains composure.*) Yes, folks. Nuclear atomic power is our tomorrow. Nuclear atomic power is the answer to all our energy needs. This is our future.

(*Enter two masked cleaners in preventative radiation suits to drag the bodies off toward left stage. G&E Rep. takes a bow and throws kisses to audience and exits right stage.*)

HOST: (*Enters to center front stage.*) Let's hear it, folks, an applause for the Grave New World!

(*Kazoos blaring "Rocky Raccoon" tune.*)

End

Archie Bunker Goes to El Salvador

Characters

Archie
Edith
TV News Announcer
City Worker
Neto
General
Male Guerrilla
Lupe
Gloria
Mrs. Valdez
Juan Valdez
Female Guerrilla
Taxi Driver
Airport Announcer Voice
Maria
Priest

Scene I

(Scene opens. On left side of stage there is a coffee table, couple of chairs, and a box draped with cloth next to back stage drop with an empty frame big [TV] enough for two figure heads. Edith, dusting the furniture, enters stage left, singing off-key and loudly, "Those Were the Days." Knock on the door. Edith opens door.)

EDITH: Oh, hello, Mrs. Valdez.

(*Mrs. Valdez enters stage right.*)

MRS. VALDEZ: *Hola, Señora* Bunker. How are you doing?
EDITH: Fine, what brings you here? Come in and sit down.
MRS. VALDEZ: Thank you, I came because I ran out of sugar and I'm making some pies.
EDITH: Oh, you are making some pies. Please be sure you send me a piece.
MRS. VALDEZ: Of course I'll give you some. How's my prize student, Gloria?
EDITH: My daughter is doing so well. You know just a week ago she was interviewing whales at Sea World. You know I'm so proud of her.
GLORIA: (*Enters stage right door all excited.*) Mother! Mother! You are not going to believe what happened to me today. Oh, *¿cómo estás, Sra. Valdez*?
EDITH: Gloria, what is going on?
GLORIA: Mother, I'm so excited! I am not going to do anymore of that "nambe pambe" reporting that I've been doing lately.
EDITH: Gloria, I thought you liked what you've been doing.
GLORIA: Mother, at last my big chance has come. I'm going to finally get into real reporting. I'm reporting on international issues! I'm going to El Salvador!
MRS. VALDEZ: *¡Vaya!* Congratulation! *¡Felicitaciones!*
EDITH: Isn't that far away?
GLORIA: Oh, Mother, I'll be fine. But you're going to have to tell Daddy for me.
EDITH: But why El Salvador? Who will take care of you, what will Archie say?
GLORIA: Mom, I will be able to see and report the truth on what really is happening down there and I can take care of myself.
EDITH: You'll be so far away. Archie will be home soon and he will get so upset. I'll try to explain to your father but it is going to be so hard.
GLORIA: Thanks, Mom. Don't worry about me. I'll be fine. But right now I've got to run. Good-bye, Sra. Valdez, please try to console my mother and also *gracias* for giving me Spanish lessons. (*Going out the back door*) Mom, love ya!
EDITH: Gloria, write often and call if you have to and don't forget to take the pill.
MRS. VALDEZ: *Adiós*, Gloria, *buena suerte* (*faces Edith*). Don't worry about her—she is a fine young, intelligent woman, bless her heart.

(*Gloria exits stage left as Archie enters stage right door.*)

EDITH: Oh, Archie (*tries to smother him with affection*).

ARCHIE: Geez, Edith, gets off me, will ya, I'm home and that should be enough. (*Notices Mrs. Valdez as he is about to sit.*) Oh no, Edith, is Taco Bell here again? Well, you can just go home, Mrs. Valdez. We have no tacos today.

EDITH: Oh Archie, I don't think Mrs. Valdez wants any tacos today.

ARCHIE: Never mind, Edith, besides I've got good news. I've just been picked as one of the 1,500 lucky officers to be sent to El Salvador as a military adviser to the Junta. Now that ain't all, besides teaching them how to keep their country in order, we are being given 120 shares of stock from each American-owned company there. Look, they even gave me an advance.

(*Pulls out suitcase full of money.*)

EDITH: Oh, Archie, that's wonderful, but isn't it kind of dangerous?

MRS. VALDEZ: Now hold it, Mr. Bunker, how can you say or think that that's good news when the people of El Salvador are in the middle of a revolution to overthrow an oppressive, violent, greedy, filthy government.

ARCHIE: Oh geez, Edith, is she still here? (*Turns to neighbor.*) Lady, you don't know nothing. The U.S. has a lot of investments there, sees, and they've got to be protected. Besides that, we ain't actually doing the shooting, we're only giving them our experience and military gunfire.

EDITH: Oh Archie, that's what you said when you went to Vietnam.

ARCHIE: Shut up, Edith, now let me explain it to you again. You know that in America we're taught to love God and country, right?

EDITH: Oh, yes, Archie.

ARCHIE: Well, thems people in El Salvador aren't doing that, so we're going over there to teach their military junta how to make them people respect theirs God and country right or wrong, in the good ole traditional American way.

MRS. VALDEZ: Mr. Bunker, the only traditional thing in the U.S.A. as it stands today is its effort to force the masses here and in the world to live with poverty, double-digit inflation, unemployment, discrimination on the bases of sex, and illiteracy. If it could, the U.S.A. military would change its emblem from the eagle to the Klu Klux Klan. I can't stand this. I'm going home. Good-bye, Mrs. Bunker.

(*Mrs. Valdez, cursing in Spanish, exits stage right door, escorted by Edith. Then Edith returns to speak with Archie.*)

ARCHIE: Ya, you do that and while you're at it, think about why you're here in the U.S.A.

EDITH: Archie, I got something to tell you. (*Subdued.*) Our little girl Gloria has gone to El Salvador.

ARCHIE: What! Edith! Why did you let her go? What's she doing over there, anyway, that's men's work. Well, that's what she gets for shooting her big mouth.

EDITH: Well, Archie, she told me she was going over there to get the whole truth on El Salvador.

ARCHIE: Geez, Edith, I already told her the truth, it's them commies that are doing all the trouble. She don't get it Edith, "Father knows best."

EDITH: But, Archie, maybe she should find out for herself!

ARCHIE: Oh, never mind, Edith. A man comes home from work and not even a cold beer is waiting. Get me a cold beer, will ya, and turn on the TV, will ya?

EDITH: (*Turns on TV.*) Archie, you want it on your favorite program, *Ironside?*

ARCHIE: Yes, of course, geez, a man comes home from a hard day's work and is entitled to watch his favorite program. Now, will you get dinner ready?

EDITH: Right away, Archie. What's smoking? Oh no!

(*Turns to audience with worried face before exiting to left of stage back drop.*)

ARCHIE, *savors his beer*: This is the way a man's castle is run.

Scene II

(*Scene II starts with the TV turned on. A cardboard sign with "MOCO News" is on screen of square frame with big box, draped with cloth below to cover the TV person's lower body. Female newscaster enters stage left, gets behind box, puts her head within empty frame, and while removing upper cloth announces on the program* Ironside *until she is ready to report facing the audience. She also introduces a commercial where two heads are to fit within frame.*)

NEWSCASTER: We welcome you to your favorite program, *Ironside*, where every crime case is solved from the seat of authority. And every criminal is brought to justice by the exclusive teamwork of a law firm. (*Mouth music—tan ta ran tan ta ran tan ta ran.*)

NEWSCASTER: We interrupt this program to bring you a news bulletin from MOCO. U.S. troops have been sent to El Salvador. Our support is in the form of artillery equipment, training of special soldiers, and increases in agents that the U.S. government has been giving the military government of El Salvador. Recently this aid was escalated by also increasing the number of U.S. military advisors and troops in the region.

ARCHIE: (*Shouts.*) Edith! She can't hear me, need to turn down the volume. (*Turns down the volume, and Newscaster keeps moving mouth.*) Edith, did you hear that! They are talking about us advisors going to El Salvador to save the country from thems rebellious people.

EDITH: (*Enters stage left side, wiping hands on a towel.*) Archie, what's all the yelling for?

ARCHIE: Come on over here, maybe you'll learn about my importance in the world. (*He turns up the TV volume.*)

NEWSCASTER: Just now the Salvadorian military received 10 million dollars in taxpayer money from the U.S. government treasury. Our government is training three Salvadorian battalions in logistics, communications, and intelligence. It is assistance such as this that has kept the ruling junta in power. In turn the junta has used the U.S.-supplied arms against the Salvadorian people. (*Pauses, to drink water from a cup, then Archie raises fist and completes comment.*)

ARCHIE: (*Raises his fist at TV.*) Lady, you don't know anything! The military over there needs all the money they can get to fight thems communists!

NEWSCASTER: The people of El Salvador have risen against hunger, illiteracy, repression, and disease. There are rumors that the military's response has been murder and violation of basic human rights. In the 1930s 30,000 peasants were massacred by government troops. Since January 1980 over 20,000 people have met their death in the streets and in the jungles of El Salvador. The rebels have most likely caused these deaths themselves. (*Pauses, looks at notes when Archie points, comments.*)

ARCHIE: (*Points at TV.*) You see there they go, killing themselves—that's why they need us!

NEWSCASTER: The Salvadorian government's actions and the U.S. military interference are clear signs of capitalists' true interests. Compared to the U.S. northern workers the U.S. southern workers are paid low wages; however, Central American workers are paid even less: U.S. corporations pay an average of $2.40 per day.

ARCHIE: God, they can buy anything they want over there. Everything is so cheap! $2.40 per day. God, they are lucky!

EDITH: Yes, Archie, I suppose so.

(*Edith goes back to kitchen, stage left back drop.*)

NEWSCASTER: This concludes our MOCO-TV bulletin, but now a word from your local sponsor.

(Newscaster becomes a commercial announcer interviewing Juan Valdez. Juan enters, looking the part of a dumb peon; enters stage left into the frame behind the big box.)

ANNOUNCER: Yes, ladies and gentleman, we find ourselves high up in the hills of El Salvador, where the fresh mountain air flows at a special plantation. This is where they grow beans, yes, beans, coffee beans. We are going to speak to Mr. Juan Valdez, who is going to tell us how he finds the perfect bean for that perfect cup of coffee. (*Juan is still waving at the camera.*) Mr. Valdez, can you please step forward. Tell us, how do you find the perfect bean?

JUAN VALDEZ: Well, *señor,* I don't know . . . I only know is how to pick the beans.

ANNOUNCER: You beancompoop, how do you find the perfect bean to make the perfect blend of Salvadoran coffee?

JUAN VALDEZ: All I know is what my father taught me and his father taught him but no one ever told us why we pick the beans. Would you like to taste my cup of coffee?

ANNOUNCER: Yes, I would. (*Takes a drink, spits it out.*) Yuck, what is this junk?

JUAN VALDEZ: Why, coffee, of course. You see, we cannot afford to buy the beans we pick so we use the leaves of the coffee plants to make our coffee.

ANNOUNCER: (*Embarrassed, shoves Juan Valdez aside roughly.*) I say . . . next time you buy that special cup of coffee, make sure it is from El Salvador, you won't be sorry, it's a very special blend. Well, we now return you to your program, *Ironside.*

ARCHIE: (*Yells.*) Edith! Get over here and turn this TV off, will ya?

EDITH: Yes, Archie, are you ready for dinner?

ARCHIE: Geezas, never mind, it's late and I've got to leave for El Salvador tomorrow morning. Edith, it's you and me now, and it's the 1900 hour and Thursday (*giving sexual leer*).

EDITH: Oh, Archie.

(Edith giggles, starts to exit, pauses, and gives audience another giggle. Both exit to stage left and Archie is heard to say the following as he turns his back to the audience.)

ARCHIE: And Edith, please, this time, don't talk.

(Giggles, behind backdrop.)

Scene III

(All furniture from Scene II needs to be cleared from stage. Scene III takes us to El Salvador, where Gloria interviews a city worker. She will also interview a guerilla fighter deep in the jungle of El Salvador. Gloria enters stage left as if avoiding gunfire. A city worker enters stage right cautiously. They meet center front stage.)

GLORIA: This is Gloria Bunker coming to you live from El Salvador where all this turmoil is taking place. Here we have an opportunity to interview one of the everyday people in the city of El Salvador, who are in the middle of all this violence. Could you say a few words to our viewers, please?

CITY WORKER: (*Notices microphone.*) *¿Estamos en televisión?*

GLORIA: *Sí, estamos en TeleMOCO y queremos su opinión acerca de intervención norteamericana.* We would like to get your opinion as a city worker in El Salvador. Could you explain how the U.S. intervention is affecting you here in the city?

CITY WORKER: *Primero déjeme explicarle, nosotros antes éramos un país de campesinos trabajadores pero la mayoría de lo que ganamos se va a los patrones, a los dueños por que nuestro labor es de tan poco valor.*

GLORIA: (*Interpreting.*) First, let me explain: we were a country of peasant workers, but the majority of our wages go to the landlords because our labor is of little value.

CITY WORKER: *Y luego vinieron los de los Estados Unidos del Norte y dijimos que bien ahora vamos a tener trabajo, dinero, comida, y un* Cadillac.

GLORIA: (*Interpreting.*) So, when the United States of North America came we said, now we are going to have work, money, food, and a Cadillac.

CITY WORKER: *Pero a nosotros nos pagan casi un décimo de lo que se ganan los trabajadores de los Estados Unidos y apenas podemos comer. Y ahora nos encontramos peleando en contra de un gobierno fascista, que se empeña en bloquear el progreso del, trabajador Americano del Sur, el Proletariado Salvadoreño.*

GLORIA: (*Interpreting.*) But we only earn a fraction of what the North American worker gets paid. Now we find ourselves fighting against a fascist government that is set against the progress of the South American worker, the Salvadorian proletariat.

CITY WORKER: *Pero ya me voy antes de que empiecen los balazos y yo quiero comer mañana.*

GLORIA: He has to run. Well, there you have it, ladies and gentlemen, this city worker is being directly affected by U.S. intervention. Our taxpayers are supporting the Junta that is killing people who want to better society for the majority. Well, thank you very much for your opinion.

CITY WORKER: *Sí, sí, de nada, de nada.*

(*Dodging sound of bullets in the background, exits right.*)

GLORIA: (*Takes a branch out of bag to make jungle scene, then, in hiding, goes to right front stage.*) And I take you to the deep dark jungles of El Salvador.

(*Clicking in the bush is heard, as Gloria faces the audience, hunched. A guerrilla fighter enters stage left to the front, hunched, facing away from Gloria. They back into each other.*)

GLORIA: (*Alarmed, facing an armed guerilla.*) *Reportero, reportero,* don't shoot!

NETO: *¿De dónde vienes y quién eres?*

GLORIA: I'm from MOCO-TV from the U.S. of North America. I am here to do an interview on a real live guerrilla. My name is Gloria. *¿Y tu nombre?*

NETO: *Me dicen* Neto.

GLORIA: *Neto, ¿diga que piensa y como justifica usted la violencia en la jungla?* Could you give us your opinion on what's happening out here in the jungle, and how do you justify this violence?

NETO: *Señora reportera, es con un llanto y una tristeza que expreso mis sentimientos de esta causa.*

GLORIA: (*Interpreting.*) It is with sadness and grief that I express my emotions about this cause.

NETO: *La razón porque nosotros los guerrillas luchamos es porque no vemos otra alternativa. Nos estamos muriendo de hambre.*

GLORIA: (*Interpreting.*) The reason we are in guerilla warfare is because there is no alternative. We are starving.

NETO: *Nuestros hijos no tienen futuro. No luchamos por ideologías comunistas o anti comunistas, estamos peleando porque tenemos hambre.*

GLORIA: (*Interpreting.*) Our children have no future. We are not fighting for communist or anti-communist ideologies; we are fighting because we are hungry.

NETO: *Bueno, termino esta conversación diciéndole que con mucho orgullo entrene nuestro grito es ¡Revolución o Muerte!*

GLORIA: (*Interpreting.*) Well, ladies and gentlemen, he has just said that it is with great pride that they say "Revolution or Death."

NETO: *Ahora si quiere la llevo al campamento. Cuidado.*
GLORIA: Now he will lead me to their encampment.

(*Both exit stage right running for cover with the sound of gunfire in the background.*)

Scene IV

(*Three chairs, one in front and two in back, facing the audience at an angle are set up and a sign that reads "El Salvador Airport." Enter Taxi Driver from stage left.*)

TAXI DRIVER: *Ay, cómo está haciendo calor* (*fans self*). *Voy a echarle mecánica a mi esposa.* (*Lifts up the hood and checks the car engine.*) Is okay! *Ay como ando cansado.*

(*Stretches, yawns, pulls hat over face and makes self comfortable in front seat. El General enters stage right and walks back and forth, waiting for Archie to arrive. Archie finally arrives, enters stage left, and is greeted by El General in front center stage.*)

GENERAL: *Andale, levántese, huevón.*
TAXI DRIVER: *Sí, sí, mi general.* I am not lazy like you.
GENERAL: *¿Qué, qué?*
TAXI DRIVER: Nothing, my general. I did not say nothing.
GENERAL: *Prepárese que ya mero llega el asesor norteamericano.*
TAXI DRIVER: *Sí, sí, mi general, lo que usted guste.* So, you are expecting a big wig?
VOICE: (*Overhead announcing.*) Flight 101 from San Diego, California, U.S. of North America, arriving in El Salvador.

(*Archie walks in a bow-legged fashion to the front center stage, carrying a pillow.*)

ARCHIE: Geez, that was a rough flight.
GENERAL: Welcome to El Salvador, Mr. Bunker. There is a car waiting for us to take us to the military camp, please climb in.
ARCHIE: You must be Pepe?
GENERAL: My name is Pedro, *señor.*
ARCHIE: Sure, sure, Pepe.
GENERAL: My name is Pedro.
ARCHIE: Whatever.

TAXI DRIVER: *A ver si podemos comenzar.* (*Prepares to start jeep, a lot of jolting and tousling.*) This jeep was made in the United Estates de Norte America.

ARCHIE: Ooh, my hemorrhoids!

(*The car starts and they drive off. Jumping up and down, making faces, Archie holds his behind.*)

GENERAL: You must excuse the condition of the roads.

ARCHIE: The first thing to get going here in El Salvador is to build better roads.

(*Car comes to an abrupt stop.*)

GENERAL: We have arrived, Mr. Bunker. (*Turns to the driver.*) *¡Pues, abre las puertas, idiota!*

TAXI DRIVER: (*Turns to audience in loud whisper.*) *¡Mejor me voy para que no me insulten!* My moder-in law calls me *idiota* and now dis one!

ARCHIE: Hey, listen, Pepe . . .

TAXI DRIVER: My name is Pedro, *señor.*

ARCHIE: Ya. (*Turns to general.*) Well just tell me who and where we're going and I'll take it from here.

GENERAL: Well, first, Mr. Bunker, we are going to attack a group of communists not too far from here. These people are rebelling against our government.

ARCHIE: So you have lot of commies here, huh?

GENERAL: Yes, many, we have the Frente Democrático Revolucionario and the followers of Farabundo Marti. These are the greatest threat to the Junta Revolucionaria.

ARCHIE: Do you have any named *¿Chile con Carne?*

GENERAL: (*Sarcastically.*) Ha ha, very funny, Mr. Bunker, but come, we must not waste time.

ARCHIE: Oh, just a little humor. (*Pats his sore rump.*)

GENERAL: We have yet another car to catch to get where we are going.

ARCHIE: Oh geezas, didn't I tell you about my hemorrhoids?

(*Archie and General exit stage left and taxi driver removes his car from the stage.*)

Scene V

(*Gloria, who is holding camera and bush, enters stage right alongside guerrilla, carrying an old rifle. They meet Maria, who enters stage left at front center *stage with another female, Lupe, carrying a bag with bandages and a sheet used for making a gurney.)*

NETO: *Maria, ¿dónde estás?*

MARIA: (*Enters with bundled baby.*) *Toma tu niña ¿quién es ella?*

(*Neto and Lupe sit on floor to side of stage left to rest and cuddle the baby.*)

NETO: *Maria, esta es una reportera de los Estados Unidos de Norte América. ¿Cómo se portó la niña?*

MARIA: *Tu híja está bien.* (*Turns attention to Gloria.*)

GLORIA: (*Turns to Maria.*) *¿Cómo puedes con esta niña? Debe estar en su casa. ¿No tiene mamá? Perdone, María, mi nombre es Gloria.*

MARIA: I speak English and yes, the baby's mother is dead. What is it that you seek?

GLORIA: Well, we in the United States of North America understand that your movement is going against the military junta that is revolutionary.

MARIA: The military junta states it is revolutionary, reformist, liberating, and that it stands for freedom except that in its quest for power greed takes over. It becomes a dictating military junta that sets out to kill in the name of democracy and calls itself revolutionary.

GLORIA: You also call yourselves revolutionary. What is the difference?

MARIA: The military junta supports only the interests of a few. We support the interests of the majority of the Salvadorian population.

NETO: *Sí, creemos en la libertad de palabra, y el derecho a la felicidad para todos.*

GLORIA: You sound just like our country's constitution. We also believe in freedom of speech and the pursuit of happiness for everyone.

MARIA: If the taxpayers in your country have any morals they would not support your government giving aid to an oppressive military dictatorship.

GLORIA: But our taxpayers do not have the whole truth of what is going on.

(*Enter rushing from stage right a Priest, tired, very worried. Sits down on floor to rest.*)

MARIA: Padre, why do you look so pale?

PRIEST: (*Noticing new face*) *¿Quién es?*

GLORIA: Sir, I am a reporter. I was explaining to Maria that few people in my country are aware of what is really going on in El Salvador.

PRIEST: (*Getting to his knees.*) *Yo les pido en el nombre de Dios pongan alto a la represión contra al pueblo Salvadoreño.* (*Sits back down.*)

MARIA: He brings up a point. Gloria, if your country claims to be a people that love God, why is so much violence against the Salvadorean people allowed to continue?

GLORIA: Our news media and your military government claim that the Salvadorian people are communists and have no God, no respect for the divine spirit.

MARIA: All humans are made of divine spirit. We all have what is called a soul. The military government makes us out to be less than human in order to justify their stealing of our lands and paying us pitiful wages.

PRIEST: (*Standing up to address Gloria.*) *Puedes dar tu servicio como reportera exponiendo la verdad. Nosotros luchamos por la dignidad del ser humano individual como también los derechos de todo el pueblo Salvadoreño.*

MARIA: He agrees, like I do, Gloria, that you can be of service to us by exposing the truth as a reporter. We fight for the dignity of the human individual. We take a stand for all the rights of the Salvadorian people to be respected.

PRIEST: *Me siento muy mal.* (*Covers face with hands.*)

NETO: *¿Qué pasa, padrecito?* (*Notes priest's sadness.*)

PRIEST: *Tengo malas noticias. La junta militar ha asesinado al Arzobispo Romero.*

LUPE: *¡Mataron al Arzobispo Romero!* (*Blesses herself and cries.*)

MARIA: Archbishop Romero has been assassinated! (*Crying.*) What a loss to our cause.

GLORIA: Archbishop Romero was a leader of your popular movement, was he not?

PRIEST: *Lamentamos la muerte del Arzobispo Romero pero su muerte no ha sido en vano.*

(*Lupe gets up to cry on Priest's shoulder, they weep in silence.*)

GLORIA: (*Interpreting.*) The Salvadorian people weep for the death of Archbishop Romero, but his death shall not be in vain.

PRIEST: *Nosotros continuaremos la lucha contra este gobierno sangriento y fascista. Mataron a nuestro hermano pero no a la voz de la justicia.*

GLORIA: (*Interpreting.*) We shall continue our struggle against this fascist and bloody government. Our brother has been killed but not the voice of justice.

(*Shots are heard overhead and everyone onstage gets in protective lower position.*)

NETO: *Maria, ten la niña mientras indago de donde vienen los balazos.*

MARIA: Yes, go ahead. I'll hold the baby.

(*Lupe gets Gloria's bush and uses it to hide Maria and child, then exits with the rest.*)

PRIEST: (*Gets his rosary and blesses the bush.*) *Voy con ustedes.*
GLORIA: Maybe we can distract them also by conducting an interview.

(*Everyone except Maria and baby exits behind backdrop stage left. Archie and General enter stage right, arguing.*)

ARCHIE: You numbskull, you just shot a most beautiful bird in a tree.
GENERAL: There was a noise. I could not take a chance. If birds or any kind of animal or nature gets in the way of my cause, it is doomed to die. (*Aims and shoots Maria in back of neck. She falls forward, holding baby in her arms.*) You see, this is how we treat these dangerous communists.
ARCHIE: But this is just an unarmed woman.
GENERAL: (*Turns Maria's body over with his weapon, when he hears the crying, exposes bundle of baby, and shoots it; crying stops.*) They don't deserve to live.
ARCHIE: Geeze, did you have to do that?
GENERAL: Everything the Junta does is necessary. I will go now and report another victory.
ARCHIE: Well, you just go and brag about killing women and children.
GENERAL: Stay as you wish and pray for their evil souls, I will be back. (*Exits.*)
ARCHIE: (*Almost frozen, falls to his knees.*) I think I've been shot. And I didn't feel it until now! (*Reaches out to the bundled dead baby and lies on floor.*) Sorry, little one.

(*Enter Gloria, Lupe, Priest, and Neto, who clutches his dead child and begins crying silently. Priest attends Maria, who starts to moan with pain, blood on neck. Gloria lifts up Archie's head.*)

GLORIA: Oh, Daddy, you've been shot. (*Crying.*)
ARCHIE: (*Moaning.*) Ahh, geeze, it's you, Gloria, my baby daughter. Listen, tell Edith that I love her, and of course you know that you are my favorite little girl. (*He passes out.*)
NETO: (*Gets up slowly, grief-stricken, holding dead child.*) *¿Por qué hacen esto?*
GLORIA: Why do they do this? Oh, Daddy, Maria, the child, oh no, no, all this is not right.

(*Priest stands over Archie's body and gives him the last rites; Archie starts to move.*)

PRIEST: *Este hombre está conciente, reportera. Maria, yo te sostengo.*

(*Priest and Lupe start tending Maria's neck wound*)

GLORIA: (*Hopefully.*) Daddy's alive? Keep breathing, Dad! I'll help you, please hold on.

(*Enter Female Guerrilla.*)

FEMALE GUERRILLA: I heard shots and fired back, but one got away.
GLORIA: Yes, it was my father. He is a military advisor. I plan to take him home and tell our taxpaying citizens what is going on here.
FEMALE GUERRILLA: (*Lowers head.*) I will help you with your father.

(*She helps Gloria get Archie onto a stretcher, which is a white sheet set out on the floor.*)

ARCHIE: Ahh, geez, this is worse than my hemorrhoids! (*Clutches chest and passes out again.*)

(*Neto holds onto his dead child; Priest and Lupe hold onto Maria as she struggles up on her feet. Gloria kneels at Archie's side. Except for Female Guerrilla everyone comes to a standstill.*)

FEMALE GUERRILLA: (*Facing audience.*) I ask you, what would you do in the face of poverty and hunger? We do not want to live in misery and oppression. We are no different than you or any other human on earth. Listen to our cry, Revolution or Death! Listen with your open heart and have compassion for your fellow humans. Join us in our struggle for universal human rights!

(*Everyone on stage raises fist in the air and states*)

"¡Seguiremos adelante! ¡Revolución o Muerte!"

End

ADDENDUM

Reunion of Teatro de las Chicanas

(Written in 1979)

The idea of reorganizing and reinstating the women's *teatro* has been discussed amongst a few of the old members. The reconstruction of the *teatro* is not only seen as a creative vehicle but also because we see the necessity of clarifying the issues affecting the working class on a local, national and international level, as well as the issues that affect women in daily life.

In the past our *teatro* has been involved in these aspects:

A.) professional: the *teatro*
B.) political: the educational phase
C.) personal: our lives and problems

Unfortunately, it seemed the *teatro* dealt more with the personal aspects of our lives. This is not to say that our personal lives are less in respect to the other sides. But it became more dominant than the political or professional aspects.

We want to reinstate the *teatro* utilizing our past mistakes and positive experiences in order to build a progressive and refined *teatro*. The foundation from which the *teatro* is built must be defined.

Therefore the precedents upon which the *teatro* is built are as follows and are the POINTS OF UNITY.

1. Recognition, implementation, and protection of the Rights of women, equal pay for equal work!
2. An end to price hikes and to all attacks on the living standards of the workers!
3. Full employment at the expense of the military budget; jobs and peace. Unemployment compensation to commensurate with the number of children to extend to all urban and rural workers. Nationalize welfare and equalize funds to all welfare recipients to commensurate with the number of children!
4. Free universal medical care!
5. Equality for all national minorities—No national privileges!
6. Equal, Quality and Integrated education for all children. Bilingual education wherever there are non-English speaking students. Nationalize Education!
7. Free quality 24 hour childcare for working families!
8. Outlaw the KKK, Nazi Party and all other fascist groups!
9. Oppose draft to imperialist wars!
10. The rights of workers to organize into unions and to strike. Repeal Taft-Hartley and other anti-labor legislation!
11. Independence, Freedom, and Regional Autonomy for the Peoples of all nationalities and territories oppressed by USNA IMPERIALISM!
12. Nationalize the energy industry! (NO NUKES)
13. Guaranty of Decent Housing through government financing and the expansion of the public sector of housing for the people!
14. Prohibition of work by children under 16!
15. Stop deportations. No documentation papers for required of any workers!
16. An end to compulsory overtime! Strict enforcement of a 35-hour week. No speed-up!

The Teatro de las Chicanas has been an outgrowth of movements during the late 60s. In particular the Chicano Movement. It was apparent that the question of "La Chicana" was being ignored. The struggle was seen as "Viva La Raza," which at the time the movement took on a very nationalistic attitude. However, as Chicanas we saw that our contributions to the movement were very typical female roles as always. Our jobs were either typing papers, making coffee, making signs, etc.

The questions of "La Nueva Chicana" did take its toll. We no longer wanted to take the back role. We wanted to be seen and heard as leaders. As this point we organized a conference, we saw the necessity to relate our goals with our mothers. We held a conference for our mothers so they could understand what the issues were as women and relate our struggle to the issues affecting us at a local, national and international level.

As mentioned earlier it seemed the *teatro* dealt more with the personal aspects of our lives. But as stated earlier to reinstate the *teatro* by utilizing our past mistakes and positive experiences in order to build a progressive and refined *teatro*. After ten years of working as a collective group, the *teatro* is not only seen as a creative vehicle but also because we see the necessity of clarifying the issues affecting the working class. So, therefore our Points of Unity might seem a bit to the extreme, but we live in very dangerous and changing times. An example of this is point 6—education—not only quality education but integrated education and Bilingual education are in the headline almost every day. The propaganda that the media portrays is very negative in relation to these issues.

This is a very important issue not only do they (the establishment) use these issues as scapegoats but they use this type of tactic to divide and conquer the working class. Another, example would be point 15. Again, we see how this question has been pushed to the extreme. When the economy fails the establishment again uses their tactics to divide the working class people. The question of undocumented workers has been used as a scapegoat for the same reasons mentioned above, the failure of our government.

ADDENDUM

Bylaws of Teatro Raíces

(Written by Delia Ravelo, 1979)

Article 1. Full-time Members

Full-time participants must follow the set criteria to qualify as a member of the *teatro* with voting rights and full privileges.

A. Community Involvement. A full-time member must belong to a valid and recognized organization within a given community. This organization, while not necessarily agreeing with the *teatro*'s goals, must not be in direct conflict with *Teatro*'s aims, i.e., KKK, Nazi Party or Anti-Busing Organization. The community organization cannot be solely a social or "fun" club.

B. Study Groups. Each full-time member will participate in a *teatro* study group. Topics will be chosen at group's discretion and according to needs of group's education. These study groups will be held once every other week. These meetings are mandatory, and are excused only by calling another *teatro* member ahead of time, in an extreme emergency of illness.

C. Acting Ability. Acting ability is of utmost importance in a street theater. Each new member will be screened and auditioned for acting ability. If the individual is found to be lacking in talent, said person will participate in *teatro* workshops, practices, and "outside" workshops. They will not receive acting parts until they have achieved satisfactory results in practices. They will understudy all parts of a play.

They may occasionally have "walk-on" parts. A new member that has no acting ability after attending workshops and practices will not be dismissed from the *teatro*. If the member is sincere in her efforts and willing, she will be able to participate in other aspects of *teatro*, such as:

a) Writing plays
b) Wardrobe mistress
c) Makeup
d) Treasury
e) Transportation
f) Booking agent
g) Child care
h) Typing
i) Fundraisers

These tasks are subject to the approval of *teatro* in general.

D. All *teatro* practices are mandatory, excusable only in extreme emergency, serious illness of yourself or child, and husband only near death or disorders, death in family, or employment.

E. Tardiness is a reflection of your seriousness and commitment to *teatro*. Meetings and practices are set up for all members' convenience. Voice your objections at once if you can't make it on time. Continued tardiness will be dealt with by entire *teatro*.

a) fines
b) expulsion

Article II. Part-time Members

A. Part-time participants are individuals who want to contribute to the *teatro* but cannot make a full commitment because of personal reasons. They may not agree totally with *teatro*'s aims, or they may sympathize with our beliefs but cannot actively participate. A part-time member can take part in *teatro* by:

a) Typing plays
b) Fundraisers
c) Child care
d) Props
e) Makeup
f) They can specify what talent they want to contribute.

B. If a part-time member has unusual or exceptional acting ability. They can take a part in acting for a specific performance, only if the *teatro* overwhelmingly agrees on acting talents, and she must attend all practices from the time she agrees to perform, subject to excuses as stated in Article I, Sections D and E.

C. A part-time member can participate in *teatro* meetings, offer suggestions and ideas, but has no voting rights.

Article III. Probation

A. Full-time members. There is a six-month probationary period from the time a prospective new full-time member (has expressed an interest in the *teatro*), has read aims and goals of the *teatro*, has read Bylaws and has been interviewed by the *teatro*. There is mutual agreement and understanding between both parties of rules, duties, and commitment, and an acting ability audition has taken place. These criteria can be met in one or two meetings, not more.

B. Part-time members. Part-time members will read aims and goals of *teatro* and Bylaws. There will be no probationary period. There will be no interview with entire *teatro* but with full-time member not on probation who introduces part-time member to *teatro*. There must be mutual agreement and understanding between both parties of rules, duties, and commitment. Criteria can be met and discussed at discretion of Full-time member. Part-time member must be introduced to *teatro* formally at the incipience of process.

Article IV. Grievance Procedure

A. In any given organization there are problems that arise daily, particularly in Teatro Raíces, where many of the members are married, with children and have full-time employment, and other responsibilities. Our problems arise from our class background as well as social, and peer pressures mounting against our involvement in a Women's *teatro*, dealing with social and political issues, affecting the working class. This brings about the necessity of the study group clarifying our position on issues and the importance of our participation in the struggle and in the *teatro*. Personalities may not always interact pleasantly, but personalities in this *teatro* are secondary. Our propaganda, our political message is the utmost task of the Teatro Raíces. This must supersede all personal antagonisms or friendships. If a member feels she has been treated unfairly or without respect, she has the right and the responsibility to deal with the grievance in a fair and honest way. A general meeting of the *teatro* must be called by member or members with grievance to discuss openly the problem amongst all parties involved. Dealing with problems openly and honestly in a group will bring about the solutions or understanding to continue membership for personal or political reasons. In this way we do not destroy the unity of the group or waste our energies unnecessarily. We would continue working towards our goals without much disruption.

Article V. Loyalty

Each member is expected to follow rules and regulations of the *teatro*, to bring about the unity and cohesiveness we need to deal with the daily pressure working against our involvement and our lives. It is critical if a member is found to be spreading lies or rumors, or dealing with *teatro* problems outside of the group. She should be made aware of the serious nature of her actions against the *teatro* and she should be dismissed. If a person wishes to be petty and play games, we cannot play along and nurse these children. We have enough of our own.

Article VI. Autonomy

The *teatro* is an autonomous organization. We are not part of any political or social organization or club. Our ideals and goals have grown from our personal experiences in this society, our studies, and our hope to build a better society in which we and our children can live decently.

All members have the right to bring forth new ideas in the *teatro* where we discuss and deal with them. Simply because a member or members belong to the "P.T.A." or the Guadalupanas does not mean the *teatro* is a part of the organization. We *are* an organization in itself. We may sympathize with the struggles of other organizations and perhaps perform for them but we are not a part of them.

KEY SPANISH TERMS

abrazos: Hugs.
abuelitos: Grandparents.
actos: Skits.
Adelitas, Juana Gallo, Valentinas: Name given to women fighting in the Mexican Revolution of 1910.
alambres: Literally "wires," breaking through the wire fence.
amiga: Friend.
argüende: Hoopla.
batos: Dudes.
bodega: Small grocery store.
bola(s): Slang for "testicles."
bromas: Jokes.
cariño: Affection.
carnala(o): Sister, brother.
carnalas: Sisters.
carnales: Brothers.
chavalas: Young girls.
Chicano/a: Political term identifying people of Mexican descent living in the southwest United States.
chichis: Slang for "breasts." (see 'bolas' 'huevos' & 'jainos')

chingado: Fuck.
chingazos: Clashes.
chingonas: Bad-asses.
chola: Street-wise girl.
choques: Conflicts.
chuntaros: Lowlife.
círculo vicioso: Vicious cycle.
comadre(s): Godmother of one's child; dear friend.
coyote: Smuggler of undocumented immigrants.
güeras: Light-skinned women.
híjole: Wow!
huaraches: Mexican sandals.
huevos: Slang for "testicles."
imagínate: Imagine that.
jainos: Slang for "boyfriend."
La Causa: Literally "the cause," referring to the Chicano social movement.
la peligrosa: The dangerous one.
La Raza: Literally "the race." Colloquialism for Chicano people.
macha: Slang for an assertive woman.
malcriadas: Ill-mannered.
m'ija: Contraction for "my daughter."
m'ijo: Contraction for "my son."
mujeres: Women.
negrita: Little dark girl.
"No sabe nada" girl: Naïve girl.
pajarito: Small bird.
pendejadas: Foolishness.
picaramente: Mischievously.
platanos: Plantains.
rebozo: Mexican shawl.
revolucionaria: Revolutionary.
rucas: Street-wise girls.
sofrito: Fried tomato and onion sauce.
tamalera: Woman who sells tamales.
teatro: Theater.
tía: Aunt.
tío: Uncle.
tristezas: Sadness.
vagones: Wagons.
vámonos: Let's go.

BIOGRAPHIES

DELIA RAVELO REYES (1952–2002) was a cofounder of the Teatro de las Chicanas. She was born in Kenosha, Wisconsin, and moved to the blue-collar town of National City as a child. She earned a Bachelor's degree in Liberal Arts and a Master's degree in Literature from San Diego State University. She was an international humanitarian, a global citizen, and a proud union member. She is survived by her husband, Michael Reyes, and children, Michael, Malina, and Isela.

PEGGY JOSEPHINE GARCIA was born and raised in the San Diego area in California. She is a third-generation Chicana. Peggy earned a Bachelor of Health Science degree from San Diego State University and a Bachelor of Science degree in Nursing from Eastern Washington University. She lives in Spokane, Washington, where she dedicates her spare time to her family and community. Peggy presently works as a registered nurse in the Washington prison system. She has one son, Gabriel Martin Garcia. She loves to dance.

LAURA E. GARCIA (La China) was born in Sinaloa, Mexico. She migrated in 1964 to Brawley, in the Imperial Valley. She graduated from Northeastern University with a Bachelor's degree in Latin American and Latino Studies. Laura is on the editorial staff of the *Tribuno del Pueblo,* a social bilingual publication featuring political analyses of issues such as immigration, homelessness, and workers' and women's rights. Laura lives in Chicago with her husband José Garcia, a union organizer. She is the proud mother of two sons; Emilio and Adrian.

GLORIA BARTLETT HEREDIA was born in Calexico, California. She graduated from San Diego State University with a Bachelor's degree in Spanish Literature. Gloria also earned her elementary teaching credential, and a Master of Science degree in Counseling. Gloria is an academic counselor with the San Diego Community College District and a resident of San Marcos, California. Gloria has been married more than twenty-five years and has a daughter, Christina. Gloria is looking forward to her retirement.

TERESA OYOS was born in San Diego California. She is a third-generation Californian. She works as a recruiter for the HIV Neurobehavioral Research Center at UC San Diego. She is also on the advisory board for Latino services at the San Diego Lesbian Gay Bisexual Transgender Community Center. Teresa is very active in her A.A. recovery program. She and her partner, Rose, have recently celebrated their twentieth anniversary. She loves to cook, dance, and spend time with her daughter Tina, granddaughter Jenica, and Rose.

KATHY REQUEJO attended San Diego State University, majoring in psychology. She moved to the Los Angeles area and became an advocate and fighter for workers' rights. After obtaining a paralegal degree with an emphasis in labor law, she became president of her local union, the Communication Workers of America, Local 9505. A cancer survivor, she dedicates her time to her family and the fight against breast cancer. Her only son, Marcus, gives her the inspiration to live each day and life to its fullest.

CLARA RODRIGUEZ CUEVAS graduated from San Diego State University in 1980. She also earned a multiple-subject teaching credential. She has been in the teaching profession for twenty years. She has served children in the Central Valley Professional Civic Service. Clara is a member of her local California Teachers' Association and has served as vice president for two terms. Clara has three children: Julianna, who has chosen a career in teaching; Steven, who has chosen to go into the medical profession; and Jaime, who has gone into the field of technology. Retirement is something she looks forward to so she can pursue her love for travel.

VIRGINIA RODRIGUEZ BALANOFF was born in Indio, California. She resides in Chicago, Illinois, with her husband, Clement Balanoff, and works as a hospice nurse. She is a registered nurse and holds a Master's degree in Community Nursing. At present she is pursuing a second Master's degree in theology to enhance her hospice work in her retirement. Virginia is proud of her children, Clement and Monica.

SANDRA MERAZ GUTIERREZ was born in Indio, California, and now lives in Pasadena, California, with her husband, Luis R. Torres, a journalist and playwright. She is proud of her son, André Miyao, a UC Berkeley graduate. She has a Bachelor of Science degree in Applied Management and earns a living as a communications project manager.

MARGARITA CARRILLO was born in Pine Bluff, Arkansas, and raised in Indio, California. Since the late 70s she and her husband, Manuel, have lived in the San Diego area. She works for the San Diego School District and is an active union member of the California School Education Association. She is an advocate for workers', parents', and students' rights.

HILDA GONZALEZ RODRIGUEZ was born in Mexico and migrated to the Coachella Valley in California in 1965. She currently resides in the San Diego area. She has worked for the San Diego Community College District for more than twenty-six years and has had the great satisfaction of seeing more than 2,000 nurse graduates. Hilda is very proud of her two children, Ray and Krystal, for completing their educational goals. Hilda plans to retire and continue to indulge her passion for the arts.

DELIA RODRIGUEZ was born and raised in a rural community of San Diego, California. She completed a Bachelor's and a Master's degree in Spanish Literature at the University of California, San Diego. During the thirty years of Delia's teaching career, she traveled and worked in Guadalajara, Mexico, Louisiana, and Oregon. Delia is a cancer survivor. Nowadays, Delia is interested in math and science and wants to study Biometrics. She is an avid reader and loves to travel.

GUADALUPE CAVAZOS BELTRAN (Lupe) was born in Phoenix, Arizona, and raised in Gilroy, California. She currently resides in Chula Vista, California. Lupe opted for quick vocational training to become a medical assistant when her husband, Fernando, was diagnosed with kidney failure and she became the head of the household. She now attends Southwestern College in Chula Vista. Lupe is proud of her sons, Fernando Jr. and Arturo.

MARÍA JUAREZ (La Cubana) obtained a Bachelor's degree in Spanish Literature, with a minor in Mexican American Studies, from San Diego State University. She has lived in the San Diego area for more than thirty-six years. She is originally from Havana, Cuba. She enjoys skiing, camping, and traveling. She is proud of her son Nelin and her daughter Felicia.

GLORIA ESCALERA was born and raised in Brawley, California. She has a vocational education credential in business occupations in computer applications and multimedia productions. She teaches multimedia productions at Otay Ranch High School, and has been an employee of Sweetwater Union High School District for thirty years. During those years she was a union site representative and bargaining negotiator for the Service Employees International Organization and California School Employees Association, a past member of several teachers' organizations, including the Association of Mexican American Educators, and was past president of Professionals in Adult Continuing Education. Her volunteer work includes starting a MEChA club at Granger Junior High and being past ASB advisor for Chula Vista Adult School. In the community her volunteer history includes the Committee on Chicano Rights, Union del Barrio, and Friends of the Undocumented.

EVELYN DÍAZ CRUZ is an Assistant Professor in the Theatre Arts Program at the University of San Diego. Evelyn earned her Master of Fine Arts degree in Playwriting from the University of California at Los Angeles and is a member of the New Dramatist Guild, the Association of Los Angeles Playwrights, and the Association of Theatre in Higher Education. Originally from the Bronx, New York, Evelyn currently resides in Chula Vista, California, with her husband and three children.

FELICITAS NUÑEZ was born in Brawley, California, and now resides in Bermuda Dunes, California. Felicitas earned a Bachelor of Arts degree in Liberal Arts and her Registered Nurse accreditation. She and Delia Ravelo were the cofounders of the Teatro de las Chicanas. She's a member of Democrats of the Desert and as a hobby takes classes at the College of the Desert.